The Art of
Ama Ata Aidoo

Vincent O. Odamtten

# THE ART OF
# AMA
# ATA
# AIDOO

Polylectics and Reading
Against Neocolonialism

UNIVERSITY PRESS OF FLORIDA
Gainesville • Tallahassee • Tampa • Boca Raton
Pensacola • Orlando • Miami • Jacksonville

Library of Congress Cataloging-in-Publication Data
Odamtten, Vincent O.
The art of Ama Ata Aidoo: polylectics and reading against
neocolonialism / Vincent O. Odamtten.
p.   cm.
Includes bibliographical references and index.
ISBN 0-8130-1276-7 (cloth). — ISBN 0-8130-1277-5 (paper)
1. Aidoo, Ama Ata, 1942– —Criticism and interpretation.
2. Women and literature—Ghana—History—20th century.
3. Developing countries—In literature.   4. Ghana—In literature.
I. Title.
PR9379.9.A35 Z8   1994
828—dc20        93-35009

All quotations from the works of Ama Ata Aidoo have been reprinted
in this volume by permission of the author.

The University Press of Florida is the scholarly publishing agency
for the State University System of Florida, comprised of Florida
A & M University, Florida Atlantic University, Florida International
University, Florida State University, University of Central Florida,
University of Florida, University of North Florida, University of
South Florida, and University of West Florida.

University Press of Florida
15 Northwest 15th Street
Gainesville, FL 32611

to Peace,
Yawo, Indira-Josina, Yom,
and all the women
who fathered the mother
in me, thank you

# CONTENTS

Preface
ix

Introduction: Polylectic Criticism
and African Literature
1

1 · A Bird of the Wayside Sings
14

2 · *Anowa*: In History
42

3 · Back to the Present;
or *No Sweetness Here*
80

4 · For Lovers and Others,
Not Just Another Version
116

5 · Poetic Interlude—Retrospect
and Prospect
133

6 · A New Tail to an Old Tale
160

Notes
175

Bibliography
191

Index
197

# PREFACE

The gestation of this work has been long and painful—for myself, for those close to me, and, in a less ego-centered way, for those who read these remarks. The work's immediate cause was the desire to publish my doctoral dissertation; the original project, however, was conceived out of love and anger, many years ago. The love came naturally enough from reading Ama Ata Aidoo's works, for these were dramas, poems, and stories that gave me pause to think and reflect, to laugh to keep from crying. These were African tales, tales insisting that we examine our own histories and look long and hard at what we have become. Yet, as I read the criticism on her works in particular, and on that of other African writers in general, I was plagued by the gnawing feeling of dis-ease. Initial attempts at identifying the cause of this dis-ease were frustrating, and my anger rose. It was not until 1985, when I found myself caught at a confluence of history, so to speak, that the nature of the dis-ease became more luminous. The occasion was the Second Annual Women's Scholarship Conference at the State University of New York at Stony Brook, where I had been invited to give a commentary on the literary representation of African women. It was out of my need to address such representations critically, in the contexts of gender, class, and culture, that I started to identify the cause of my anxiety.

I realized that part of my discomfiture was a result of the *partial* readings of Aidoo's works, which many of the critics actively encouraged. Gradually, I came to understand that this fragmented dialogue was a manifestation of these neocolonial times, and if I was to be at ease, to find more truthful meanings, I had to try reconstructing the omissions or erasures of the dialogue between Aidoo's texts and her audience(s). I have approached Ama Ata Aidoo's works with as much humility and candor as I could muster. The alleviation of the dis-ease can only be effected through a more complete reading of the conditions of the text-life as it speaks to my (our) life. To this end, my approach to her works encourages what I call a *polylectic reading*, or what might be seen as a revitalized contextual reading; however, I have tried to do more than merely revitalize a received critical methodology.

The polylectic method as demonstrated in this study of Aidoo's works demands that the critic not only acknowledge the importance of the under-girding orature but attempt to conjoin that aesthetic to the whole critical enterprise. In the process, one must recognize the intrinsic risk of overpar-ticularizing or overgeneralizing. For instance, throughout this work I have tended to extend the implications of the Akan matrilineage to the whole of Ghana, even though many of the other nationalities adhere to a patrilineal system. Such generalizations must be taken with due caution; however, one must keep in mind that the historical reality of Akan hegemony and in-fluence over many of the other groups has produced an intricately layered situation. Indeed, some groups, such as the Ga, were initially thought to be matrilineal. Similarly, one might be persuaded, after reading the study, that all personal and interpersonal ties and conflicts are overdetermined by ideological impositions. Yet I have sought to demonstrate that such over-determination, within the context of economic relations, does not preclude the autonomous behavior of individuals.

I am grateful to my students, whose reactions to their readings and my lectures helped me modify and sharpen my own ideas about African litera-ture. I wish to thank my dissertation committee, as well as Kofi Anyidoho, Lemuel Johnson, Vicky Vernon, and all those who read various parts of this labor of love for their warm encouragement and friendly criticism. I am forever indebted to my wife, Peace Enyonam Agbley of Peki Dzake, for all her tears and sacrifice, her invaluable linguistic abilities, and her dis-passionate advice. I am especially proud of our children, who put up with me as this project came into its own. Finally, I extend many thanks to Ama Ata Aidoo for her generosity and to our ancestors, whose wisdom is so wonderfully expressed by her talents.

*Vincent O. Odamtten*

# INTRODUCTION

# Polylectic Criticism
# and African Literature

The relationship between a literature and the critical
comment that develops about it is never static. Any new
literature or literary movement of value is not only subject
to existing critical approaches but may itself act as a
powerful agent in modifying those approaches; there is a
continuous dialogue between literature and criticism.
—Edgar Wright

African literary criticism and its objective—the critical evaluation of African literary texts—has been dominated, until recently, by men. In the 1950s and early 1960s, the criticism of contemporary African texts was produced almost exclusively in the former colonial metropolises by Europeans. Despite their sometimes sympathetic, or occasionally disparaging, treatment of the texts, written generally by Western-educated African men, the critics exhibited a decidedly Euro- and phallocentric bias that often resulted in gross distortions and misreadings. The reasons for this critical processing of African texts have their roots in specific historical configurations that are, in the main, well known. Chinua Achebe summed up the solution and problem succinctly: "The European critic of African literature must cultivate the habit of humility appropriate to his limited experience of the African world and purged of the superiority and arrogance which history so insidiously makes him heir to."[1]

With the emergence of more African texts following political independence, the site of the critical enterprise shifted from the former colonial centers to the newly independent nation-states in Africa. This phase of critical evaluation, while partially freeing itself from a Eurocentric perspective, was trapped in an older tradition—patriarchy. As Mineke Schipper points out: "In reality, male reactions to women's liberation efforts in African society are often alarming, especially when the future of the society as a whole seems critical or hopeless. . . . In African literature as a whole woman hardly has a mouth yet. The image of women in the novel is also very much a male writer's business, and often sadly stereotyped."[2] This situation and the fact that Ama Ata Aidoo has been speaking most vocally and eloquently to readers of African literature since 1964 make a critical assessment of her major literary productions long overdue. With the exception of writers such as Nadine Gordimer, extended or book-length studies of a single African woman writer's work are nonexistent.[3] Indeed, critical studies of the products of African women writers tend to focus on five or more authors. Such packaging may be due, in part, to considerations of unequal power relationships and "marketability." The problem is loaded with complex ideological and historical considerations with which this introduction is not directly concerned.

Precisely because of such determinations, however, a radically different kind of critical investigation becomes urgent. Awareness is growing regarding what may be seen as the repression or conscious avoidance of more challenging ways of reading African literary texts. Dissatisfaction with the current state of African literary criticism, and the perceived need for a criticism that might liberate the critical project from the constraints of the hegemony of Western discursive practices, is most convincingly argued by Kofi Owusu:

> African (written) literature is, on balance, in a healthy state. It is the critical discourses on the imaginative literature that more often than not exhibit unhealthy symptoms. . . . One is the literal-mindedness which appears to be potent enough to interfere with the literary appreciation of African literature. A second is the timidity which translates into critics' insistence that they not be surprised by the "unfamiliar" and the "unexpected." Consequently, the freshness of potentially new discoveries is lost on critics who dare not abjure the

comforting familiarity of [their favorite critical discourse] . . . for "uncertain" knowledge. And, third, there is the symptomatic failure to connect various critical discourses to informing systems, models, or theories that may be comparable to, but need not be, "imported" or "foreign" ones.[4]

Thus this calculated interruption of the often circular conversation of African critical discourse is a vital contribution to a more inclusive critical appreciation of African literature. One hopes that this analysis will act as a catalyst, prompting African literary criticism to realize its fullest potential. Such an investigation should avoid the reproduction, in critical terms, of the exclusive and/or sterilizing dichotomies characteristic of colonial and neocolonial (and many precolonial) social and political relationships.

The motivation for this study was the need to avoid, on the one hand, readings based on conscious or unconscious phallocentric bourgeois preconceptions of African women–authored texts, and, on the other, an often necessary, yet more problematic, desire to valorize a "feminist" perspective without due regard for what the (con)texts actually say. In the first instance we, as critics, become lazy and arrogant. The result of such critical (mal)practice is the insensitive distortion and ultimate destruction of the text-work as a historically constituted aesthetic and ideological product, unique in its portrayal of a specific condition. Such was the fate of many works by African authors at the hands of Western critics, even of some Western-educated African critics.

And, because African women writers have been caught or, more often, drowned at the convergence of predominantly male-oriented Euro- or Afrocentric bourgeois (and occasionally Marxist)[5] literary and sociopolitical traditions, the need for a recuperative feminist reading becomes all the more imperative. Yet there seems to be a marked tendency to cast African women writers and their works in an untenable either/or light. Henry Louis Gates, Jr., responds to Margaret Homans's article on Gloria Naylor's novel *Linden Hills* with a number of observations that are theoretically pertinent to our investigation.

What happens if we resist the temptation to subsume into a narrative of sexual binarism the dispersed array of subject-positions that *Linden Hills* frames—what happens, that is, if we respect another (nonmonistic) feminist injunction and refuse to impose a hierarchy of political signification? The question arises here because part of what distinguishes black women's fiction in the contemporary scene is a sense of a historical community and its peculiarities, sometimes antic, sometimes grim, but never quite reducible to a masterplot of victim and victimizer. At best, these texts are porous to history and propose an articulation of power that is more decentered and nuanced than most of us are accustomed to. Attention must be paid: master narratives of sexual oppression, crucial as they are, can so easily render the sociopolitical subtext opaque.[6]

It is precisely that clouding of subtext(s) by an incompletely theorized feminism, carelessly applied to African texts, that should be resisted. Such a feminist perspective, illuminating as it might be, may produce equally unacceptable readings of these texts.

Specifically, African women's works are either seen to champion a perspective that characterizes the evils of patriarchy as (1) not only primary but also and especially European male (that is, colonialist) impositions, or (2) no less primary oppressions arising from indigenous precolonial values and social relations. Such dichotomizing, though understandable (given the historical burden of patriarchal marginalization), leads, at worst, to the formal approval of an exclusivist feminist "protected village" type of criticism. Fortunately, this tendency has not gained much of a hold on the new criticism of African women-authored literature. Critics like Molara Ogundipe-Leslie point out, quite clearly, that the African woman's commitment to "womanhood does not *only* relate to gender . . . [but] should be [seen as] committed in three ways: as a writer, as a woman and as a Third World person; and her biological womanhood is implicated in all three."[7]

For the critic, it is essential to keep Ogundipe-Leslie's observations constantly in mind; and, more importantly, both male and female critics must be aware of and keep in check their own ideological preconceptions that impinge upon the critical project. Minike Schipper states that "the open-minded critic . . . is not bent upon including or excluding texts according to his own current value system, but . . . reads literary texts within the contexts from which they originated. Of course, inclusive criticism demands more of the critic since nothing is fixed in advance, especially when texts by authors from other cultures or ideologies, or of the other sex are concerned"(50). Implicit in Schipper's "inclusive criticism" is the specter of a relativistic claim such as that hidden in Edgar Wright's remark that is the epigraph to this Introduction. Against such a claim, Schipper's advice that with goodwill and a familiarity "with the other's culture, history, etc." the critic might not be "excessively influenced by standard Western or male (or both) dominated values" (50) may not be enough to effect a real dialogue. S. P. Mohanty, in his discussion of Peter Winch's arguments in the latter's essay "Understanding a Primitive Society," states that, in order to begin a genuine dialogue across cultures, critics must be willing to extend their own categories, since it is they who do not understand the other, rather than forcing and distorting the other's work to fit their own scheme.[8]

Instead of the usual model of a dialectical relationship between text and critic, works like Aidoo's, which draw from a multiplicity of sources and disrupt normative Western generic compartmentalization, require a new critical perspective. Such a criticism would be *polylectical*.[9] A polylectic critical method demands that we approach a work of art in a self-interpellative manner, bringing to our reading and critique enough knowledge that our evaluation may account for as many of the complexities of the specific (con)text of the literary/cultural product as possible. Thus we would begin to see the text and its environment as part of the personal, local, and global dynamic. Simply put, a polylectic criticism acknowledges the *interdependencies*, even as it recognizes the *overdeterminate autonomies of writer, text, audience, and social whole*. To quote Schipper again: "African critics who have the experience of values being dictated by Eurocentric exclusive criticism may have a head start on Western critics, as they would have seen how objectionable exclusive criticism can be. Unfortunately, there is no guarantee that this will be the case"(50). Kofi Owusu's remarks quoted earlier emphasize the problem that African criticism must confront and from which it must liberate itself.

Ngugi wa Thiong'o, in *Writing against Neocolonialism*, states that the African writer since the late 1940s has gone through three stages or phases that more or less correspond to "the age of the anticolonial struggle; the age of independence; and the age of neocolonialism."[10] Such a characterization is, because of the simple clarity of its conception, still valid as we enter the 1990s. We may quibble about this or that detail; however, it must be understood that *Writing against Neocolonialism* is a general guide to the aesthetic-ideological nature of African writing in the last half-century. It not only charts the various histories of selected African writers, but it also outlines the political tendencies that have marked the history of contemporary Africa.

As responsible and responsive social beings, we are challenged by Ngugi's closing remarks:

> The African writer of the eighties, the one who opts for becoming an integral part of the African revolution, has no choice but that of aligning himself with the people: their economic, political and cultural struggle for survival. . . . Such a writer will have to rediscover the real languages of struggle in the actions and speeches of his people, learn from their great heritage of orature, and above all, learn from their great optimism and faith in the capacity of human beings to remake their world and renew themselves. (19–20)

Such compelling words urge us not only to discover a means by which we can more critically read those works that trace the footprints Africa's histories have left us but also, as readers, to confidently find those works that recognize, as Ngugi writes, "that the eighties and nineties will see a heightening of the war against neocolonialism" (19). If there are writers who are writing against neocolonialism, there should be reader-critics who complement their work. Therefore, it would seem necessary that we also learn, like committed writers in the application of their craft, *to read against neocolonialism*. To critically read, in this way, is to read in opposition to Africa's neocolonial arrangements and to begin to develop a polylectic understanding of Africa's economic, political, and cultural actualities.

Such a project is breathtaking in its implications. We shall risk a few generalizations as we examine, as closely as possible, how the major works of Ama Ata Aidoo, looked at from this new perspective, help us *to read against neocolonialism*.[11] It is appropriate that one of the narrators from Aidoo's work *Our Sister Killjoy* should remind us:

> Things are working out
>
> towards their dazzling conclusions . . .

> . . . so it is neither here nor there,
> what ticky-tackies we have
> saddled and surrounded ourselves with,
> blocked our views,
> cluttered our brains.[12]

As neocolonial subjects showered by the ideological hailstorm of shared histories of oppression and exploitation—the "ticky-tackies we have / saddled and surrounded ourselves with" (5)—as well as of resistance and struggle, we find ourselves at what seems to be a significant historical gathering of forces and tendencies.

From this vantage point, we are more able to review and evaluate the consequences of colonialism and its effect on the postindependence phase of our history. In addition, as we grapple with the complexities of neocolonialism in order to move beyond the present undemocratic and exploitative arrangements on a new trajectory, we will fully realize that

> we
>  no
>   more
> fear
> these images of
> hell.[13]

In order to reach that point at which "these images of / hell" really hold "no / more / fear" for us, we must start at that point in our recent histories at which we were paralyzed by such "images" and more.

The title of a prior incarnation of this critical study characterized the body of Aidoo's work as a developing art. My intent was not to suggest a hierarchical relationship between a developed art (or, indeed, a socioeconomic and political group) and an underdeveloped one. Although a diachronic progression exists between the production of Aidoo's first text, *The Dilemma of a Ghost*, and her most recent novel, *Changes—A Love Story*, a synchronic analysis enables us to highlight those elements of Aidoo's art that actively seek to engage the consciousness of her primary audience in a radical process of *reading*.[14] This developing of her readership's self-education toward a more complete understanding of our varied histories, complex presents, and possible futures becomes the objective toward which Aidoo's creative project is impelled. In short, Aidoo's works constitute aesthetic-ideological products, the value of which arises from the neocolonial subjects' (our) active and critical reading of the various texts.[15] One is thus able to more completely account for the nature of the complex structures of each of these texts in their inter- and intratextuality against the background of their interrelated contexts.[16]

Ama Ata Aidoo was born in the central region of Ghana (then Gold Coast) on 23 March 1940. Like many colonized subjects of the Gold Coast, she was educated in an environment that exhibited the multiple contradictions evidenced in a traditional matrilineal society in which tendencies toward patriarchy (an insidious precolonial manifestation) and patrilineal privilege (a more overt colonial imposition) are being consolidated. The process of conflation and consolidation had begun, in the Gold Coast, with the de facto domination of the coastal region by British and European imperialist interests during the nineteenth century.[17] This process, however, did not go unchallenged. Oppositional forces arose because, in large measure, the matrilineal underpinning of the precolonial society had not been displaced during the succeeding years of colonial rule. Thus, certain precolonial social and ideological relations remained more or less intact, even if politically weakened. Of great import was the belief, still persistent in contemporary Ghana, that a woman—even within a marital relationship—should aspire to economic autonomy. The consolidation of colonialism, and its preference for a male-dominated educated African elite, led to disruptions and escalating tensions in a socioeconomic system that, with regard to the election or appointment (enstoolment) of political leaders (chiefs), gave the voting power almost exclusively to women (the Queen-Mother and her female relatives). This arrangement kept the society from becoming overtly antifemale.

Nevertheless, the perks and protection British colonialism afforded the average African male meant a consistent erosion of such preexisting social arrangements. In the Gold Coast of Aidoo's formative years, and in contemporary Ghana, the ratio of educated Ghanaian males to females thus disproportionately favors the males. If avenues for educational advancement during the colonial and neocolonial phases of Ghana's history were restricted for women by British educational policy, however, other avenues for social advancement were not so easily closed or narrowed. Women quickly moved into the economic sector, especially retail trade.

It is in recognition of these conditions, rather than in rejection of "feminist" theories of male oppression, that Aidoo asserts in her introduction to Ayi Kwei Armah's first novel, *The Beautyful Ones Are Not Yet Born*, that

> there have been other ridiculous parallels, especially in the area of what exactly the African woman is, the assumption on the part of most Westerners being that the poor African woman was a downtrodden wretch until the European missionary brought her Christianity, civilization and emancipation. This may apply in certain areas of Africa, but certainly, for most Ghanaian women, the question of their emancipation is not really a problem to discuss since it has always been ensured by the system anyway. Nor is this an idealized view. It is there for anyone to see who is prepared to observe a society instead of imposing on it his own prejudices and syndromes.

In addition, prevailing social attitudes toward a woman's economic independence are fairly well entrenched. For a Ghanaian woman to be wholly dependent, economically speaking, on her husband (or, more often in today's context, on a "sugar-daddy") would mean that the woman was not a woman. In the same introduction, Aidoo states that, "in [Ghanaian] society, women themselves believe that only two types of their species suffer: the sterile—that is, those incapable of producing children—and the foolish. And by the foolish they refer to the type of woman who depends solely on her husband for subsistence." This is not to say that the sterile woman is undeserving of sympathy or support. On the contrary, because she has no children, an issue addressed in Aidoo's early works, *The Dilemma of a Ghost* and *Anowa*, she has limited economic potential. Also, since in a matrilineal society her children *belong* to the mother, the childless woman has no security in old age. And yet "it is also a fact that the only group of females in the country [Ghana] who may not be sure of themselves are the educated."[18]

This admission by Aidoo underscores her realistic characterization of educated women like Sissie in *Our Sister Killjoy* and of Ghanaian women in general, educated and uneducated. For the Ghanaian woman exposed to a Western-oriented education and ideology that disseminated idealized models of womanhood at variance with indigenous models, the confusion of identity and purpose becomes all the more problematic. The hegemonic influence of British colonialism and Western ideas made the acquisition of education desirable even as its effects on individuals were devastating, particularly on women. Fortunately, many Ghanaian men (Gold Coasters) also actively supported the education of women, in spite of the colonial policy of female discrimination. Aidoo's father, Nana Yaw Fama, like Kwame Nkrumah and like Kwegyir Aggrey, the noted Ghanaian educationist and nationalist, believed that to educate a woman rather than a man was to educate a whole nation. As childbearers and rearers, and all things being equal, women effectively controlled the ideological reproductive apparatus and determined the cultural and ideational direction of the traditional society. Social conditions are not static, however, and societies are always in flux. Aidoo's works investigate that dynamic relationship and suggest the need for a radical restructuring of our view of Ghanaian society and, by implication, of all societies in order to change ourselves and those societies for the better.

Aidoo's tertiary education at the University of Ghana, Legon, although overdetermined by the colonial Oxbridge model, did allow her to break, in part, from Western (male) normative aesthetic and ideological perspectives. This break was encouraged partially by Efua Sutherland, whose concern with traditional folk materials and forms may be discerned in Aidoo's writings; although such influence should not be overstated.[19] In addition, the period between September 1964 and June 1966, when Aidoo was a Junior Research Fellow at the Institute of African Studies, University of Ghana, Legon, was to reinforce Aidoo's commitment to the effective and radical use of traditional oral forms and strategies in her work. Neither should we ignore her interest in the pan-Africanist and socialist ideas current in Gold Coast between the mid-1950s and the 1960s.[20] The climate of critical debate that characterized those times enabled Aidoo to avoid a romanticization of Africa's past as some exotic golden age similar to that invoked by the negritude of such African male writers as Camara Laye and Leopold Senghor.[21]

This period immediately preceding and following political independence also produced problems in the literary works of many African writers other than the mystical valorization of Africa's precolonial past. In her essay "The Function of Radical Criticism Today," Molara Ogundipe-Leslie addresses these problems and raises some critical issues germane to the present study of Aidoo's works. Generally speaking, African-authored texts, through the use of proverbs, legends, folk tales, literal translations from indigenous languages, and so forth, have sought to create an authentically *African* literature. Much of this body of literature, however, has also revealed a philosophical perspective that carries the inscription of "the post-Romantic and existentialist twentieth century message of the 'otherness' of the Other, the unknowability of him or her, a difficulty in communication between persons"(Ogundipe-Leslie, 1987, 12). Aidoo's specific immersion in the general ideology of Gold Coast/Ghana, her unique background, and her education seem to have made her particularly sensitive to the possibility that her literary work might yield this kind of ideological message. The textual ideology, the message that arises from the interaction of form and content, style and idea, may in fact contradict the supposedly conscious authorial ideology—the writer's expressed or implicit agenda or intention—thus producing works that are bifocal even as they collapse textual and authorial ideologies. They fuse oppositions such as "negritudinous African romantic primitivism with Western philosophical perceptions of existence [exemplified by] the romantic individual." These authors usually make their protagonist an artist, "the most acute example of such individualism [whose psychological character exhibits a] flight into irrationalism and pessimism in an increasingly turbulent world which Marxists see as revolutionary but liberals see as chaotic and incomprehensible" (14). Aidoo's texts do not offer a world in which the possibility of communication, of change, and of radical sociopolitical transformations has been closed or erased. The possibility of such closure or erasure is radically and continually questioned by Aidoo's deployment of specifically disruptive formal and rhetorical elements, like the dilemma tale convention and the self-conscious, protean raconteur. Thus, by means of a technique comparable to ironic undercutting of statement or idea, Aidoo avoids the conflation of authorial and textual ideologies.

These disruptive elements and interpellative tactics, much in evidence throughout her work, have their origins in the precolonial as well as the peasant and proletarian cultures of contemporary Ghana. Further, these appropriations are not made to add local color in order to satisfy Western aesthetic or ideological prescriptions. In fact, they are there precisely to thwart such impositions as narrowly conceived anthropological, psychological, and even Marxist or feminist readings. The textual frustrations should be seen as among Aidoo's tactics in an overall strategy of resistance. There are arguments that identify Aidoo's exposure to Western (American) feminist ideas during the 1970s as responsible for the perceived shift of emphasis to women's concerns in some of her short stories and, more especially, in the Ghanaian novel *Our Sister Killjoy*; such arguments quickly lose their force, since *all* of Aidoo's works, pre-1970s and after, evidence a consistent regard for women's issues. These issues are always and already addressed within a larger web of ideas, beliefs, and practices (Mohanty, 15) that resists an exclusivist confinement. Consequently, each of Aidoo's works must be read and evaluated with particular attention to context— the work's relationship to the historical ground it narrates or depicts, and its relationship to other Aidoo texts. In short, we must recognize the complexity of the historical matrix in which Aidoo's work is embedded. We must also understand that each of Aidoo's works, in addressing specific ideological and sociopolitical issues, exists as both a development from and a developing to another ground. That ground, in an ultimate sense, is conditioned by the neocolonial reality in which the texts are rooted, which overdetermines both artist and audience.

This study examines the evolution of Ama Ata Aidoo's concerns as an artist and a woman who is an active participant in the ideological and sociopolitical life of Ghana in particular, and Africa and the Third World in general. The discussion focuses on six of Aidoo's works: two plays, *The Dilemma of a Ghost* and *Anowa*; a collection of short stories, *No Sweetness Here*; a stylistically radical novel, *Our Sister Killjoy, Or Reflections from a Black-Eyed Squint*; an equally challenging collection of poetry, *Someone Talking to Sometime*; and her latest novel, *Changes—A Love Story*.

Her work actively seeks to engage her audience in a process of self-criticism and education. The desired objective of the engagement between audience and Aidoo's (con)texts is the radical transformation of the former's consciousness of personal and public history. This study reveals how her innovative use of structural and thematic elements gleaned from

Ghana's orature radically transforms the Western literary genres in which she appears to be working.[22] In addition, we may see her work as progressing toward an increasingly complex vision of Ghanaian society and global politics. That her vision remains firmly anchored in the struggles of all oppressed peoples is a testimony to her commitment and maturity. In her work, we see multiple forms of oppression, exploitation, and domination reproduced in ways that necessitate a more sophisticated understanding of *colonized attitudes* that prevent any escape from the marginalized spaces dictated by global power relationships. The study calls for a more complete reading of Aidoo's varied literary output by applying an equally flexible, open, materialist critical perspective, that is, a polylectic criticism. This critical perspective, while correcting earlier misreadings of Aidoo's works, builds upon previous criticism and to a degree corrects and preserves that criticism. The study contends that the six works that are its object constitute an ideologically and aesthetically linked series. Each work, individually and collectively, speaks of the urgent need of the victims of these inequalities and injustices to find ways to establish a new type of society.

# A Bird
# of the Wayside Sings

Ama Ata Aidoo was twenty-two when her first major work, *The Dilemma of a Ghost*, was performed by the Student's Theatre, at Commonwealth Hall's Open-Air Theatre, University of Ghana, 12–14 March 1964. Aidoo arrived on the national and international scene as a promising young writer when the play was published the following year. As her literary debut, *The Dilemma* received mixed responses from critics and reviewers. Despite the popularity of the play in Accra, Lagos, Ibadan, and elsewhere in Africa, some of the critical authorities echoed C. J. Rea in tone: "It [*The Dilemma*] is less successful as a play, because Miss Aidoo lacked an experienced stage director to help her work out a final version before publication. In this she suffers the same lack as all dramatists in West Africa, where there is no professional English-language theatre group."[1] Rea's paternalism and incipient racism demonstrated many of the problems discussed in the Introduction to this study that prevent a genuine dialogue between the ex-colonialist critic and the ex-colonized's cultural products. Although more often praised than censured, the play tended to be faulted for what were seen as "technical" weaknesses. For example, Karen C. Chapman states that, "among the technical faults [of the drama] playing time is less than an hour for the five acts into which the play is broken; the issues raised in the play, complicated as they are, tend to disintegrate and lose climactic rhythm, especially in the last two acts; and characters appear or reappear without clear dramatic reasons—some disappear altogether, just at the point when the audience begins to identify with them sympathetically."[2] Chapman's complaint about characterization focuses on one of the main consequences of using the dilemma tale convention. By preventing the audience's *sympathetic* identification with the characters, the narrator further stresses the need for continued disinterested discussion of the issues raised in the drama.

More recent criticism seems divided. On the one hand, some still seems to echo many of the initial misgivings about the drama. On the other, the commentaries of a growing number of critics provide new and useful insights about *The Dilemma*.[3] What becomes apparent is that the highly critical responses came from those who still believed in the hegemony of a Western master narrative. Further, these critics did not or could not take into full account *the conflictual nature of the text at a presentational level* (that is, that of the characters themselves) as well as *the play's relation to the historical context that it narrates,* which is at a higher level of generalization.

Although Chapman is not the only critic culpable of privileging Western paradigms over more culturally context-sensitive ones, her "reading" of Aidoo illustrates certain aspects of the problem faced by non-African readers and critics. As she notes in her introduction:

> Miss Aidoo has treated human problems with an understanding unavailable to many dramatists twice her age. There is no romanticizing of negritude or violence. In her writing, none of the tedious, quasi-anthropological, quasi-sociological treatment of Africa's past (or future) geared naively to attract anti-white audiences. She is soberly aware of human truths. While her play is firmly wedded to the social world it embodies—today's fragmented Africa—it is always reaching toward something more universal and, as such, beyond the color barrier. (Chapman, 30)

Again, Chapman's remarks tell us more about the suppositions of the critic and the general ideological character of her society than they do about Aidoo's drama. The desire of Chapman and other bourgeois critics to render Aidoo's play more palatable for Western audiences not only distorts the artwork but limits the cultural and ideological horizons of Chapman's own readership. The need to see the drama as "always reaching toward something more universal and, as such, beyond the color barrier," in the context of the United States during the late 1960s and early 1970s (when Chapman's introduction was first published), makes understandable the social interests that her critical appropriation of *The Dilemma* serves.

Neither should we be persuaded that a narrowly formulated (Western) feminist reading will yield a more comprehensive view of *The Dilemma*. We should be cautious about seeing Aidoo's drama as simply "a woman's perspective of cultural conflict" (Nicholson, 59). In fact, the view that Aidoo's first play is a feminist celebration, the quintessential drama in praise of traditional African womanhood, also limits the text. This is not to say that Aidoo does not recognize the significant role of women in a society like the one depicted in *The Dilemma*. But strictly *unqualified* feminist readings lead to oversimplifications of a complex work. The issues of race and gender and their amelioration are not exclusive or primary, since Aidoo focuses our attention on the whole society. She is not diverted by the dubious need to substitute one set of hierarchies for another, as one of the play's central characters, Eulalie, seems so willing to do. Part of Aidoo's literary inheritance, specifically that bequeathed by African male writers, was a distorted and distorting one. As Merun Nasser notes:

> Anglophone African writers have always included women in their writings. However, for the most part, women have been portrayed in the literature in a subservient role quite unlike their traditional role. The traditional role of the African woman has always been a complementary role and evidence of that fact has been widely supplied by social scientists. For instance, in the traditional African village community, men fell the trees with the help of the young boys while women remove and burn the felled trees. In addition, women sow, plant and weed the fields. And while in most societies the males reserve the right to land, the females reserve the right to surplus derived from cultivation; women may store, exchange or sell the surplus. The economic autonomy of the woman thus limits the relationship of dominance and subservience between the sexes.[4]

It is in this regard that I find partially theorized feminist readings of Aidoo's works problematic. Nasser's article reveals that the social questions we have

been asking recently are directed toward understanding how African literature perpetuates stereotypes of female subservience.[5] If we wish to combat such distortions, we should try to understand the causes, to grasp the
totality of the problem. Narrowly constructed readings, regardless of their
ideological foundations, often hide more than they reveal. For instance,
Nicholson concludes her discussion of *The Dilemma* by asserting that

> even in her first work, which has a male as its central character,
> Aidoo's major concerns are undoubtedly issues that define the place
> and status of women in Ghanaian society. The theme of cultural con-
> flict, then, is subsumed under the more focal issues of the place,
> role, and status of Eulalie, Ato's Black-American wife in her new
> society. . . .
>
> Without straining to make the mother figure into a super woman,
> or idealize her, Aidoo nonetheless shows that the African mother is
> the support and strength underlying the family. The quiet wisdom,
> humanity, resilience, and all the positive qualities that Esi Kom is
> invested with become the hallmark of most of Aidoo's women char
> acters in her subsequent works. (Nicholson, 84–85)

Nicholson seems to downplay the operative social and ideological dynam
ics that were and are part of the colonial and neocolonial reality that *The
Dilemma* dramatically narrates. Despite her worthy intentions, her need to
read the text as especially affirmative of women's roles tends to produce a
partial view of what Aidoo's work actually presents.

That women's roles in the traditional society were more complemen-
tary than they are now speaks not so much to the "affirmation of African
womanhood" as to the ravages of colonial oppression. It reveals how colonial domination can alter the precolonial social relations of many African
societies. Only when we take this larger view of Aidoo's authorial project
do her works in general, and this play in particular, make sense. As Aidoo
herself has remarked, "You come to literature or things like that, and it's
then that you really understand a term like neocolonialism. . . . Because
of the colonial experience we still, unfortunately, are very much lacking in
confidence in ourselves and what belongs to us. It is beautiful to have independence, but it's what has happened to our minds that is to me the most
frightening thing about the colonial experience."[6] Aidoo is concerned with

what happens to people under conditions of colonialism and neocolonialism, not just with the recognition of the African woman or mother as "the support and strength underlying the family." That she chooses women as a center should not be taken for an overriding feminist concern that subsumes all else. The literary and cultural context in which Aidoo was to make her debut as a writer was dominated by men. Quite often, the works of her contemporaries expressed a degree of ambivalence even as they attempted to unite a surfacing nationalism with aspects of Western bourgeois culture. It is partly in light of this literary inheritance that we begin to understand Biodun Jeyifo's characterization of *The Dilemma* as one among "certain plays [that] deal exclusively with the political, social and cultural problems of the emergent elites."[7]

In Aidoo's reaction to her literary inheritance she anchors her play in a fuller, more comprehensive context; by doing so, particularly in her use of the chorus of the two neighbors, she is able to focus attention on the major dilemmas of our age: gender, race, and class. Further, the play has been characterized as exhibiting "realism," which Jeyifo applies "to those plays that deal with 'real' people in 'typical' situations, with plots that seem credible or probable in relation to the daily rounds of life and the cycles and passages of time within a given human community" (Jeyifo, 56). The audience or reader is never allowed to forget that, although what is being seen or read is a fiction, it is rooted in a shared objective reality. Put another way, despite the obvious differences in terms of historical experience and geographical location, we, as social and political beings, must contend with the economic and ideological determinations and articulations of class, race, and gender.

Further, Aidoo's first play, though situated in modern Ghana just after the heady days of Independence (circa 1960), is both structurally and thematically related to the traditional dilemma tale, the pertinence of which is foregrounded in the title. Essentially, the dilemma tale is a narrative whose primary function is to stimulate serious, deep-probing discussion of social, political, and moral issues that confront human beings in their everyday lives. Aidoo uses the dilemma tale neither to satisfy the expatriate anthropological critic nor to provide local color. The immediate task her drama confronts is the focusing of our regard, by means of the dilemma tale device, on contemporary Ghanaian and African problems. Although dilemma tales have been the object of inquiry by many Western anthropologists, their purportedly scientific investigations do not result in particularly insightful conclusions. For instance, William R. Bascom, who is more open than most anthropologists in the field, prefaces his documentation of these "riddle-cases of conscience" with this apologia:

> It is their intellectual function and their relevance to ethical standards, *rather than any literary merit,* that make the dilemma tales interesting. *No elaborate plot or surprising denouement is necessary to present a dilemma, and some examples barely qualify as prose narratives.* . . . It is perhaps in part because *many dilemma tales have little literary merit*—a shortcoming greatly exaggerated in my summaries which follow—that they have been relatively neglected by American folklorists; *this neglect also reflects the general indifference of American scholars to African folklore, of which dilemma tales seem to be particularly characteristic.* (italics added) [8]

It is interesting to note that, in Sembene Ousmane's *Tribal Scars,* the stories are connected by a protean narrator/storyteller whose critically sensitive concerns center on the problems of why and how we have become what we are in the postcolonial era.[9] The written text ends with the title story, which is begun by the narrator of the other stories but finished by Saer, a character whose question precipitates the story-telling occasion among his audience of male tea drinkers (Ousmane, 1974, 102). "Tribal Scars, Or the Voltaique," however, as a *telling event* that attempts to solve the riddle of the origins of "tribal scars," is unresolved by the time we close the book. We are left dissatisfied, although Saer's story, within the larger frame opened by the nameless narrator, comes to a definite conclusion: "And that is how our ancestors came to have tribal scars. They refused to be slaves" (Ousmane, 1974, 116). The nameless narrator does *not* provide a closing frame for Saer's powerfully moving explanation and so leaves us in an aesthetic-ideological quandary. Do we accept the ending provided by Saer? What are the implications if we do? Why does the nameless narrator refuse to close the frame that he intentionally opened, and that strategically includes us in the narrative? "In the evenings *we all go* to Mane's place, where we drink mint tea and discuss all sorts of subjects, even though *we know very little about them*" (Ousmane, 1974, 103; italics added).

I suggest that this ploy achieves, among other ends, "a fidelity to the oral, [so that] these texts can instead be 'heard' to declare the precedence of 'real' human—therefore essentially untextualizable—voices and meanings over the putative political and historical hegemony of the word" (C. Ward, 89). To this end, there is always an irresolution (on one or more levels of signification) that creates a tension with the tale's formal closure. Those present are compelled to resolve what is unresolved in the performance outside the theater or text, in order to achieve a sense of aesthetic-ideological satisfaction. In fact, the telling of dilemma tales in particular, and of other oral narratives in general, affords excellent opportunities for raising issues that may be in unacknowledged conflict with the dominant ideology.[10] It is in this regard that we should begin our examination of *The Dilemma* and the rest of Aidoo's works. Whether looking at "performance" or "text," *we must learn to read against neocolonialism*.

It should be noted that the traditional raconteur has never been only a creative artist or performer, but also one whose performance has been *licensed*. That is to say, the nature of the performance (the choice of material, genre, and so on) legitimized the criticism or challenging of the status quo or perceived social and political injustices. The dilemma tale achieves a detachment from its fictive content, if handled in a competent way, because it is a more critical mode of literary discourse than, say, the traditional Kwaku Ananse folktale. This ability to signify the "not-said" of its content—by way of self-reference to its ideological determinations through its very structure—separates it from the traditional oral folktale in the same way that literary criticism, as a mode of discourse, is separate from the literary texts that are its objects. As valid as is Terry Eagleton's critique of Pierre Macherey's overdependence on the concept of "absence" and apparent negative formulation of the relationship between the general ideology and the text, in the case of the dilemma tale Eagleton's cautionary remarks seem inappropriate.[11] When one considers the dilemma tale, it becomes evident that the relationship between the general ideology and the "whole text" *prevents* an uncritical reading, by simultaneously foregrounding and making unsatisfactory such critically negative reproductions of the textual-ideological relationship. In the dilemma tale, especially as it is deployed in Aidoo's play, the formal structure and the significance of its content are inseparable. Thus, *The Dilemma*'s performance value lies in the fact that, as a fixed and truncated part of a larger whole, the dilemma is always extended out of the text and into the context of the audience. It can never remain within the "partial" text of the written form. This is what makes a polylectical materialist criticism of *The Dilemma* necessary for a full understanding of the text, one that avoids misreadings similar to those indicated earlier, which are characteristic of bourgeois criticism.

In the specific example of *The Dilemma*, which incorporates elements of a literary mode of production (a dilemma tale) rooted in precapitalist, precolonial African societies' general modes of production, we have a text. Having a text, however, indicates the influence of other determinations as well: namely, the emergent traditions of modern African literature that have been overdetermined by the realities of colonial and postindependent Ghana. This text belongs to a literary practice or tradition that is both Western *and* African. The multiple determinations that have produced its specifics throughout Africa are various; the particular form it assumed in the Ghanaian context, however, is our initial concern, although the discussion has significance for the rest of Africa. Lloyd Brown notes that "among contemporary Ghanaian dramatists, male and female, only Ama Ata Aidoo compares with Sutherland in exploiting oral literature, especially folk drama, in modern theater. Like Efua Sutherland, Aidoo has taught extensively in her field. . . . Both as a writer and teacher she has always demonstrated a special interest in the kind of oral literary traditions that so strongly influence her own plays" (Brown, 1981, 84). Perhaps the demands of her activities as a teacher have made Aidoo more aware of the implications of her art. We see in her literary products a consistent effort to avoid those complications that her male precursors left only partially addressed; namely, the expression in their works of a bifocal vision, a complex cultural dualism that sought to unite a Romantic precolonial primitivism and a post-Romantic neocolonial existentialism. They undertook this partially realized effort toward unity to describe the historical division and trauma of the Western-educated African. Their ultimate objective was the amelioration of what has been called "cultural schizophrenia." [12]

*The Dilemma* is concerned with the return of Ato Yawson, a young Ghanaian who has been studying in the United States of America. This return is the cause of various conflicts that move the action, particularly because Ato has not informed his family of his marriage to an African-

American, Eulalie Rush. His very traditional family, epitomized by his mother, Esi Kom, ignorant of this marriage, is naturally surprised and even antagonistic to Eulalie and all she represents.[13] They consider her a "wayfarer," "the offspring of slaves"; in other words, a person without history, a tree without roots (17–19). Eulalie comes to Ghana carrying the heritage of the "New World," its histories of invasion, slavery, and racism, its myths and misconceptions about the "Dark Continent."

More precisely, Aidoo's play has as its underlying concern the dilemma of a ghost. On one level it is the dilemma of the Ghanaian petit bourgeois intellectual who is confronted with the problem of what Chinua Achebe and others have called "the clash of cultures." The site of this fray occurs in perhaps the most immediate and intimate of contexts—marriage and family. On another level, the drama examines, through the formal elements of the dilemma tale, the reactions of the participant-audience to the confrontations at both the presentational level and the general ideological one.

A brief overview of the Ghanaian climate in which *The Dilemma* was written and produced will help further our appreciation of Aidoo's work. Under the leadership of Dr. Kwame Nkrumah, the former British colony of Gold Coast had become the independent "Black Star" of progressive African politics during the late fifties and early sixties. As a relatively wealthy nation Ghana had a significant educated elite, an aggressive agricultural cash-crop policy, and systematic exploitation of mineral resources, factors that contributed to the heightened optimism that marked the transition from colonial to independent status. Progressive intellectuals and activists from all over the globe were making trips to Accra.[14] Yet, even in those days, there was an inkling that things were going awry.

Partly because of Aidoo's authorial ideology and partly because the drama is structurally and thematically related to the traditional dilemma tale, the play is more able to reveal its own ideological determinations than, for instance, Wole Soyinka's *The Lion and the Jewel* or *The Road.*[15] Both Aidoo and Soyinka use material, whether formal-structural or mythological-religious, gleaned from the orature of the Akans and Yorubas, respectively. Mildred A. Hill-Lubin has observed, however, that Soyinka's works tend to be closer in design to the Western literary tradition and relatively more accessible to the Western critic.[16] In *The Road*, Soyinka focuses on the dregs of Nigeria's urban population with the one exception of the character of the Professor. The Professor seems to have made the revolutionary leap that Ato Yawson, in *The Dilemma*, is incapable of making. Following the lead of Frantz Fanon, it is likely that Soyinka is actually echoing the old idea that society's urban dispossessed need guidance and leadership "from *without* by already revolutionized cadres" (Jeyifo, 19). The Professor, however, assumes this leading role because "he dominates, mystifies and bedazzles them with his torrential verbal salvoes and the brilliance of his talents" (Jeyifo, 20). His desire to be "a man of the people" originates from his hopes of gain and profit.

Despite what may appear to be a revolutionary step, or a mad Orphean descent into the hell of urban Africa, our reading discloses Soyinka's rejection of the possible transformative role of the revolutionized petit bourgeois intellectual. Perhaps Ngugi wa Thiong'o's assessment of Soyinka's artistic vision more precisely locates the problems:

> Confronted with the impotency of the elite . . . , Wole Soyinka does not know where to turn. Often the characters held up for our admiration are (apart from the artists) cynics, or sheer tribal reactionaries like Baroka. The cynicism is hidden in the language (the author seems to revel in his own linguistic mastery) and in occasional flights into metaphysics. . . . Although Soyinka exposes his society in breadth, the picture he draws lacks depth, it is static, for he fails to see the present in the historical perspective of conflict and struggle. It is not enough for the African artist, standing aloof, to view society and highlight its weaknesses. He must try to go beyond this, to seek out the sources, the causes and the trends.[17]

At variance with Soyinka's position, Aidoo's play dramatically challenges the assumption or rejection of this role by the Ghanaian intellectual. Aidoo's deliberate choice of traditional oral materials and forms, her authorial ideology, and the general radical ideological climate during Ghana's immediate pre- and post-Independence era seem to have enabled Aidoo to avoid a "static" depiction of her society.

Even when a critic like Lloyd Brown recognizes the influence of African orature in the works of Aidoo, he is unable to grasp the full significance of the traditional dilemma tale as it bears on the concerns of the play (Brown, 1981, 84–121). A somewhat detailed analysis of the prelude, with reference to subsequent developments in the play, will show how Aidoo deploys an African orature within and beyond the drama. The play opens with a direct address to the audience:

> I am the Bird of the Wayside—
> The sudden scampering in the undergrowth,
> Or the trunkless head
> Of the shadow in the corner.
> I am an asthmatic old hag
> Eternally breaking the nuts
> Whose soup, alas,
> Nourished a bundle of whitened bones—
> Or a pair of women, your neighbours
> Chattering their lives away.[18]

By calling herself the Bird of the Wayside the narrator is, in the traditional context of tale-telling, making a disclaimer, for this title suggests an out-cast, a stranger to the community who, ignorant of the community's laws and customs (ideological practices), may inadvertently offend in the telling of the tale. At the same time, this characterization of the narrator, taken together with the self-descriptions that follow, foregrounds the mutual determinations that exist between the ghost of the title and the inability of the principal characters in the drama to resolve their conflicts. After her disclaimer, the narrator alludes to herself in the first three instances as immaterial: "the sudden scampering in the undergrowth," "the trunkless head," and "the shadow in the corner." These references to the intangibility of the narrator—who, as traditional raconteur, is all characters—suggest that the principal characters in the drama are unable or unwilling *to see* the ideological underpinnings of their own actions. As audience-critics to whom this is addressed, however, we are to be made aware of these de-terminations by the very structure of the dilemma tale. That is to say, the drama does not end with the choral singing of the children—

> Shall I go to Cape Coast
> Shall I go to Elmina?
> I can't tell
> Shall I?
> I can't tell

> I can't tell
> I can't tell
> I can't tell.
> (52–53)

—because, in the words of Louis-Vincent Thomas, their song, which poses a question, only serves as the point "of departure for interminable palavers between young and old" (Bascom, 3). The dilemmas that confront the characters are simultaneously seen and not seen, contained and not contained, within the performance.

In the context of bourgeois (dramatic) literary practice, the narrator is usually absent from the text, certainly from the drama's performance. In Aidoo's play, however, the narrator is not only present but, in the opening address to the audience, points to her absence (or potential absence). Although arising from different historical contexts, the consequence of this duality is similar to the Brechtian alienation effect: "A representation that alienates is one which allows us to recognize its subject, but at the same time makes it seem unfamiliar. . . . The new alienations are only designed to free socially-conditioned phenomena from that stamp of familiarity which protects them against our grasp today."[19] Aidoo's use of the oral tradition in *The Dilemma* allows us, indeed forces us, to be distanced from the dramatic action. We are aware of it as performance; yet our "interminable palavers" and the stark realities of our daily lives root the play in the now— our historical present.

In contradistinction to the first self-descriptions, the next two place the narrator, as an "asthmatic old hag," in the position of a transhistorical figure whose actions are unproductive: "Eternally breaking nuts / Whose soup, alas, / Nourished a bundle of whitened bones." In the next characterization, the narrator is placed within the same historical moment as the audience—"a pair of women, your neighbours"—whose actions are also unproductive: "Chattering their lives away." The dilemma tale would have been useless if it gave rise only to an "interminable palaver" over the choices to be made. As audience and participants in the "whole performance," we cannot and do not have all of eternity to make our choices; like the ghost at Elmina Junction, mentioned in the children's choral song, we have only until the dawn.

Having established the location of the play by means of the alienation

effect, Aidoo further heightens the situation by a series of juxtapositions
that illuminate the narrator's relationship with the audience:

> I can furnish you with reasons why
> This and that and the other things
> Happened. But stranger,
> What would you have me say
> About the Odumna Clan? . . .
> Look around you,
> For the mouth must not tell everything.
> Sometimes the eye can see
> And the ear should hear.
>
> (lines 11–19)

The confidence of the narrator's assertion that "I can furnish you with
reasons why" speaks of the creative ability of the raconteur as well as her
knowledge of the neocolonial society. But the narrator undercuts this confidence by asking the audience ("stranger"), "What would you have me
say / About the Odumna Clan?" The complexity of this utterance cannot
be overemphasized, despite its apparent simplicity. In keeping with the
character of the traditional raconteur, the narrator is assuming a posture
of humility; in effect, she is asking the audience to be patient with her telling of the story. After all, anything a Bird of the Wayside's performance
will speak of can only be hearsay; ironically, it is the narrator who is the
stranger. But in the actual phrasing of the question it is we, the audience-
critics, who are now excluded and labeled the "stranger." This reversal of
our position with respect to narrator and the play foregrounds the reversals that are to take place during the actual performance. We wish to be
entertained, perhaps to escape the all too familiar dilemmas that confront
us daily, but the narrator will not allow us such an easy way out:

> Look around you,
> For the mouth must not tell everything.
> Sometimes the eye can see
> And the ear should hear.
>
> (lines 16–19)

We are enjoined to be attentive, critical, and distanced, because that is the
only way we will truly understand *The Dilemma*.

The narrator-raconteur then proceeds to describe the locale of the play and its social background, situating the Odumna Clan house with respect to the town, and offering a brief historical overview of the events that lead up to the first act. The socioeconomic prominence of the Odumna Clan, the home of Esi Kom and her family, is referred to in the next few lines:

> Yonder house is larger than
> Any in the town—
> Old as the names
> Oburumankuma, Odapadjan, Osun.
> They multiply faster than fowls
> And they acquire gold
> As if it were corn grains—.
>
> (lines 20–26)

The hegemonic position of the Odumna Clan within the semifeudal and semicapitalist society of Ato Yawson's hometown is emphasized by the clan's rapacious acquisition of wealth (lines 24–26). The reference to "the Three Elders"—"Oburumankuma, Odapadjan, Osun"—legendary heroes of the Fanti, ironically accentuates the failure of leadership embodied in Ato Yawson's inaction.[20] The transition from a semifeudal aristocracy to a neocolonial capitalist ruling class is not easy, and the price is a heavy one (lines 27–39). The emergent neocolonial social order demands leaders of a new type—"the making of / One Scholar"—who will solve the problems that are an inevitable result of that change. The superior individual is to lead the inheritors of the old colonial order to victory; for, as the clan's praise singer–historian chants, "We are the vanguard / We are running forward, forward, forward." But, one might ask, into what? Where will the new leaders, the Western-educated national bourgeoisie take us? Can we be sure that they will not be blinded, that "the twig shall not pierce [their] eyes" (line 36)? Or that the masses—the peasants and the proletariat—will not take the struggle further, "the rivers prevail o'er us" (line 37)? Set against this public dilemma are the private dilemmas of Ghanaian Ato Yawson, his African-American wife Eulalie Rush, and her in-laws, which are the immediate concerns of the play.

The central trope that concertizes the concerns outlined in the prelude is expressed in the song "The Ghost." We first hear this song in act 3, which, like act 2, begins with what could be taken as the dramatic externalization of Ato's internal existential and ideological dilemmas. On the other hand, it can be a material happening, as Aidoo's stage directions indicate. Either or both, the game the two children are engaged in not only symbolizes Ato's predicament, and by extension that of the Ghanaian petit bourgeois intellectual, but also signifies the underlying philosophical assumption of the dilemma tale (28). This teasing can be taken as Aidoo's scene setting, the authentication of the children's play activity, and the simultaneous underscoring of the importance of children in African societies. The question the children attempt to answer is: What is to be done? They decide on the game of "Kwaakwaa"—hide-and-seek—but they cannot agree on who should hide and who should seek. Their intransigence leads to an escalation of verbal insistence or hostility. Ultimately the boy resorts to violence: he strikes the girl. As a result of the girl's crying, however, the boy reconsiders: "Oh, I did not mean to hurt you. But you too! I have told you I want to hide. . . . Let us play another game then. What shall we do?" (28). Significantly, the girl's next choice is to sing "The Ghost," which involves holding hands and dancing, a communal act. Seen in this way, not only does the childish banter become a paradigm of the structural or formal rationale of the dilemma tale (that is, the positing of a dilemma that leads to "interminable palaver" and, one hopes, a consensus for action), but it also encapsulates the relationship between Ato and Eulalie up to this point. Ato and Eulalie wish to return "home," to "play" in this new—relatively speaking—society that is neocolonial Ghana; they cannot decide, however, who is to find whom. Or what. And we must decide whose values are to guide them in the context of shifting social, political, and ethical standards.

Unfortunately, Ato's arrogance and intransigence, in the face of changed or changing objective conditions, is the way to a self-condemned marginality and, ultimately, to historical irrelevancy. The communality and gender reconciliation expressed by the choices made and the actions of the boy and girl heighten, ironically, the ghost's paralysis at the junction (28). Moreover, the isolation of the ghost, confronted by the dilemma of which way to go or what to do, contrasts with the dilemma faced by the boy and the girl and their solution to their problem. Ato's dishevelled entrance, the disappearance of the children, his agitated state of mind and admission that, as a child, he "loved to sing that song" serves to further identify him with the ghost and the paradoxical status of being concurrently central and marginal to the drama and the narrated history.

In the monologue that immediately follows the exit of the children, Ato admits that as a child he was curious about many things. "I used to wonder what the ghost was doing there at the junction. And I used to wonder too what it did finally. . . . Did it go to Elmina or to Cape Coast? And I used to wonder, oh, I used to wonder about so many things then. But why should I dream about all these things now? . . . Probably I am going mad?" (29). The dream, if it ever was a dream, is disturbing to Ato because it obliges him to remember the critically questioning consciousness of childhood, however random and eclectic it might have been. It is a denial of Fanon's prayer at the end of *Black Skin, White Masks*: "O my body, make of me always a man who questions!"[21] As such, it evidences a time previous to the accretions of bourgeois values symbolized by Ato's apprenticeship in America. His dismissal of these uncomfortable thoughts and questions speaks of the almost pathological insistence on internalizing all dislocations and on relocating the causes of frustrations and so on in the mind of the victim himself—"probably I am going mad" is Ato's rhetorical explanation (29).

The entrance of Ato's uncle, Petu, from the farm at this point emphasizes the distance between the two, not only in generational terms, but in class and occupational terms. Uncle Petu is a peasant, a farmer very much aware of the necessity of producing food for survival. He probably wakes up before dawn to go to his farm; and so, when Ato asks him if he has been to the farm, Petu's reply to "my master" carries a great deal of sarcasm (29). Uncle Petu's attitude is a telling comment on Ato's behavior, which generally belittles the physical activities and values of rural life. At the same time Petu's comment reflects the general or popular characterization of the educated Ghanaian as a parasite. Similarly, the implication of a forced marginalization echoed in Petu's statement, "I have to relieve the wayside herbs of their dew every morning" (29), serves to remind us that the peasantry, the so-called illiterates, and the workers are those whose labor supplies the society with the necessities of life. Yet Uncle Petu's generalized animosity toward the national bourgeoisie is tempered with a personal concern for his nephew: "Do not be disturbed. Although I do not like afternoon dreams myself. I will tell your grandmother and hear what she has to say about it" (30).

Meyer Fortes notes that, "the maternal grandmother holds a special position as she is often the female head of the domestic group and this gives her great influence in the bringing up of children. She is the guardian of morals and of harmony in the household. . . . The grandparents are felt to be the living links with the past. They are looked up to with reverence, not only as the repositories of ancient wisdom but also as symbols of the continuity of descent."[22] In this light, Petu's intention to seek the advice of Nana about Ato's "afternoon dream" becomes doubly significant. It not only affirms the reverential regard for Nana as "the guardian of morals and of harmony in the household," but it also links her emblematically, as the grandmother of the family, with history and "the continuity of descent" and reminds us of the figure of the "asthmatic old hag" in the prelude. Her connectedness stands in opposition to the isolation of Ato at the end of the play. Ato's unacknowledged guilt concerning his Westernization leads him to covertly practice birth control; his practice threatens the continuity of both the family and tradition.

Yet we cannot put all the responsibility for the possible discontinuity of descent on Ato or even on Eulalie, though she shares it. The characters who symbolize the non-Western traditions need to ask the right questions and understand the real nature of the problems they face. Aidoo's stage directions are particularly illuminating. After Ato's Uncle Petu leaves and Eulalie enters, we are instructed to acknowledge her anxiety over the possibility of yet another meeting with "the whole lot of them [Ato's family]" (30). Instead of seizing the moment to frankly and openly discuss the significance of the Ghanaian concept of family, marriage, and gender roles with Eulalie, Ato, revealing his pride in "progress and development," suggests that the two of them go to see "the new Methodist School" (30). Aidoo emphasizes the extent of their Westernization by indicating that the pair walk "hand in hand," sightseeing like tourists. Such a gesture, in the Ghanaian context, would smack of pomposity.

This kind of behavior is aptly encapsulated in the term *been-to,* which in most neocolonial African societies has come to refer to people, like Ato Yawson, who have been educated in Europe, America, or other Western countries. Been-tos are seen as harbingers of the desiderata, what Ayi Kwei Armah refers to in his novel *Fragments* as the conduits through which Western commodities or the "cargo" is brought back for the benefit of the "loved ones" (the family and, finally, the whole society).[23] The been-to is usually characterized as suffering the double estrangement of the *sujet-en-*

*soi:* [24] rejected by or rejecting his or her "African culture" by virtue of higher education on the one hand, and simultaneously rejected by or rejecting Western bourgeois culture by virtue of his or her color. The been-to is thus a paradox who, for the "loved ones," augurs the possibility of surmounting the restrictions and limitations of their neocolonial reality. To those who cannot share the benefits of the bourgeoisie, however, the been-to symbolizes their oppression and is a person to be envied and even despised or resented.

The prose passage that precedes the dialogue between Eulalie Rush and Ato Yawson "on a University Campus; never mind where," gives us more information about the specific historical moment into which the dramatis personae are inserted and, incidentally, that moment of which Aidoo too is a part. The narrator gives us an indication of the attributes of the operative social relations and ideological preconceptions that, in a significant way, determine the actions of the characters:

> Thus, it is only to be expected that they [Esi Kom's family] should reserve the new addition to the house for the exclusive use of the One Scholar. Not that they expected him [Ato Yawson] to make his home there. No . . . he will certainly have to live and work in the city when he arrives from the white man's land. . . . But they all expect him to come down, now and then, at the weekend and on festive occasions like Christmas. And certainly, he must come home for blessings when the new yam has been harvested and the Stools are sprinkled. (8)

The dichotomy between the semifeudal expectations of the tradition-bound Odumna Clan members and the demands of the emergent neo-colonialist socioeconomic order, which are to overdetermine the choices of Ato Yawson, are realized in the separation of the old and new wings of the Odumna Clan house and the ritual visitations expected of the "One Scholar," "the vanguard" of the new dispensation. Yet the narrator-raconteur is acutely aware of the two contesting socioeconomic formations. Implicit in this awareness is the partially acknowledged admission— at least by the narrator and, possibly, by the critical audience—of the inherent weakness of the traditional, semifeudal society in its confrontation with the emergent socioeconomic formation: "The ghosts of the dead ancestors are invoked and there is no discord, only harmony and the restoration of that which needs to be restored. But the Day of Planning is different from the Day of Battle" (8). The narrator-raconteur then reminds the audience of the fictive nature of the drama, even as she stimulates our curiosity: "And when the One Scholar came . . . I cannot tell you what happened. You shall see that anon" (8). Within the context of traditional oral performance, such an utterance would be followed by the demands of the audience-participants urging the raconteur to proceed with the performance and not waste time. That most oral presentations are given at night adds to the distancing effected by the Bird of the Wayside's admission that "it all began on a University Campus; never mind where. The evening was cool as evenings are. Darkness was approaching when I heard the voices of a man and woman speaking" (8). The dialogue raises a number of difficulties, which are to be made more specific during the remainder of the play. These are the predicaments that must be solved by the various characters and, ultimately, by the audience; for the play, loyal to the oral form on which it is based, does not give any pat answers. In the context of the foregoing remarks it is germane that Eulalie, the first to be overheard, should ask: "But who's a graduate? What sort of creature is it? Why should I have supposed that mere graduation is a passport to happiness?" (8). Paradoxically, the question reflects revealingly on the protagonists—Ato Yawson and Eulalie herself.

The two are united by their common Western education and, as such, are part of the "vanguard" whose "destiny" is to lead the people "forward." The narrator's choice to start the dialogue at this point and Aidoo's own choice of these particular characters, "one American, one African, frees the emotionally charged subject of cultural conflict of the racial overtones it acquires in a lot of the African [literary] approach[es] to the subject" (Nicholson, 61). As illuminating as Nicholson's observations are, however, Aidoo's choices do more than overcome "the racial overtones" or accentuate the historical and psychosocial legacy of European contact with Africa "for black people all over the world" (Nicholson, 61). These choices and the questions raised by Eulalie spotlight the important problem of what Western education means to those who have been nurtured as sujet-en-soi by Western imperialism's local (national) reproduction of bourgeois culture and the remnants of the semifeudal society. A major characteristic of a sujet-en-soi is the lack of a critical self-consciousness that allows the individual-as-subject to grasp fully the nature of his or her conditioning by different and conflicting ideological practices or discourses, that is, the semifeudal and neocolonial Ghana. Unlike Althusser's proposition that *"individuals are always-already subjects,"* [25] here the concept of individuals-as-subjects marks those individuals whose specificity has resulted in a critical consciousness that allows them to perceive and take action against their existential condition by what Althusser terms the "Ideological State Apparatuses."

Ato Yawson's evasion of this question from his bride-to-be, Eulalie Rush, points to his inability to become a "subject." In fact, we might say that at this point in the play Ato Yawson is less than sujet-en-soi, for he even denies the materiality of the demands of the semifeudal society that his traditionalist family represents. This is clearly seen in his immature outburst: "How often do you want to drag on about African women? Leave them alone, will you. . . . Ah yes they talk. But Christ, they don't run on in this way" (8). He does not wish to be reminded of his "other" self, that self that his traditional upbringing has shaped. This denial is all the more keenly felt in his exaggerated sensitivity to Eulalie's "American-ness": "This running-tap drawl gets on my nerves" (8). Eulalie's response, "I only speak like I was born to speak—like an American!" (3) at least shows that she recognizes herself as a conditioned subject, a product of a specific society: *she is an American,* relatively speaking. On the other hand, Ato wishes to ignore the differences that history and geography exert on the development of the neocolonial sujet-en-soi. He wishes, like Alexander Blackburn, the protagonist in Orlando Patterson's novel *An Absence of Ruins,* to stand "outside of race, outside of history, outside of any value." [26] One is reminded of Ngugi's assertions about the effect of what he describes as imperialism's "cultural bomb, . . . [which] annihilate[s] a people's belief in their names, in their languages, in their environment, in their heritage of struggle, in their unity, in their capacities and ultimately in themselves. It makes them see their past as one wasteland of non-achievement and it makes them want to distance themselves from that wasteland." [27] Ato wishes to be happy, and, because of this desire, he envisions the future as a transcendental romantic never-never land (10).

It is significant that, although Eulalie has "tourist brochure" (9) images of Africa, she is the one who keeps questioning the actions of Ato, his family, and herself. In short, she is, throughout most of the play, very much aware of herself as sujet-en-soi—a person caught between two conflicting ideological practices. This awareness forces upon her the beginnings of a critical consciousness; however, she never becomes a "subject" or "individual-as-subject" in the sense that I have defined it. Her desire to "belong somewhere again" (9) is a desire to be a person, to be a subject, and thus fulfill her historical and existential calling to be more completely and consciously human. That throughout most of the play her in-laws referred to her as the "wayfarer" speaks to her marginality and oppression in both America *and* Ghana as an African-American woman. This appellation also alerts us to the de-centered aspect of her character, while hinting at the reversals of subject-positions (between herself and Ato, and between her and the narrator) that are to take place as the drama proceeds. Her eagerness at the beginning of the play to accept Ato's views of the Ghanaian reality underscores the limitations of her awareness of the multiple determinants of her existence (9). She merely wants to substitute one set of cultural practices for another without critically questioning what such a substitution would mean for her becoming a fuller person, or "individual-as-subject."

The solemnity of the latter part of Eulalie's affirmation of her lasting love for Ato and her wish that his gods become hers (4) could be construed as derivative: "The Bible is an evident shaping-force throughout African literature style. There are frequent biblical allusions in *The Dilemma*, all of them placed judiciously and skillfully, to reinforce Miss Aidoo's dramatic vision. They bring the universal applications of the play's dilemma into sharp relief. . . . And [referring to the previous quotation] towards the end of the prelude, one finds echoes of the Book of Ruth" (Chapman, 35–36). A discussion of the origin of Aidoo's "solemn" language is less interesting to me than that Eulalie's requests have the tone of marriage vows, in the Western sense, and that Ato's affirmative replies are contradicted by his subsequent actions in the play. Furthermore, even if we take the language as biblical or as direct transcription from Fanti,[28] it only confirms, in the first instance, the overdetermination of the Christian ideology and colonialism in the lives of the two protagonists, and of Aidoo, the writer, and, in the second instance, points to Ato's desire for the flight or escape from his society I mentioned earlier.

Another important question that Eulalie raises pertains to having children and the role of a mother and a wife in the Ghanaian/African context. She is obviously very anxious about the consequences of her wish to postpone having a child, for she is aware that this might cause conflicts, either with Ato or with her in-laws. Ato is completely oblivious to her justified fears (10). His dismissal of them and her acceptance of his superficial assurances indicate the complexity of their conditioning. Ato's replies clearly reflect both his cultural-nationalistic arrogance and his male chauvinism. He is unable to appreciate the import of Eulalie's doubts, and, in his dismissal of those doubts, he reaffirms our suspicions about his reluctance to honestly confront his history. He falls into the trap of assuming the posture of the "benign" paternalistic oppressor. Eulalie reveals the limitations of her own subjective discomfort in relation to taking on the roles of Ghanaian wife, mother, and family member. Her willingness to acquiesce to Ato's better judgment brings to light her double oppression as a woman and a miseducated African-American, a "wayfarer." Both characters are unable to see beyond the limits of their own historical and ideological determinations. To paraphrase Kwame Nkrumah, a woman in the grip of neopaternalism is not mistress of her own destiny (Nkrumah, 1966).

In the second scene of act 2, Eulalie is apparently talking to herself (23–25); this scene can be taken as a soliloquy or a "dialogue of disembodied voices," however, delivered as a monologue. The latter view would emphasize the marginal status of Eulalie in relation to the Odumna Clan — "this / Black-white woman. / A stranger and a slave" (22)—and would echo the insubstantiality of the protean narrator of the prelude, the Bird of the Wayside, cementing the link between Eulalie and the narrator. Eulalie's cigarette smoking, her lighter, her ashtray, and her bottle of Coca-Cola remain symbols of her Americanness. On the imaginary and more emotive level, the disembodied dialogue is a conversation between Eulalie and her dead mother. Therefore, on the symbolic level, the exchange illustrates Eulalie's attempt to confront her own history. Yet this chat, set against the background of African drumming, can only be a half-hearted engagement, rooted as it is in a subjective, antiracist racism: "Ma, ain't I telling the whole of the States to go swing! Congress, Jew and white trash" (24). She is still being "hailed" by that which she seeks to escape. Her resistance to the racism of Euro-America is a personal-cultural one; yet this desire for a pristine Africa—"the very source" (24)—uncontaminated by the racist oppression of the United States is problematic. Alternatively, Eulalie's admission that "I adore the old one [Nana]"(24) might appropriately be characterized more positively. Nana represents the living link with the past and the future; thus Eulalie's attraction to her opens up the possibility of escaping the ideological reach of her American past and the frustration of her neocolonial present.

When the sound of the drums interrupts her tête-à-tête, we suddenly see how scared she is of the new reality (25–26), a reality as intimidating as the American reality she has sought to escape by marriage to Ato Yawson. But this is only because she cannot fully understand either reality. She still has images "of the jungle and the wild life. . . . And I haven't seen a lion yet!" (24) she admits to herself. Nevertheless, she can understand that life in the United States, particularly for a black person, can be tenuous. "Sugar, don't let them do you in," her dead mother warns. Eulalie understands that those suffering the triple oppressions of class, race, and gender have little chance of creating a wholesome life for themselves. "And how can one make a family in Harlem? Ma . . . with her hands chapped with washing to keep me in College" (24). Similarly, in a more unconscious way, her dialogue with her dead mother symbolizes the connection with the past and present cultural traditions (ideological practices) of Africa. Aidoo shows that this is a tie that the Middle Passage, the forced transportation of Africans to the Americas, never severed. In many respects, such a proposition anticipates Amilcar Cabral's observation that "a people who free themselves from foreign domination will be free culturally only if, without complexes and without underestimating the importance of positive accretions from the oppressor and other cultures, they return to the upward paths of their own culture, which is nourished by the living reality of its environment, and which negates both harmful influences and any kind of subjection to foreign culture."[29] This cultural link becomes all the more important because of Eulalie's intuitive fondness for Nana, the Old One, who knows that the domain of the ancestors is really one end of a continuum of which we are a part. It also foregrounds the reconciliation and acceptance of Eulalie into her Ghanaian family—it is what motivates Esi Kom, at the closing moments of *The Dilemma*, to say:

> We must be careful with your [Ato's] wife
> You tell us her mother is dead.
> If she had any tenderness,
> Her ghost must be keeping watch over
> All which happens to her. . . .
> [There is a short silence, then clearly to EULALIE]
> Come, my child.
> [And with that, Esi Kom supports Eulalie through
> the door that leads into the old house].
>
> (52)

This emphasis on the restorative function of culture, in the context of neo-colonial oppression, is underscored by Aidoo's grounding of the drama in history.

In contrast to Eulalie's attempts to immerse herself in her adopted culture, uncertain and tentative though they are, Ato's reaction to her fear and disorientation only serves to confirm further my earlier characterization of him as sujet-en-soi. The juxtaposition of Eulalie's observation that coconuts are "much cooler, sweeter and more nourishing" (26) and Ato's awkward admission that he also is thirsty and would like "gin and water" (26) goes to further emphasize his alienation from the culture that nurtured him. His arrogant sexism and contempt for his own culture underlie his dismissal of Eulalie's request to start a family (27). Ato cannot grant Eulalie enough respect even to admit that her change of mind is due to observation and rational thought. The implication of his utterances is that women are all emotion—"They are always getting feelings"—and that he, a man, is intellectual, cerebral, and logical. In this respect, Ato Yawson is like George Andrews, one of the protagonists and narrative voices in Gloria Naylor's *Mama Day*. Interestingly, Andrews is an orphan who is brought up in an institution, the Wallace P. Andrews Shelter for Boys, and believes that "only the present has potential."[30] Ato, haplessly, has none of these potentially redeeming virtues, although both are, in a sense, living without histories. Ato's denial of his wife's request to start a family is unforgivable, especially since he had earlier promised that "we should postpone having children *for as long as you want*"(10; italics added). The reversal of his promise is really not unexpected, for Ato, the petit bourgeois intellectual, is, in Fanon's terms, a black man trapped behind a white mask. The logic of his assumed white identity dictates that he need not respect any agreement made to an inferior person, if such an agreement does not advance his self-interest or protect his ego.

The ideological assumptions of both Eulalie and her new Ghanaian family give rise to the seemingly irreconcilable encounter between the West and Africa. The dialogical exchange cannot take place, because the culturally distanced linguistic and social practices of the two principals, in their struggle toward meaning, paradoxically prevent the possibility of mutual comprehension. Each makes irreconcilable claims. Eulalie's involve her being an (African-)*American,* and thus insisting on her right to the benefits of that nation's hegemonic practices; Ato's status of the One Scholar to him necessitates an insularity beyond the pressure even to communicate. Ato Yawson, historically chosen as mediator by his traditional upbringing and Western education, is too immature, vacillating, and confused to be an effective arbiter. He is unable to see what is really at stake behind the all-too-pressing problems of childbearing, infertility, and exogamy, which threaten the very stability of the society to which he has returned.

In marrying Ato, Eulalie Rush, "the daughter of slaves," seeks to reestablish her roots, *to become and to belong;* yet her upbringing and education have ill prepared her for this humbling and traumatic encounter with her past and possible future. To her, Africa is simultaneously a "Promised Land" and the "Dark Continent" of popular fiction. Even as she craves the consumerism of the United States and the West, she recognizes that capitalism and its bourgeois ideology (in all its global variants) dehumanizes her. She wants desperately to understand her continued oppression and victimization and to reach some reconciliation with her past. Her inability to effect such a transformation on her own prompts her to hide within herself. She attacks those around her, thinking they are the causes of her problems, yet she is unaware that this offensive has the same ideological-material bases as her earlier subordination and present confusion (46–48). Despite her own efforts, she recognizes that, even in the "Promised Land," her marginalization seems to be proceeding unabated and undebated under the (mis)direction of her "Moses," her husband (41–45).

The final act begins with a confrontation between Eulalie and Ato. In this act thematic threads are brought together in the tradition of Western drama; however, true to the dilemma convention, the complications are not fully resolved. Eulalie's bitter accusations are directed against Ato, rather than against the traditions and the values of the family on whom he has turned his back. Eulalie's repeated reference to Ato as "Moses" not only emphasizes his intimate emotional relationship to Eulalie as her savior—the one to lead her from her American bondage to the promised homeland—but also signifies his symbolic role as a leader of his people out of the prison of neocolonialism. Ato typifies the petit bourgeois vacillation of the Ghanaian intellectual, who simultaneously sees himself as leader of "my people" (47) and eschews the responsibility of leadership because he is a "damned rotten coward of a Moses" (47). Ato's self-identification with "my people" is sustained only as a temporary defense against the accusations of Eulalie. It is Ato's arrogance toward his people that is the real target of Eulalie's vitriolic tirade, rather than a sense of superiority vis-à-vis the members of the Odumna Clan. Eulalie's outburst comes out of a refusal to be further dehumanized, to be treated as an object by Ato, who sees himself as superior to both his family and his wife.

Unlike the opening scene of act 3, in which the boy and girl dispute over what game to play, this scene does not end with a reconciliation. The two scenes parallel each other, however, in that the verbal combat quickly escalates into physical violence and ends with Ato (the boy) hitting Eulalie (the girl). Later, the two neighbors come out after having been awakened by Ato's cries. They see his figure as it crumples onto the terrace, and the second woman remarks, "It looks like a . . . ghost" (48). The midnight chat reveals the attitude of villagers, which goes beyond mere curiosity or gossip and has its basis in a genuine concern for harmony and peace (48–49). The recognition by both neighbors that the "game" has only begun also indicates a shifting of sympathy toward Eulalie—the stranger. This indicates the displacement of Ato from the emotional center of the drama and foregrounds the "reconciliation" between Esi Kom and Eulalie.

The midnight confrontation between Ato and his mother emphasizes Aidoo's rejection of the ideologically untenable position of the Ato Yawsons of neocolonial Ghanaian/African society. Esi Kom's sarcasm is not aimed at Eulalie, whom she now sees as an unwitting victim of her son's spinelessness and chauvinism, but at Ato's cowardly arrogance: "Why did you not tell us that you and your wife are gods and you can create your own children when you want them? . . . and yet who can blame her [Eulalie]? No stranger ever breaks the law. . . . Hmm . . . my son. You have not dealt with us well. And you have not dealt with your wife well in this" (51–52).

It is this realization of her son's inability to be more than a "shadow in the corner" that allows Esi Kom to see him as a traitor, as it were, since "before the stranger should dip his finger / Into the thick palm nut soup, / It is a townsman / Must have told him to" (52). Esi Kom's attitude, coupled with the knowledge that Eulalie's mother has died, makes the reconciliation between Ato's mother and her daughter-in-law all the more plausible. And yet this embrace, this emotional meeting of precolonial and neocolonial ideologically opposed subjects, should not overshadow the significance of the play's ending with the petit bourgeois intellectual, Ato Yawson, center stage, albeit reduced to a confused and ineffective ghost, unable to decide whether to go to the East or the West—to Cape Coast or Elmina. Historically, both Cape Coast and Elmina (the mine) were staging posts for the penetration of the hinterland. Cape Coast, the former capital of colonial Gold Coast, was and is regarded as an intellectual and educational center as well; while Elmina, as the Portuguese name suggests, was the conduit through which the human and mineral wealth (slaves and gold) was channeled to the centers of European imperialism and the New World.

In "Generations in Conflict," John Nagenda disapproves of the ending, asserting that it is "artificial and unconvincing." He further complains that "by itself, each speech works, [but] there isn't enough interplay between them to make them into a complete play" (107–8). It seems that Nagenda's verdict is based on the assumption that all "complete" plays (and one suspects that he also implies *good*) must conform to Aristotelian descriptions of properly constructed dramas, or, at least, to Shakespearean or more generally speaking European models.

So Ato Yawson, the petit bourgeois intellectual, the "Moses" of the Ghanaian/African people, stands at the crossroads, and he must choose which road to take. At the very moment that things threaten to "fall apart," it is Ato's mother, the uneducated villager, who holds things together by reaching out and embracing Eulalie, the "unwilling prodigal." Ato Yawson, left outside in the dark—between the old and new wings of the Odumna Clan house—becomes the "wayfarer," the bird of the wayside. It is this change that confirms the relationship between Ato and the ghost at Elmina Junction.

His indecision serves to underscore Aidoo's use of the dilemma tale as a means to draw attention to the nature of the conflicts that characterize Ghanaian neocolonial society. The apparent resolution of the family dilemma, seen in Esi Kom's embrace of Eulalie, is itself tenuous, especially in the context of a society and future that are indefinite: "The young people of the coming days / Are strange . . . very strange. / Fear them, my sister" (38). The One Scholar whose education has cost so much, whose return is seen as a deliverance (7–8), has become a ghost incapable of choosing his destiny. Such immobility on the supernatural level is, for a ghost, ominous, for the fast-approaching dawn will signal the end of whatever power or authority such an insubstantial entity once had. On the sociopolitical level, Ato Yawson, the representative of the neocolonial intellectual, is paralyzed; he is unable to decide about his role in the struggles that have arisen as an inevitable consequence of the antagonistic contradictions during the immediate postindependence era.

Aidoo's deployment of the dilemma tale convention vitally alters the nature and experience of the drama itself; such use forces the audience to eschew simple answers to the problems of gender, race, and class as they come together in the public and private interstice of the social relations of the major characters. So, even though the struggle seems to be centered on Ato, the end of *The Dilemma* destroys that image. Ato Yawson is unable to make a choice because he refuses to confront his and our history honestly, to answer unequivocally the hailings of both the antagonistic ideological material practices and the characters within the drama. Aidoo in her first drama effectively uses the traditional dilemma tale to expose the problems that are symptomatic of neocolonial Ghanaian society; at the same time, she forces the audience to adopt an engaged position vis-à-vis the issues raised by the conflicts between and within the characters. The open-endedness of the drama prevents the audience from remaining on the emotional or imaginary level of reconciliation. The uneasiness that most audiences will experience forces a distancing and a recognition that the ideological-material struggle is not over, as the first woman of the chorus observes in the final act: "And this is only the beginning" (49). Yet the drama actually ends with the erasure of the petit bourgeois protagonist and the fading echo of the children singing the ghost's song of indecision.

# *Anowa*: In History

*Fere ne owuo efenim owuo.*
(If it is a matter of choosing
between disgrace and death,
then I shall prefer death.)
—Akan proverb

Aidoo's first play, *The Dilemma of a Ghost*, is only a beginning. It takes off from the experiences of her Ghanaian audience, primarily composed of petit bourgeois intellectuals and a few members of the national bourgeoisie and working classes. It deals with what was and, in certain respects, still is the most fundamental sociopolitical problem for this audience. In exposing the bankruptcy of Ghana's intellectual leadership, Aidoo brought to the immediate attention of her audience the dilemmas that arise from the complex articulations of gender, race, and class issues within a neocolonial context. Such reminders, and the attendant questions left unanswered, need an appropriate response: How are we to change our circumstances when all we experience seems so onerous? As the potential leaders of what must be a revolutionary transformation of society are we condemned—like Ato Yawson—to a spectral contrapuntal immobility? Are we deaf to the competing voices that demand to be heard and answered? Although the contemporary issues left unresolved in Aidoo's first play are more fully addressed in her later works and will be discussed later in this study, the play *Anowa* requires immediate attention, since its historical character helps to illuminate Aidoo's subsequent works.[1]

A major contributing factor to Ato Yawson's failure in *The Dilemma* was his inability to honestly confront his own and the people's histories; in *Anowa*, her second play, Aidoo takes us back to a moment in which we may more honestly confront those histories. The play's action draws upon the historical circumstances that significantly contributed to the situation presented in Aidoo's first drama. *Anowa* enables us to better see how, as social beings, as both producers and products, we are implicated in the transmission and perpetuation of our past in our present and possible futures. Without the deliberate recovery of these histories, in the context of the struggles of *real people*, Aidoo's audience will have only an abstract notion of why the perplexities of neocolonialism so circumscribe our lives and seem to continually narrow the horizon of our expectations. Must we hang about in the darkness not knowing whether to go West or East, to the old wing or the new wing, to Elmina or to Cape Coast? And yet the formulation of this choice may itself be false, because "[we] can't tell" (*The Dilemma*, 53) without confronting the history, the road that led to our arrival at this particular junction. That is, until we can resituate Aidoo's ideological problematic within the social and political history of Ghana, the actions depicted in her first play remain mere abstractions or fictions.

We must place the text in the real world and comprehend it as part of the creative rendering of historical processes that have not yet ended. *Anowa* concerns a specific period of Ghana's colonial past and attempts to delineate the evolution of the ideological repercussions and the life narratives dramatized in *The Dilemma*. In terms of the general history of the geographical area now called Ghana and, more especially, of the coastal area between Accra in the east, Sekondi-Takoradi in the west, and Kumasi to the north, *Anowa*'s time line starts in the fifteenth century. This period marks the beginnings of a shift, in what may be characterized as a wholly African trade, toward a transoceanic and emergent global commercial network.[2] By 1471 the Portuguese had reached Elmina, and in the decades that followed there developed a more or less mutually beneficial and respectful trade in African gold, ivory, and pepper for European manufactures. Although originating as a direct and limited importation into Europe, the trade in slaves quickly expanded, as the expropriation of land for the development of plantations in the Americas and the Caribbean became systematized.[3] Among the many consequences of this early trade was the additional stimulation of the political and economic ambitions of coastal western African states. The Denkyira, who had been the dominant power in the area, soon found themselves subjugated by their northeastern neighbors, the Ashanti. These military and commercial ambitions were often realized at the expense of smaller states like the Fanti. During a series of wars between the 1660s and 1750s, under the leadership of the first three kings of the Oyoko Clan—Obiri Yeboah, Osei Tutu, and Opoku Ware—the Ashanti extended their nominal authority south to Elmina, north to Dagomba, and east to Akwamu.[4]

The rise of the Ashanti did not go unchallenged, for others among the Akan had similar political and economic aspirations. By the beginning of the eighteenth century a series of independent Fanti states, which stretched from the Ga State in the east to the River Pra in the west, had formed a political union (July, 1974, 147). This union was not as hierarchically or centrally organized as the Ashanti nation, which was an ever-present threat to the independence of the union's membership. Along the coast, however, a number of forts, castles, and trading posts testified to the long and complex history of European contact with the Fanti in particular, and other peoples of the Gold Coast. After the Portuguese came the Dutch, Danes, English, French, Brandenburgers (Prussians), and Swedes; however, by the 1790s only the Dutch and the British were a significant non-African presence in the area. The Ashanti, after defeating Denkyira, had become trading partners with the Dutch, and eventual controllers of Elmina Castle.[5] Meanwhile, the Fanti were in a worthwhile partnership with the English, who used the Cape Coast Castle as a major trading and administrative base, in addition to several forts along the Fanti-controlled coast. By the end of the first decade of the nineteenth century, the Ashanti Empire exerted influence over most of present-day Ghana, and some important areas of modern Ivory Coast and Togo felt the consequence of its hegemony.

The political, military, and commercial situation along the coast during the latter part of the 1700s was one of brinkmanship. The British government distrusted the Ashanti for military and commercial reasons; however, the British were in no position to do much about either Ashanti power or their own merchants' desire to profit. The desire of English traders to acquire wealth was to benefit the Fanti in their struggle with their kinspeople, the Ashanti. Always suspicious of Ashanti expansionism, the Fanti states were able to draw the often unwilling British government into their disputes with the Ashanti over sovereignty and trading rights. This climate of distrust, fear, and manipulation led to a succession of small-scale clashes, which were followed by treaties and, eventually, a series of full-scale wars between the British and the Ashanti.[6]

The delicate balance of power between the Fanti, Ashanti, and British was radically altered in 1806 when Osei Bonsu, the new Asantehene, attacked and defeated the Fanti army in the state of Abura. The antagonistic forces of local politics, economic demands, and imperialist ambitions (both British and Ashanti) were to collide in open war; the result was the defeat of the Ashanti and British penetration into the interior of what is modern Ghana at the close of the nineteenth century. The events that immediately preceded the establishment of de jure colonial rule by the British are pivotal to an appreciation and understanding of Aidoo's second play.

In *Anowa*, Aidoo deploys the convention of the dilemma tale in a seemingly less obvious manner than in *The Dilemma*. This more covert use of the dilemma tale, coupled with the overt use of a traditional tale or legend, has led many commentators of *Anowa* to see it as "more indebted than . . . the first play to oral literature" (Brown, 1981, 90).[7] Aidoo, in an interview with Maxine McGregor, remarked that "[*Anowa*] is very different from *The Dilemma*. This is set in the latter part of the nineteenth century in what was then the Gold Coast, and it's more or less my own rendering of a kind of . . . legend, because, according to my mother, who told me the story, it is supposed to have happened" (Pieterse and Duerden, 23). The disobedient daughter tale, in its starkest outline, is common in many West African societies, but Aidoo's treatment of it differs from standard versions in many respects. Most relevant here is that Aidoo has chosen to place the action "in the latter part of the nineteenth century in what was then the Gold Coast." The play is thus set against the background of rising British colonial ambitions in Fantiland. Aidoo's second drama more clearly than the first shows the connection between sexual oppression and colonial domination. She succeeds in delineating the convergence of forces, both internal and external, that accelerated the marginalization of women in colonial and neocolonial Africa. What comes through in Aidoo's play is that the issues of gender oppression are materially based, that the dominant social relations that arise and are part of the economic production relations of a given society, at a particular historical moment, produce specific modes of behavior or cultural practices. These practices may not be the result of deliberate or malicious intent by individuals in that society. But neither is it one's destiny to accept cultural practices that one finds abhorrent or counter-productive.

As I have already suggested, Aidoo does not abandon *the techniques* of the oral tradition just because she has opted to use a traditional legend as the basis of her second play. True to the dilemma tale convention and Aidoo's authorial need, the drama's resolution—in a double suicide—is illusory and unsatisfactory. Just as the traditional dilemma tale lacks a clear-cut termination, so *Anowa* lacks any specific resolution or anagnorisis. The drama has two possible endings. As Aidoo indicates in the play's prefatory production notes: "It is possible to end the play with the final exit of ANOWA. Or one could follow the script and permit THE-MOUTH-THAT-EATS-SALT-AND-PEPPER to appear for the last scene. The choice is open" (63). This option is offered because the contradictions, the multiple modes of ideological and economic domination typical of the advent of classical colonialism in the then Gold Coast, still hail us in this age of neocolonialism. The director's or reader's choice speaks of the same forces, though modified and disguised, that lead to the tragedy of *Anowa*. We are left with a haunting historical legacy that must be demystified, along with more pressing problems to be resolved, by our own animated discussions and actions *after* the performance.

By 1816 the Ashanti finally gained the upper hand over the Fanti. This clear-cut victory resulted in the British government or, more correctly, the British Company of Merchants (BCM) signing a treaty that recognized the Ashanti as overlords of the Fanti. In addition, the British governor or his representative was to investigate all complaints made by the Ashanti against their Fanti subjects.[8] The British government gave the BCM de facto control of the castles and European-African trading contacts along the Fanti coast. In return, the government expected the BCM to put an end to both the transatlantic and domestic slave trade in the area. The BCM could do very little, without military support, about the problem of slavery. Ultimately, profit and the maintenance of the status quo determined that the British Company of Merchants did nothing to antagonize the foremost military power in the area.[9]

By the start of the second decade of the nineteenth century, politics in England led to the revocation of the BCM's control of affairs along the coast of Fantiland. After the abolition of the company, Sir Charles Macarthy, governor of Sierra Leone, took over control of the forts in 1822. Disdainful of the Ashanti, Macarthy soon found an excuse to move against them. Apparently, an Ashanti trader insulted the governor, and a policeman, in the service of the British, replied by insulting the Asantehene. The Ashanti authorities arrested the policeman and detained him at the inland town of Dunkwa. In January 1824 Macarthy's forces confronted the Ashanti only to be routed. Macarthy was wounded and later committed suicide to avoid capture. In order to save face, the British government in 1826 commanded a combined British and Fanti army to attack the Ashanti. This expedition proved more successful, and the Ashanti signed a treaty in 1831 restoring independence to the Fanti, Denkyira, and Assin and lifting trade restrictions. With respect to one of the major issues in *Anowa*, the British demand that the Ashanti also deposit over five hundred ounces of gold and send two princes to the British as a gesture of good faith raises questions about the legitimacy of the British desire to end domestic and international slavery.[10] Then the British government formally withdrew from direct intervention in the region, allowing the English merchants and their Fanti counterparts to sort things out among themselves.

The merchants appointed Captain George Maclean, a shrewd and ambitious diplomat, as governor in 1828 (W. E. F. Ward, 189–206).[11] By slowly introducing his own police in various Fanti towns and acting as the judicial authority in local disputes, he embarked on a process of *informal colonialization*. As his personal power increased, Maclean did nothing about either domestic slavery or the illegal transatlantic variety. Eventually, complaints about what were regarded by many as his autocratic and self-serving activities prompted the British government to take action. A select committee of the House of Commons, acting on the report of a Dr. Madden, met in 1842. Rather than censure Maclean—for all the charges proved true—the British turned the de facto colonization of Fantiland by Maclean into de jure colonization under the authority of the governor of Sierra Leone.

By 1844, Maclean and the lieutenant-governor, a Captain Hill, had negotiated a number of separate but interconnected treaties with the chiefs of the nineteen Fanti states. These treaties, or bonds as they were more often called, not only legalized Maclean's imposition of the British legal system throughout Fantiland but—and this was perhaps more insidious— obligated the British to protect the signatories in case of aggression from the Ashanti, who were seen as the principle enemy of the British (and of the Fanti).[12] Collectively, these treaties were subsumed under a very brief document, rather dubiously perceived by some British historians as the Magna Carta of the Gold Coast but more popularly known as the Bond of 1844.[13] It is striking that 6 March, the date in 1844 on which the bond was signed by almost half the nineteen Fanti chiefs, was the same date that marked Ghana's independence from British rule in 1957.

Between the signing of the bond and the death of Fanti politician John Mensah-Sarbah in 1930 the Fanti people received a number of conflicting signals from their so-called British protectors.[14] In 1865, a British government committee advised that, excepting Sierra Leone, all West African "colonies" were to be cut loose to "encourage in the natives the exercise of those qualities which may render it possible for us more and more to transfer to them the administration of all Governments."[15] In 1868, however, when King Aggrey of Cape Coast and the other Fanti rulers formed a confederation as the initial step toward complete independence and an organized platform for the protection of their rights, the British opposed it (Kimble, 192–221). Under the leadership of Sir Garnet Wolseley, the British finally defeated the Ashanti in 1874, converting the former protectorate and the Ashanti domains into the British crown colony of the Gold Coast. This action was vehemently opposed by a coalition of the traditional rulers and the intelligentsia of the various micro-nations, including the Fantis.[16]

It is in and against this context of rising nationalism and aggressive British imperialism that we must situate *Anowa*. In many ways this drama echoes and modifies the popular folk tale of the disobedient daughter, a tale which has received varied treatment from writers like Amos Tutuola and Efua Sutherland.[17] Anowa, the strong-willed titular heroine, refuses to marry any of the bachelors in her hometown of Yebi. Anowa, to the chagrin of her mother, Badua, chooses a less than exemplary young man, Kofi Ako, with whom she elopes. The young couple start a trading business between the hinterland and the coast. Anowa's indefatigable energy is a major factor in their eventual prosperity; however, their relationship deteriorates as rapidly as their wealth increases. The clash of personalities and values leads to mutual recriminations and ends in madness and death.

Unfortunately, critical reactions to *Anowa* have focused attention on certain aspects of the content of the drama without taking a fuller account of the formal characteristics of the play, its wider historical significance, and its relationship to Aidoo's first drama. This critical response has been limited to a handful of reviews and short critiques and even fewer longer studies. Like those of Aidoo's first play, these critiques reveal more about the critic's ideological assumptions than about the drama. To be fair, many of these works avoid the gross misreadings typical of the first wave of criticism concerning *The Dilemma*. In fact, the most significant feature of the longer critiques is that each attempts a radical interpretation of *Anowa*. They range from quasi-materialist critiques that incorporate a relatively larger contextual framework surrounding a normative humanist analysis indicative of mainstream Western scholarship, to radical feminist perspectives, to limited orthodox Marxist-nationalist approaches. Of course, each strategy evidences an overlap of ideological perspectives.

In his critique of *Anowa*, Lloyd Brown comes close to a genuinely revealing appraisal of Aidoo's second play, more thorough than that of many other critics. Yet despite his insights into the historical complexities of the drama, he ultimately restricts *our* perception of the play by insisting that Anowa, the character, is the morally superior woman who valiantly resists the abuse and misuse of *power* by men (and some women) in a society that supports and encourages sexist exploitation and oppression. We are led to believe that Anowa's struggle is the measure of individualism and freedom (Brown, 1981, 95, 98). Brown seems to be unaware of the ideological assumptions implicit in his own assessment of the central issues of Aidoo's play. He posits a Western imperialist celebration of what only *seems* to be subjective individualism in its most positive aspect of validating individual choice, as opposed to what is seen as traditional African values that deny the possibility of choice. This occlusion of other tendencies in the social and cultural world of *Anowa* may explain why, in spite of Brown's frequent references to the historical circumstances that precede the events depicted in Aidoo's drama (Brown, 1981, 91–94, 98–99), he fails to realize the full extent of the power of the ideological determinants of *the specific historical and socioeconomic confluence at which the characters are caught*. By so doing, his analysis lifts *Anowa* out of the historical context that gives particular significance to the dilemmas and actions faced and effected by the characters of this drama. Brown's conflation of past and present leads him to an ahistorical valuation of the drama's significance for Aidoo's primary audience. Such an interpretation prevents a "symptomatic reading" (Althusser, 249–58) of the text.

Aidoo divides her play into three parts or "phases." These major divisions are bracketed, if we take the text-performance to the "last" page, by the arguments and observations of The-Mouth-That-Eats-Salt-and-Pepper, the play's internal chorus/audience. The Old Man and the Old Woman together constitute the chorus and audience of the unfolding drama in which we also participate, the locus of the ideological struggle is temporarily de-centered. The text-performance, framed as a dilemma tale, demands our critical participation in exploring the problematic of knowledge and of what constitutes the consciousness of a sujet-pour-soi or subject—not only within the play, but also outside it, among us, the audience. The dual speakers of the prologue call forth this critical polylectic consciousness from the audience *before* the chronological unfolding of the play's action.

The prologue and coda—the "last" scene of phase 3—directly involve the external audience in the performance. Each of the phases or parts ends with either the Old Woman or the Old Man having the last word; Aidoo thus sets up a complex dialectic between female and male, as well as between the voices that support either the status quo or progressive change. These structural repetitions that precede, follow, and punctuate the realistic action focus our attention on the conditions that determine the personal fates of Kofi Ako and Anowa, even as we recognize that their lives arise from a specific sociohistorical context. This attenuation of our consciousness prevents us from oversimplifying the problem that, in the real world, still confronts Aidoo's contemporary audience.[18]

Consistent with the historical rootedness of this play, the prologue of *Anowa* is dominated by a chorus of two elders, male and female, rather than by the protean transhistorical figure of the Bird of the Wayside. The Old Man and the Old Woman—collectively referred to as The-Mouth-That-Eats-Salt-and-Pepper—represent the antagonistic contradictions of traditional society. These local contradictions are part of a global polylectic which expresses the opposition between the matrilineal gerontocracy of semifeudal Fanti society during the ascendancy of British colonialism. The Old Man also symbolizes the progressive tendencies within that social dynamic, while the Old Woman stubbornly clings to the status quo, even in the face of the changes overtaking that society. This unity of opposites, as chorus, reverses and completes the obverse relationship of Anowa and Kofi Ako, while also reflecting the relatively subdued relationship between Osam and Badua, Anowa's parents.

The Old Man's opening address to the audience is calculated to give an objective though partial view of the larger historical movements from which arise the peculiar circumstances that give the legend of Anowa dramatic significance. In the role of traditional raconteur, the Old Man invites the audience into the dramatic performance (65–67) in much the same way that the narrator, Bird of the Wayside, did in *The Dilemma*. The diachronic relationship between the prologues of the two plays is significant: first, *Anowa* situates the subsequent action within a spatially and temporally specific context, whereas in *The Dilemma* we are told that the action "all began on a University Campus; never mind where. The evening was cool as evenings are . . . I heard the voices of a man and a woman speaking" (8). Second, having rejected the *leading role* of the petit bourgeois intellectual—by ending her first play with Ato Yawson, the One Scholar, transformed into a metaphoric ghost—Aidoo turns our attention to the role of the trader and emergent protonational bourgeois comprador in her second play. Significantly, Anowa and Kofi Ako, by opting for a life of trading with the "white men / Who came from beyond the horizon" (68), become "wayfarers" in relation to the conservative standards of the traditional social order. Although Kofi sees himself as fundamentally at one with society, Anowa—in terms of the new social order—considers *herself* a "wayfarer" (97).

The Old Man's lyrical description of "the state of Abura" romantically recalls the religious and mythic antecedents of a land in which "everything happens in moderation" (65). He then counterbalances his mythopoetic celebration with an admission of the reality of political pressure (66): the threats to Fanti autonomy were multiple—while defending themselves against external aggression during the first part of the nineteenth century,

the Fanti also needed the "little peace" (66) in order to protect their economic hegemony in trade between the interior and the Europeans on the
coast. The Old Man goes further in his revelations concerning the Fanti
in particular, and the Gold Coast in general. He stresses that, in the past,
trade had a more sinister character:

> And yet, there is a bigger crime
> We have inherited from the clans incorporate
> Of which, lest we forget when the time does come,
> Those forts standing at the door
> Of the great ocean shall remind our children
> And the sea bear witness.
>
> (66)

This "bigger crime" is, of course, the European slave trade. Its presence in
the prologue reminds us of the prelude in Aidoo's first play, forging another
diachronic link through the thematic and structural elements of the two
dramas. "Those forts," symbols of colonial power, were and are reminders
of the complicity and active participation of African people in that degrad-
ing trafficking of human flesh. By stressing this historical connection in
the prologue, Aidoo forewarns the audience that the practice of (domestic) slavery, or panyarring, is to be an issue in the drama. The complexity
of the historical situation outlined by the Old Man, and in the brief overview given here, cannot be underestimated. As a semifeudal matrilineal,
corporate-kin society moving into an increasingly aggressive global capitalist system, the Fanti traders see their class interests firmly aligned with
those of the British imperialists, rather than with those of the Ashantis, or
even of the local traditional ruling class (66–67).[19]

The Old Man, in his double role as raconteur and chorus-audience,
understands the mutual determinations of class imperatives and personal
desires. In addition, he cautions us against the tendency to reject our own
people just because they have actively or unwittingly helped, for selfish or
personal (psychological) reasons, to consolidate colonial subjugation. For
"out of one womb [that is, the Gold Coast and Africa] can always come
a desperate breed" (67). In the context of the play, Kofi Ako represents
that "desperate breed." Implicit in the Old Man's commentary is the link
between Kofi and Anowa, who, in her own way, is also part of that "desper-

ate breed"—although her desperation arises from frustration rather than from personal greed. Anowa's dilemma is similar to that which the Ghost at Elmina Junction encountered in *The Dilemma*. She sees before her two paths that offer uncertainty and absence for her and for the generations of people she might bear (95–98). While the characters are grounded in a particular historical moment, the narrator singles out Kofi Ako in his next observation:

> O my beloveds, let it not surprise us then
> That This-One and That-One
> Depend for their well-being on the presence of
> The pale stranger in our midst:
> *Kofi was, is, and shall always be*
> *One of us.*
>
> (67; italics added)

The irony implicit in the Old Man's reference to dependence and "well-being" mirrors not only the historical complexities of the colonial encounter but also the relationship between Kofi and Anowa. As the drama unfolds we begin to see that Anowa is as emotionally, sexually, and psychologically dependent on Kofi as he is materially, economically, and psychologically dependent on "the pale stranger." The Old Man thus ends the opening part of his succinct introduction with an enigmatic question to the audience about Anowa: "But what shall we say of our child, / The unfortunate Anowa? Let us just say that / Anowa is not a girl to meet every day" (67). At this juncture, Aidoo introduces the Old Woman—the *other* of the chorus-audience, The-Mouth-That-Eats-Salt-and-Pepper—who has hitherto been absent. Her presence brings onto center stage the ideological opposites that are to struggle behind and through the actions we, as audience, are about to witness.

The character of Anowa, and the fate that befalls her and Kofi Ako, cannot be satisfactorily explained within the confines of a fictive or representational discourse. The Old Woman would have us accept, however, "[t]hat Anowa, is something else! Like all the beautiful maidens in the tales, she has refused to marry any of the sturdy men who have asked for her hand in marriage. No one knows what is wrong with her" (67). By overtly linking Anowa to the protagonists of the disobedient daughter folktales,

the Old Woman adds to the tragedy a melodramatic quality. By emphasizing the fictional correspondence between the drama we are about to
witness and actively participate in, Aidoo (through the Old Woman) sets
up a parallel link between a false consciousness (fictionalization) and the
Old Woman herself. In other words, we should not trust the Old Woman
as a reliable or unbiased narrator-participant. Further, by equating Anowa
with the fictional heroines of folktales, the Old Woman seeks to negate the
validity of Anowa's resistance to the status quo, thereby emphasizing her
unusualness and removing her from *historical* personalities who, in their
own ways, also resisted the restrictions and oppressiveness of the status
quo. The Old Woman sees Anowa as a type rather than a real character like
Dede Akaibi, the Ga Queen-Mother, who was assassinated in 1610, or Yaa
Asantewaa, the Ashanti Queen-Mother, who led the most stubborn and
effective military resistance to British colonial ambition ever witnessed in
Gold Coast.

Counterposed to the Old Woman's hostile undercutting of Anowa,
which effects a fictionalization of the fictional character, is the Old Man's
sympathetic defense of Anowa's struggle to be sujet-pour-soi. The Old
Man also insists that we take into account the actualities of history in reaching any judgment of the play and the characters. Because he is also an active
participant within the drama's temporal and cultural limits, his beliefs rest,
in part, on the assumption that there is an unbroken continuum of spiritual
and material (earthly) existence.[20] He thus asserts that Anowa is

> A child of several incarnations,
> She listens to her own tales,
> Laughs at her own jokes and
> Follows her own advice.

> (67)

Anowa has this privileged status because she is "a child of several incarna-
tions," or a spirit child.[21] The Old Man asks, "It is not too much to think
that the heavens might show something to children of a latter day which
was hidden from them of old?" (101) in a discussion with the Old Woman
about Anowa's "unusual" birth and life. The cultural (mystical) explanation
of Anowa's birth is shared by her father, who had always wanted her to be a
priestess. Osam asks his wife, Badua, "*Did you not consult them over and over*

*again when you could not get a single child from your womb to live beyond one day?*" (71; italics added). Anowa's eventual birth and growth into a young woman would be seen, given her mother's history of difficult births, as miraculous. Therefore, it would not be untoward to consider a child such as Anowa *unusual* in her "unusualness." From her mother's point of view she would be special, and this would lead to the general view voiced by the Old Woman that "Badua has spoilt her [Anowa] shamefully" (67). As soon becomes clear, however, Anowa is not "spoilt . . . shamefully." She is very independent-minded; it is perhaps this trait that prompts the Old Man—as the voice of the chorus who supports the upward paths of traditional Fanti culture and the critically mediated incorporation of positive aspects of foreign ideological practices—to so consistently support Anowa in his discussions with the Old Woman. The ideological position upheld by the Old Man is directly opposed to that of the Old Woman and Badua. Unlike Anowa, these two women seem to be satisfied with social relations as they are; therefore, they are sujets-en-soi because they are uncritical and even defend *the negative ideological hailing* of Fanti culture at this crucial historical juncture. In fact, both women can only explain Anowa's resistance to being satisfied with life as sujet-en-soi, as they are, by recourse to suggestions of vanity, witchcraft, and overindulgence (67–68).

Even though the prologue ends with the Old Woman having the last word, the Old Man's closing speech is of some importance to an appreciation of the drama that is about to be played out. The Old Man begins by calling the audience's attention to the fact that the play's chief characters are to be the center of the self-reflexive action (68). The implication is that (narrative) commentary is going to be absent, or at least minimized, a supposition immediately contradicted by his next utterance, and by the play itself. The dramatic discourse, predicated upon the dilemma tale technique, assumes the character of an "always-already-given structure" that effects its own deconstruction and, paradoxically, its reconstruction.[22] This is achieved by the foregrounding of the historical significance of the action by the Old Man's narrative commentary and by the realism of the activity of the characters. We have, in *Anowa*, a process of continual centering and de-centering of the action by the chorus-audience's participation and commentary in, and beyond, the formal ending(s) of the drama. The Old Man's final words in the prologue thus suggest the historicity of the fiction:

But here is Anowa,
And also Kofi Ako.
It is now a little less than thirty years
When the lords of our Houses
Signed that piece of paper—
The Bond of 1844 they call it—
Binding us to the white men
Who came from beyond the horizon.

(68)

The private drama of Anowa and Kofi Ako takes place during the 1870s against the public machinations of the rival European imperialist powers and the threat of Ashanti invasion. This reference to the European presence at the beginning of the play, and its specification in phase 3 by means of the ever-present portrait of Queen Victoria that hangs over the redundant fireplace in the central hall of Kofi Ako's Cape Coast house, emphasizes the importance of this historical moment in Ghana's colonial past. The Old Man's remarks in the prologue are generally spoken from a temporal space that comes after the "end" of the action about to be performed; they act as an ironic counterpoint to the Old Woman's and Badua's conventional observations about the *baffling* character of Anowa. These latter commentaries, however, occupy a temporal space anterior to or simultaneous with the start of the action in phase 1 of the drama (67–68). The Old Woman, who has the last word in the prologue, predicts that "the gods will surely punish Abena Badua for refusing to let a born priestess dance!" (68). This seemingly vatic utterance also reveals the narrowness of a society that would strictly impose (as always already given) certain prescribed roles for individuals. The overdeterminacy of such ideological prescriptions, however, should not be taken as totally oppressive and restrictive; for, on one level, the Old Woman's prophesy in the end proves false. Abena Badua basks, for a limited time, in the reflected glory and success of her daughter and son-in-law; further, Anowa and Kofi Ako are the ones who end ingloriously.

The distancing elements of the drama that are foregrounded by references to the Atlantic and domestic slave trade, the Bond of 1844, and the transformation of traditional Fanti society, which would ordinarily alert one to the objective ideological problematic, are displaced by such readings as Brown's. Having displaced the problematic, Brown can proceed to assert confidently that

> if Kofi and the Old Woman are traditionalists in the narrow and suspect sense of repeating the errors of the past, then Anowa and the Old Man represent another kind of historical continuity. They embody the persistence of humane perspectives on the problems of power and identity in their culture. Taken together, both sides reflect the essential ambiguities of history itself, which is a continuous succession of events, legends and conventions that depend upon the individual capacity for humane wisdom or abusive power. In effect, both sides constitute the process, intrinsic to the play itself, of interpreting and responding to the continuum of social history. (Brown, 1981, 99)

On the contrary, history has *no* "ambiguities." Rather the conflicting interpretations and distortions of the facts of history to serve specific ideological interests lead one to conclude that it has. Further, we begin to sense Brown's bourgeois intellectual bias, which is evidenced in the apparent dissolution of real work into abstraction, in short, a detachment from history. Thus he views this "continuum of social history" as separate from and external to the individual's existence. History becomes just "a succession of events, legends and conventions" that only elicit a *response from or an interpretation of* history's ontological status by the individuals who "embody the persistence of humane perspectives on the problems of power and identity in their culture."

Yet Brown points out that dramatists like Aidoo and Sutherland

> are concerned with that concept of theatre in which the dramatic art, like the art of oral literature, will be experienced and judged on the basis of its integration with both established and changing customs. In this sense, theatre as a living tradition does not depend on those familiar criteria of permanence and fixed meanings which are often offered as the only significant characteristics of "major" literature.

This view of theatre is more consistent with the oral artist's custom of combining a sense of permanence with a process of continual change. (Brown, 1981, 99)

So while Brown's analysis points to an intimate relationship between Aidoo's use of her oral literary heritage and her secondary immersion in a formal Western literary tradition, Brown seems unaware of the potentially radical implications of this synthesis—both for the audience-critic and the drama itself. This blind spot leads him to the conclusion that "all of her [Anowa's] significant actions and judgements are rooted in the assumption that humaneness and moral integrity are *the crucial lessons to be derived from a full understanding of history*" (Brown, 98; italics added). Such an assertion could have been avoided if Brown had resisted conflating the textual and authorial ideologies and thus investing Anowa, the character, with a consciousness that rightly belongs to Aidoo. In short, it would be impossible (given Aidoo's conscious re-creation of, in her own words, a "sort of legend") for the protagonist of that drama or legend to have the kind of consciousness that Brown claims for the character. Anowa's tragedy arises precisely because her "significant actions and judgements" and her desires are overdetermined by the ideological contradictions and the economic transformations of *that particular historical moment* of which she is an active, though initially only a partially articulate, participant.

Sharing ideological ground with Lloyd Brown, Mary Nicholson shifts from a humanist viewpoint to a feminist one. Through this theoretical optic, she highlights some of the positive aspects of Anowa's character. Yet, like Brown, Nicholson seems to lift the play out of its historical moment and to present Anowa as a transhistorical figure representative of the "unusual" woman, a "heroine [who] lived ahead of her time. She is the foremother of the modern day articulate and assertive woman" (118).[23] This elevation of Anowa as the sole repository of tendencies already historically evident leads Nicholson to see the outcome of Anowa's struggle as predestined: "Her life could not have been otherwise. Her world was not ready for talented females like her" (119). Nicholson, impelled further by the logic of her own theoretical assumptions, equates the contradictions that frustrate Anowa's "creativity"—her "unusual" character and personal "tragedy"—with "the struggle of women for emancipation, the world over, [which] has been going on for centuries" (119). In *Anowa*, Aidoo eschews a narrowly conceived proposition that male domination and oppression is, *in the last instance,* determinate. In fact, by being so tenacious in her presentation of Anowa as a morally superior victim of a sexist social order, Nicholson appears to discount or minimize the complex articulation of the economic and ideological factors evidenced in Aidoo's "tragic" drama of *Anowa*.

Phase 1 takes place in Yebi and opens with a mime scene that is important in three major respects. The scene involves four characters: Anowa, Kofi Ako, and an anonymous couple who are the principal actors in the mime. Anowa walks on stage and sits down facing the audience. Kofi Ako creeps up behind her and startles the young woman. Then an anonymous woman carrying a tray of foodstuffs crosses in front of Anowa and Kofi. This woman is followed by her husband. As they exit, the woman keeps looking back at Kofi and Anowa, then trips and falls. Anowa and Kofi, as audience viewing a slapstick routine, burst into laughter. The woman's husband helps her up, and they gather the contents of the overturned tray and exit to the continued laughter of Anowa and Kofi. As short as this scene is it has multilayered implications.

First, it is an encapsulation of the period before the success Anowa and Kofi experience after their elopement, while at the same time it suggests the future development of their relationship. On one level it represents their naïveté and innocence in the face of life's harsh realities—accidents *do* happen. The woman's constant backward glances at Kofi and Anowa lead directly to her falling over and upsetting the tray of foodstuffs. In a similar way, Anowa's backward glances at her people's history and her husband's underdeveloped sensibility lead, in part, to the disruption of her relationship with him. Second, the scene depicts a nonantagonistic division of labor and a harmonious social relationship. When the accident does happen, the woman's husband readily and quickly assists her. This action contrasts sharply with Kofi Ako's behavior toward Anowa during the latter half of phase 2 and all of phase 3. Third, the scene recalls the complex nature of the relationship between the boy and the girl in Aidoo's first drama, *The Dilemma*. This intertextual echo illustrates Aidoo's ability to economically express the historical and ideological nexus that links fictional time (times past and future) with the real time (time now) of her dramas and the experience of the Ghanaian/African audience participants.

The next scene not only gives us an insight into the characters of Osam and his wife, Badua, but it also reveals in a direct manner exactly how high the ideological and personal stakes are. Even when it comes to such everyday considerations as choosing a marriage partner or occupation for one's daughter, neither Osam nor Abena Badua can assume the outcome. Osam is a man on the defensive and, like his wife, accepts the status quo, although for entirely different reasons. He is definitely sujet-en-soi and does not wish to be otherwise. All he wants is a "little peace"—an easy way out of any problem. So, in regard to Anowa's "wildness," her independent spirit, he tells his wife: "I have always asked you to apprentice her to a priestess to quieten her down" (71). For Osam all problems can be neatly solved by shifting the responsibility, just as responsibility for various actions and attitudes is continually shifted by each character I have labeled sujet-en-soi; further, such shifts act as counterpoints to the larger shifts in power that take place on other levels in the drama. One begins to recognize that Osam's attitude is similar to "the Lords of our Houses / [Who] Signed that piece of paper—/ The Bond of 1844" (68) to whom the Old Man referred in the prologue. Osam's reluctance to become embroiled in domestic arguments over the apprenticeship of Anowa or her marriage mirrors the quandary faced by the elders in dealing with either domestic and international slavery or the complexities of imperialist aggression—both British and Ashanti. Just as the limited foresight of the elders accepted solutions that amounted to capitulation in the face of the economic and ideological problems, so Osam's evasiveness leads him to react, rather than to act, affect his world, and effect desirable changes. In this respect he is much like Ato Yawson in Aidoo's first play, blaming others for his omissions and faults (92–94).

Abena Badua's motivations are much more subtle than her husband's, although on the surface they may seem similar. Badua also wishes to maintain the status quo, but for more substantial material gain (72). It is obvious that she wishes to bask in the reflected glory of her daughter's favorable marriage, especially if it leads to greater wealth—a productive farm (property), more children (additional labor), and political honors (a place among the elders and a captainship in the army). Osam sees that many of these material, political, and military rewards—or their equivalents—may be gained through the priesthood. Because he always seeks the easy solution to a problem, however, he fails to recognize or understand the true role of the priesthood in traditional society.[24] Ironically, Badua gives a much more insightful characterization of the social and political function of priestesses in traditional society than does her husband. She asserts that "they [priestesses] are not people. They become too much like the gods they interpret. . . . *They read into other men's souls.* . . . *But a priestess lives too much in her own and other people's minds,* my husband" (72; italics added). This realization drives her to an almost paranoid fear of priests and priestesses. Far from being a way to "quieten down" a rebellious individual, entry into the priesthood could result in that individual having an enormous effect on the course of his or her society's development. Yet both parents have only imperfectly realized perceptions of the forces at work in their society and their own daughter's character, as Osam's reply to his wife's fears testifies: "My wife, people with better vision than yours or mine have seen that Anowa is not like you or me. *And a prophet with a locked mouth is neither a prophet nor a man. Besides, the yam that will burn, shall burn, boiled or roasted*" (73; italics added). His aphoristic utterance implies an unalterable social situation, one which, even if it were possible, does not obtain in Aidoo's dramatic "history." The limits of Osam's and Badua's understanding is illustrated in the allusions each makes during the course of their argument, which immediately follows Anowa's revelation of her intention to marry Kofi Ako. The domestic realism of the argument masks the ideological significance of the exchange (75). Like the Old Woman in the prologue, both parents metaphorically consign their "real" daughter to the realm of fiction; in their own minds they thus displace or neutralize Anowa's single-minded revolt against the values and practices they so blindly defend. In a sense, Kofi Ako is like the trickster Kwaku Ananse, but despite the resemblance, Kofi is too unprincipled and dissembling, for he eventually becomes inextricably enmeshed in a web of his own making.

The return to the dominant realistic mode of phase 1's domestic complications is exemplified in the natural escalation of verbal abuse between husband and wife, and between mother and daughter. Badua's concerns, although selfish, are the genuine concerns of a mother for her only surviving child and daughter. Even though she has an almost intuitive fear of the power of the priesthood, her emotional exclamations are ideologically overdetermined. Osam's reluctance to become too embroiled in the arguments between mother and daughter is poignantly expressed when he earlier asks Badua: "Which is your headache, that she is not yet married, or that she is wild?" (71). And later, after preventing Badua from hitting Anowa, he asks in desperation: "Tell me what has come over this household? And you too Badua. What has come over you" (78); it is too late, however, for reasonable discourse and civil settlement of family squabbles.

This disruption of domestic harmony is rather poorly handled by all concerned. It stands in contradistinction to the sincere attempts at arbitration evidenced in Aidoo's first play. In *The Dilemma* the extended family (particularly Uncle Petu and Ato's grandmother, Nana) attempts to correct the apparent barrenness of Eulalie Rush, in order to save the marriage and guarantee continuation of the lineage. All the parties in Osam's household, however, behave *immaturely*. The question of mature and appropriate behavior is of primary importance, if we are to understand and appreciate Anowa's development ("a young woman who grows up") during phases 2 and 3. Unfortunately, Osam's reaction only confirms our earlier impression of him, and, having failed to resolve the domestic impasse, he blames the women, particularly his wife. His concern with the surface, rather than the substance, of issues is unambiguously expressed in his final words to his daughter: "Anowa, you must not leave in this manner" (79). He resigns in silence and a temporary limbo, Anowa's "father who smokes a pipe," unable and unwilling to understand "what has come over [his] household." Abena Badua, on the other hand, is able "to weep quietly." Even though her weeping is precipitated by self-pity, her demonstration of emotional engagement elicits a measure of sympathy from the chorus-audience.

Abena Badua is naturally disconcerted when her daughter finally chooses her own man: "Of all the mothers that are here in Yebi, should I be the one whose daughter would want to marry this fool [Kofi Ako]?" (74). As a result of the almost hysterical objections of Anowa's mother and some of the townsfolk, represented in the drama by the Old Woman, the young couple decides to seek their fortune on the road. Before they leave, Anowa defiantly vows never again to set foot in Yebi, their hometown in the state of Abura (79). Nicholson rightly points out that, in a matrilineal society, it is unusual for a woman to help her husband acquire wealth and property, since "a husband's property is inherited by his nephews [and nieces] rather than his wife and children" (102). As true as this is, in general terms, in situations when one or both partners are only children (as in Anowa's case), then marriage ties tend to be closer. The reason for this apparent contradiction of conventional practice might be found in the nature of matrilineal societies, where sibling relationships tend to be defined in opposition to other relationships, even conjugal ones. The husband would thus usually confide his private material and spiritual concerns to his sister rather than to his wife, for instance. An understanding and appreciation of such mores would forestall the kind of feminist distortions that, in effect, consign all women (except the "unusual" ones) to the role of deviously scheming wives who, "in prosperous marriages . . . exploit the fondness of their husbands in order to entice a share of the riches out of their husbands" (Nicholson, 102). Rather, as we see in the play, it would be natural for Anowa, who does not have siblings, to regard her husband, Kofi Ako, as both husband and brother (87, 96).

Anowa's claim to assist her husband thus carries implications beyond her psychological need. First, it is addressed to Badua, who readily accepts the prevailing ideological (cultural) prejudices and belief of her time and is thus likely to agree with the conventional stereotypes of others (92). Second, the knowledge that Kofi Ako belongs to the Nsona House Clan (75) would call to mind the stereotypical images associated with Nsona people, especially the men: witty masters of the oral arts—something Kofi Ako definitely is not. In addition, they see themselves as the best and the greatest human beings ever born, another claim that Kofi Ako has been unable to substantiate (75, 77, 79). They are also considered to be dreamers rather than agents; therefore, one marries such a person at the risk of one's present and future health, wealth, and sanity. It is in this context that Anowa's choice of mate, although considered imprudent by some, stresses her need to question and even go against conventional wisdom in the pursuit of a more meaningful life.

Just as conventional wisdom would censure Eulalie Rush's rejection of the safety of life in the United States for the uncertainty of life with Ato Yawson, so Anowa's rejection of traditional ideological practices—symbolized by her mother and the Old Woman of the play's internal chorus-audience—might be considered foolish. Nevertheless, we must see it as an attempt to cope with and understand the changing circumstances that are slowly but surely affecting traditional Fanti society. As part of this social development Anowa's actions may also be viewed as the affirmation of the right to personal choice—however disastrous. The order of things is never to be the same, and Anowa's last words in phase 1 have truer prophetic implications than she can possibly imagine: "Mother. I shall walk so well that *I will not find my feet back here again*" (79; italics added). For Anowa, to go back to Yebi would be to return to the past, to the status quo, and so she would be condemning herself to being sujet-en-soi—an historical footnote. Yet, *Anowa is "dramatically" in history,* and so it seems there have to be those nostalgic backward glances.

Phase 1 ends with an exchange between The-Mouth-That-Eats-Salt-and-Pepper. Like the two gossips, "your neighbours" in Aidoo's first play, the Old Man and the Old Woman (now occupying the same space-time as the rest of the drama's action) comment on the preceding action and stress the ideological issues at stake. We no longer have the temporal shifts that characterized their utterances in the prologue. This allows for a closer auditing of their exchange in relation to the thematic and structural (formal) concerns of the drama. Scene 5 opens with the Old Woman voicing the complaint that seems characteristic of all generational conflicts, no matter the cultural specificity of the context: "What do the children of today want? . . . The days when children obeyed their elders have run out" (79–80). The generational issue is neither limited to nor uniquely focused on the conflict between Badua and Anowa, that is, mother versus daughter, as Kofi Agovi stresses.[25] In keeping with the generalized complaint of the Old Woman, one notes that the Old Man's reply and rhetorical questions show a more critically mediated response to generational conflicts. Behind such questions lies the sense that some overwhelming change is being effected by youth that does not auger well for their parents. At the same time, through aphorisms and telling questions, the Old Man stresses the complex determinations involved in considering the nature of any relationship (80). His remarks also indicate that he does not consider social roles innate, biologically determined behaviors or attributes. In short, the Old Man questions the tendency to assume a privilege that is located solely in one's genes. Can one claim privilege and abdicate responsibility because one has discharged one's semen and fertilized an egg or carried the fetus to term? These are fundamental questions concerning human social, political, economic, and biological reproduction, production, control, and organization. They are the substance underlying our discussions of the literary work that depicts real characters dramatizing their stories in history, rather than just being or performing (as in a possession or fictions).

For the Old Woman, as for Badua, the principal issues are conformity and the upholding of traditional values, exemplified in the obedience of children to their parents and elders. The Old Man nevertheless insists that what is at issue is not the maintenance of the status quo versus anarchy but the necessity for individuals to seek and effect meaningful change in their lives: "Abena Badua should have known that *Anowa wanted to be something else which she herself had not been*" (80; italics added). In fact, both Osam and Badua recognize that their daughter must live a different life from their own, but what is particularly irksome is that they cannot accept the nature of that difference—the result of change and growth. Echoing the earlier conversation between Osam and Badua about Anowa's unwed state and her "wildness," the Old Man asks: "Are people angry because she chose her own husband; or, is there something wrong with the boy?" (80).

The Old Man's defense of Kofi Ako, that one should not judge "a man of name by his humble beginnings" (81), should be seen in the same manner as Nana's defense of one of her grandnephews, Ebow, (and Ato Yawson) in *The Dilemma*, when Esi Kom criticizes Ebow's disrespect and immaturity. In essence, the Old Man cautions against hasty value judgments and malicious rumor-mongering: "We all talk too much about those two [Anowa and Kofi Ako]. And yet this is not the first time since the world began that a man and a woman have decided to be together against the advice of grey-haired crows" (81). It is significant that the Old Man does not assume that "the advice of grey-haired crows" is better, or even wiser, than the apparently impulsive decision of Anowa to leave Yebi with "her man." Concurrent with his participation in the drama, the Old Man is able to maintain a self-critical distance from the action; the audience thus sees him as a reliable observer-commentator. The Old Woman, however, is seen as being too subjectively involved with the action to be reliable. In fact, her critical outbursts and gnomic statements are viewed as even more impulsive than the original actions of those she verbally castigates:

OLD WOMAN: What foolish words! Some people babble as though they borrowed their grey hairs and did not grow them on their own heads! . . . [She exits noisily.]

OLD MAN: I'm certainly a foolish old man. But I think there is no need to behave as though Kofi Ako and Anowa have brought an evil concoction here. Perhaps it is good for them that they have left Yebi to go and try to make their lives somewhere else. [As lights go out, a blending of the *atentenben* with any ordinary drum.] (81)

The Old Woman's exits, such as the one above, show little respect for the views and opinions of others and are blatantly immature and irresponsible for one so advanced in years. In contrast, the signature that closes phase 1 and functions as musical commentary to the Old Man's final utterance is a tempering of the extreme (the *atentenben*) with the middle path (the ordinary drum).

Phase 2 focuses on the appropriate and inappropriate behaviors of Anowa and "her man," now that they are "on the highway," free from parental authority and the ideological hailing of traditional Fanti society, represented by the village of Yebi. They are at a spatial and historical juncture—neither here nor there—a temporal node, much like the ghost at Elmina Junction in Aidoo's first play. A number of years have been collapsed into this phase; and, although there is a temporal foreshortening, the pace of the dramatic action in the first scene slows as Aidoo draws attention to the evolving dynamics of the relationship between Anowa and Kofi Ako. Sustained by Anowa's vision of a better life, imprecise as it might be, and her untiring determination to succeed, rather than by the sole efforts of her husband, Kofi Ako (a "man who [*only*] expands"), they establish a profitable trading business. As the business grows, Kofi Ako first contemplates and then buys slaves (bonded men) to help the business expand further. The combination of material wealth and power is too sweet for the nouveau riche appetite of the former "good-for-nothing cassava-man," as Badua called him. His arrogance, which finds expression in male chauvinism, and his deliberate blindness to the injustices of domestic slavery prove too much for Anowa, whom he describes as "shamelessly . . . rak[ing] up the dirt of life," and being "too fond of looking for the common pain and the general wrong" (99).

Anowa is willing to sacrifice the comforts of today in order that tomorrow may be better for all. Kofi, on the other hand, would rather have immediate gratification, immediate security. Perhaps Anowa assumes, like Aba (the second woman in the chorus of neighbors in *The Dilemma*), that another wife and children are an economic asset, a source of labor and therefore future social security. Based on this assumption, she urges Kofi to marry another woman because she thinks she cannot bear children. Kofi, however, is curiously reluctant and defensive about contracting a second marriage. Anowa's suspicions are aroused. Traditionally, if a wife agrees to a husband marrying another woman then the man is obligated to do so, unless there is a just cause or reason to prevent such a contractual union (84). Aidoo returns to this issue in her second novel, *Changes—A Love Story*. Monogamy was perhaps less a measure of fidelity and love than an indicator of the economic status of the marriage partners; that is, the poor were monogamous, while polygamy was enjoyed by the wealthy. Kofi's behavior leads Anowa to broach the possibility of some psychosomatic supernatural explanation for his timidity. Thus Anowa has every right to think the worst of her husband. After all, had not Badua described him as "this fool, . . . this watery male of all watery males," (75) earlier in the drama?

Anowa knew, from the start of their relationship, that Kofi lacked the confidence and strength to pursue a task to its conclusion through honest labor. Both she and her mother knew that he had never amounted to anything before Anowa met him (76–79). Later, Kofi Ako admits his lack of confidence, implying at the same time that he has procured medicines for protection against the witchcraft of others, and to secure a prosperous future (85). Kofi's paranoia and Anowa's justified suspicions are grounded in the still commonly held belief that special medicines—*sikuduro*—protect the procurer against the supernatural machinations of others (particularly family members) and guarantee the acquisition of material wealth.[26] Anowa points out that all such protection is bought at a great price. In this context we begin to understand the complex psychosocial pressures that bear upon the "wayfarers" of the highway from Yebi. Anowa discerns the sinister implications of Kofi Ako's words, although it becomes progressively obvious that Kofi does not fully comprehend the consequences of his own ambitions, actions, or words. Kofi's reply to Anowa's concern about her apparent inability to have a child is, to say the least, callous. In order not to have their argument focus on his guilt, he tries to suggest that her opposition to sikaduro is the cause of their problems (85–86). Kofi's faulty logic and assumption that he knows what Anowa thinks shows how close he is in character to the protagonist of *The Dilemma*; he is, in many ways, Ato Yawson's economic and psychosocial forebear.

Our knowledge of the play's culturally and politically complex contexts should caution us against imposing our own late-twentieth-century assumptions and prescriptions on *Anowa*. Such caution would prevent us from constructing the artificial problems Lewis Nkosi finds in Aidoo's play. While Nkosi's Marxist-nationalist reading identifies issues similar to the ones I have outlined, his application of a materialist dialectic is caught in a colonialist manichean dichotomy. He remains unable to synthesize the discrete facts of the drama into a new critical whole. For Nkosi, *Anowa*

> hints at a world psychologically in conflict with its realistic mode. The play seems to be about the corrosive effects of acquisitiveness and slavery; it also seems to be a protest about the situation of women in African society. Nevertheless, Anowa's attack on her husband, Kofi Ako's materialism, on his exploitation of slaves as well as his "conspicuous consumption" of wealth, is deprived of much of its force by the fact that Anowa's source of dissatisfaction is not clearly brought out. In the end we are left with the vague impression that Kofi Ako's sexual impotence, the cause of which is mystically attributed to his cupidity in the pursuit of material wealth, matters more to Anowa than their ideological conflict which stems from Ako's views on slavery and the subjection of women.[27]

Nkosi is disturbed by the seeming lack of resolution in this play, and what he sees as "a dimly perceived wrong done to women." He fails to appreciate the text-performance, *Anowa*, as extraordinary. For while Anowa is critical of her husband's materialism, vanity, and exploitative character—thereby suggesting, to Nkosi, a high degree of understanding of the situation in which she finds herself—the aesthetic demands of the drama necessitate a resolution of those ideological conflicts on their own aesthetic territory.

The aesthetic solutions—the suggestion of a mystical/psychosexual cause of the problem and the resolution in madness and double or solitary suicide—are not unsatisfactory because Aidoo has presented "an imperfectly realized vision of society" (Nkosi, 181). Nor is the resolution problematic because Aidoo "has not yet succeeded in devising plots and characters whose interaction add up to a coherent view of society, which can reveal to us in dramatic form what she wishes African society to become in the light of its traditional past" (ibid.). Nkosi would like to see, in the character of Anowa, "a fully developed consciousness of what their disadvantaged position might mean, what causes it and what might alleviate it" (178–80). His prescriptive assumptions lead him to demand that the writer has a specific ideological duty to perform in the production of creative work. Such a demand requires, according to Nkosi, a resolution in the play itself of the ideological contradictions of the *author's* (and, in a sense, Nkosi's) social and historical moment. This demand impoverishes our appreciation of the text-performance by the premature collapsing of the categories (for a materialist criticism) into a mechanical dialectic.[28]

Nkosi's reading, in fact, corresponds very closely to Sigmund Freud's characterization of the analyst's reading of the "dream-work," and Pierre Macherey's negative expression of the textual-ideological problematic referred to in chapter 1 concerning Aidoo's deployment of the dilemma tale convention. The resolution *is* unsatisfactory because "a text does not merely 'take' ideological conflicts in order to 'resolve' them aesthetically, for the character of those conflicts is itself overdetermined by the textual modes in which they are produced. The text's mode of resolving a particular ideological conflict may then produce textual conflicts elsewhere—at other levels of the text, for example—which need in turn to be 'processed' " (Eagleton, *Criticism*, 88). It is apparent that Nkosi has not integrated the function of Aidoo's peculiar deployment of the dilemma tale convention into his critical methodology. Had he taken this into account, he could have avoided echoing the textual-ideological relationship which, in Macherey's model, acts as a bridge between Marxism and what is, in essence, a literary formalism.[29]

The dramatically and ideologically important second phase's opening scene ends with Kofi's soliloquy, a monologue that confirms our earlier demonstration of the extraordinary ties between Anowa and Kofi: "Wherever we go, people take you for my sister at first. They say they have never heard of a woman who helped her husband so. . . . 'Your sisters are the only women you can force to toil like this for you.' They say that however good for licking the back of your hand is, it would never be like your palms" (87). Anowa's hardworking attitude and her close marital relationship would be considered extraordinary in a matrilineal society; one should recognize, however, the significance of the second part of the quotation, which ends with the proverb. Sibling relations, especially among siblings born of the same mother, are considered next in strength to the bond between a mother and her child within the matrilineage. A saying among the Akan graphically expresses the nature of this relationship: "Your brother or your sister, you can deny them *nothing*." This is true even when the conduct of one's sibling may be considered irresponsible. The proverb reveals the real attitude of Kofi, while it points out the persistence of matrilineal social assumptions.

In addition to the close bonding between maternal siblings, it would be a relatively lesser social and psychological stigma for Kofi to have a childless marriage than for his sister to be infertile, since she is the traditional medium of continuity of his family's descent line. Such knowledge casts a more sinister hue on the implications of Kofi's claim that "Anowa has a few strong ideas. But I know she will settle down." In fact, it becomes much easier to accept the probability that Kofi Ako would be more than willing to sacrifice Anowa's fertility, sanity, and other assets in the pursuit of his own wealth and security. This likelihood helps to explain his "sudden" change: "Perhaps if they knew what I am beginning to know, they would not say so much. And proverbs do not always describe the truth of reality" (87). Kofi's new "determination" allows him to doubt the ability of proverbs (a traditional linguistic tool of critical oral discourse) to adequately describe the emergent reality. Traditional critical dialogue proves woefully inadequate when Kofi tries to describe the changing Fanti reality and his role in that process. He senses that the continued use of outmoded methods of description and analysis (that is, proverbial wisdom) will lead to crucial misreadings of the new dispensation. As Kofi points out, even in its proverbial flexibility, language is not always the most effective medium for the description of what we see as the real. There are connections (ideological echoes) between different kinds of insight (knowledge) that challenge the orthodox evaluations of the workings of history—its causes and effects. Ironically, he is also guilty of misreading the personal and public currents that characterize the confluence of historical streams at which he and Anowa have been caught. For Kofi Ako, the effect of being a Fanti trader in the latter part of the nineteenth century can only be expressed in nontraditional ways. His actions and predicament can only be articulated by reference to the personal dynamics of the power relations between husband and wife, man and woman, colonizer and colonized.

It is not accidental that Aidoo situates the drama at this crucial period of Fanti/Gold Coast history. *Anowa* attempts to delineate the causes and effects of ideological transformations that have resulted in the present configuration of social and economic relations. Traditionally, marriage within a matrilineal society such as the Fanti was viewed as a contract between equals that "allow[ed] the conjugal relationship to be envisaged as a bundle of separable rights and bonds rather than as a unitary all-or-none tie" (Fortes, 280). In short, the advent of colonialism affords this "watery male" the de jure right to further marginalize women. This consolidation of power in the individual male, at the expense of women, is a correlate of the shift in power relations taking place in Fanti society to the benefit of British imperial expansion. In this light, it becomes clear that when Kofi Ako sees himself as "the new husband and [Anowa as] the new wife" (87), he is talking in terms of the new colony—populated by the increasingly wealthy comprador class, whose power is validated by British imperialism, symbolized later in the play by "a fireplace and above it, a picture of Queen Victoria unamused" (103). Further, it is significant that Kofi phrases his resolve in a direct manner: no gnomic ambivalence about the ways of this new world, which Kofis will create with the aid of hard-working, self-sacrificing Anowas, and, of course, the paternalism of the British Empire.

It is important to note that the inherent paternalism of the imperialist enterprise was symbolically packaged as something else—Mother Victoria, sternly protecting her dark-skinned children from the rapacious clutches of aggressive non-British males. All the while, Albert (read Gladstone, Disraeli, et al.), the new model husband/man, in the straight-laced hypocrisy of holier-than-thou religious morality and the domestic harmony of Victorian monogamy, takes care of business. We must not forget that Ako and Anowa were coming to maturity a generation or so after the Bond of 1844.

Like "the Lords of our Houses" (68) who became the agents of British imperial ambitions, Kofi Ako wishes to assume a role, not just as agent for British imperialism, but as unquestioned sovereign in his personal and sexual relations with Anowa. Such a role would effectively mask his inadequacies and insecurities. Unfortunately for him, he is unable to recognize Anowa for who she is, in much the same way the colonizer's arrogance prevents a similar recognition of the native. Kofi chooses the path of least resistance, not realizing that for the honor of being seen to be in control, one must actually surrender all meaningful control, in the end. His obsession with acquiring wealth could be described in classical Freudian terms as material substitution for his sexual impotence. His desire to have additional men working for him instead of another wife is perfectly rational (94–95): to have another wife would further test his manhood. Up against the native's (Anowa's) resistance, the platitudes of a so-called benevolent paternalism ring false; and, if the pretense is to continue, then Kofi Ako, like all successful imperialists, must continually rewrite the Other's versions of her story. We must understand that the history of the victor, even in its most benign form, is a transformation of facts into fictions—as happened to Anowa's history prior to Aidoo. Indeed, Aidoo continually warns us that if we are to rescue Anowa's story, *as her story,* from the distortions of a colonized history, then we must place Anowa back *in* history. As critical readers, we cannot valorize or privilege Anowa for immediate gains— nationalist, feminist, humanist, or any other "ist"—she must be situated in the context of a changing and highly complex social, economic, and political set of circumstances and interactions, if we are to appreciate the significance of her life, madness, and death.

In addition, by stressing her opposition to the acquisition of slaves, Anowa is upholding the right of persons, female or male, to work and enjoy the fruits of their labor, particularly since this is a time of relative peace, as is evidenced by the prosperity of their "skin" trade. By her opposition, Anowa is upholding traditional values of communalism. Such values stress cooperative production relations rather than rigid, hierarchial, competitive and exploitative ones. In addition, these traditional attitudes voiced by Anowa are preferable to the dubious benefits of domestic slavery— generally seen, at their best, as double-edged swords. Kofi—Anowa's moral and intellectual inferior—adopts the ascendant ideological and psychological violence of patriarchal and capitalist discourse in order to justify his desire for buying slaves: "What is wrong with buying one or two people to help us? They are cheap. . . . Everyone does it" (89). Anowa's rejection of domestic slavery is valid because the practice runs counter to traditionally cooperative production relations, which are possible within the structure of the matrilineal family and society. A more egalitarian alternative exists through the regulated and legitimate acquisition of another wife (or wives) and children, whose rights and obligations are socially protected and clearly defined.

The play should not be taken as a blanket endorsement of polygamy, but in historical context this practice indicates the rationale behind Anowa's pleas for Kofi to marry another woman rather than to acquire slaves. When he tries to explain Anowa's opposition to slavery and her "difference," Michael Etherton's usually perceptive observations about the actions of the characters seem to slip into an aesthetic-versus-ideology mode that establishes an ultimately frozen dialectic:

> She is restless because she is intelligent. *She is uneducated, and yet she is rational,* with an understanding too advanced for *a static society.* All her society can do is understand her as a priestess, or a prophet- ess or a witch. Indeed, how many women have been branded witch by a society unable to cope with their intelligence and rationalism? Anowa is able to comprehend the absolute evil of slavery in a way that her husband, contained within the social system, cannot. She is also able to comprehend the true significance of the relationship between a man and a woman, a husband and a wife. (italics added) [30]

Etherton's assertions occasionally reflect assumptions of colonialist criti- cism, undercutting his more intelligent observations, which unambigu- ously call our attention to the historically specific context of a drama like *Anowa.*

Anowa's predicament becomes all the more complicated because the couple's trade with the British, their only source of livelihood, is intimately related to her marriage problems. As she admits to Kofi, "I cannot be happy if I am going to stop working" (94), and despite this revelation, Kofi secretly wants Anowa to become a "housewife," in Western terms. The buying of slaves, for Kofi, means the (relatively inefficient) maximization of profit and the consolidation of his patriarchal domination over his wife. The Old Man is in fundamental agreement with Anowa's position on domestic slavery, and he observes, in scene 5 of phase 2, that "every house is ruined where they take in slaves" (99). The Sierra Leonean James Africanus Horton (1835–1883), discussing the division of labor between the sexes—admittedly from a probourgeois patriarchal perspective—notes that Fanti women tend to work harder than the men, specifically in the area of agriculture, its associated occupations and petty trading. He saw this as indicative of "a very low scale of civilization." In addition, he observed that the educated men had become "agents of English firms," or independent merchants. This latter situation, however, he regarded as a "comparatively . . . great advance in civilization, although there is vast room for improvement."[31]

Despite Horton's and Kofi Ako's wish that the women trade their labors for domesticity, Anowa struggles fruitlessly to discourage her husband from buying slaves. As a result, her motivation for living wanes, and she rejects all the trappings of their acquired wealth (94–99, 113–21). As the drama moves toward its dual endings we return to Yebi and Anowa's parents, who argue about their daughter and son-in-law's fortunes. Badua's concern for her daughter's fertility, or rather perceived infertility, prompts her to defend Anowa against Osam's unjustified accusations. Further, her suspicion that both Anowa and Kofi Ako have "sold her [Anowa's] birth-seed to acquire their wealth" (92) articulates her daughter's own fears of Kofi's duplicity (84). The shadow play between these two scenes, and between the plays *Anowa* and *The Dilemma*, is Aidoo's method for evoking in the mind of her audience the reality of historical linkages between past, present, and future. The importance of the temporal continuity of events, whether they be historical facts arising from social and political interactions or imaginative facts arising from personal and public interactions that motivate Aidoo as a writer, should not be underestimated. We should understand that the social and cultural background against which the events unfold assumes dead ancestors and the unborn to be always and already inextricably part of the moment that we call the present. It is this connectedness that the reader or audience must keep in mind, if they are to fully appreciate the complex ideological matrix that Aidoo's works, individually and severally, create and inhabit. Anowa's predicament is that of a sujet-en-soi struggling to be more *fully* sujet-pour-soi. Her suspicions about her husband's weakness and his cupidity in the pursuit of material wealth act as a catalyst impelling her toward the recognition of her own psychosexual tensions and the wider social and political contradictions of her age. She arrives at these conclusions despite her "restless soul," despite the claim that she is possessed by "a destiny that is fixed, blind and destructive [and that] she is a victim of a predestination that is rooted in the belief system of her society" (Agovi, 62–63). It is the multifarious determinations (at times conflicting and seemingly hidden) that connect the personal with the political and public realm of ideological discourses.

The ending of the third scene of the second phase, a modified replay of the previous one, enables Aidoo to demonstrate, through their dialogue, the particular mode of ideological insertion of Osam and Badua, while underscoring the distinction between Anowa and Kofi Ako. Both scenes end with an agreement not to quarrel; in the third scene, however, we are shown just how thoroughly Osam and Badua are sujets-en-soi with regard to the demands of traditional Fanti society, among other forces (93). As Anowa becomes progressively isolated and estranged from her husband, he too begins to suffer the consequences of his own actions. We begin to see what locks Anowa and Kofi Ako in their impossible embrace. Anowa knows, as unhappy as she is with having slaves, that to extricate herself from the situation by walking out on her husband would be to abdicate a commitment and responsibility that she had freely chosen. In addition, she is aware that if she leaves Kofi Ako, this Nsona man, who only "expands" like a hot-air balloon, will collapse. Thus there is a limit to how far she can push Kofi, since she has already burnt her bridges back to Yebi; if "her man" fails, her only reason for living, apart from labor, will be destroyed.

In this respect, it would be a mistake to overemphasize Anowa's "general restlessness [as being] partly explained by her quest for the means of guaranteeing her independence as a woman" (Brown, 1981, 98). Stressing Anowa's "independence" prompts a view of her as having "a strong penchant for individuality . . . [which] isolates her" (Nicholson, 87). This kind of insistence on "independence" and "individuality" does not explain why Anowa remains with Kofi Ako. We overlook Anowa's need for community and see her only from the perspective of Western bourgeois norms of "independence" and "individuality": a woman alone, a black superwoman.

Anowa desires true companionship based on equality and a shared history, a common past, but Kofi's greed and guilt blind him to this alternative. Kofi Ako's ramblings indicate his inability to come to terms with his own guilt, with what he calls Anowa's "moods," and with the implications of the confluence of antagonistic ideological practices of which he is both witness and blind participant (96–98). There no longer exists a common language with which Ako can communicate: "O it is difficult to think through anything. All these strange words!" he cries in desperation. He wants to escape from having to deal with the responsibilities that accompany the benefits of a society moving into the capitalist system. He is clutching at straws, and his one hope is the concreteness of abundant material possessions. In this respect, he is the nineteenth-century precursor of Ato Yawson. And, like his bewildered counterpart who could not help *his* wayfarer-wife, Kofi Ako cannot help Anowa. His solution only perpetuates hierarchial distances, alienation, and separation, even as he seems to offer the opposite (96).

His wealth cannot save him, and Anowa has no use for it. In this heightened state of disaffection, Anowa dreams of her recovered history under the portrait of Queen Victoria in the great hall of their big house in Cape Coast—Oguaa (104–7, 111–12). The scene ends rather surrealistically with "the voices of an unseen wearied multitude [singing] 'Swing Low Sweet Chariot'" (107). Such an anachronistic eruption into the dramatic narrative heightens the recovered histories that, in the prologue, were symbolized by "those Forts" (66). We see Anowa grow from a sorrowful victim to an individual whose awareness allows her to establish a strong sense of community with the oppressed and others who have been wronged. It is an awareness of the truth that allows her to take the offensive, to escalate the ideological and personal stakes in her confrontation with her husband. Truly, she is "a young woman who grows up."

Anowa identifies with the plight of mothers, though childless herself, a significant step toward a mature understanding of the complex nature of oppression. In this regard, her "conversations" with the couple's adopted twins, Panyin-na-Kakra, and the slave boy and girl during the third phase become a means of connecting with other displaced members of her husband's household. But this bond of shared oppression is not based on a blind biological identity, for, although Queen Victoria might be "a human woman," Anowa has seen the likes of her in other women—her mother,

Badua, and the Old Woman of the chorus. What Anowa criticizes is the socialization of women, which becomes more overt in its oppressiveness through the institution of marriage. But not only women are socialized into dehumanizing and oppressive roles: "She remembers the children." In her conversation with Kakra, we realize that the institution of domestic slavery has far-reaching consequences, for Kakra cannot remember his origins. He too is a bird of the wayside, a wayfarer, and a ghost.

In utter exasperation, having failed to elicit any logical reason for Kofi Ako's command that she should go away and leave him (115, 117), Anowa calls for an assembly of priests, priestesses, and elders to adjudicate their differences (118–19). It is significant that the climax of the private drama between Anowa and Kofi Ako should take place at this time, for "Nana Abakrampahene Kokroko is here. He and the other chiefs are meeting with the Governor." From all indications, Aidoo has situated the play during the late 1860s and early 1870s; this being so, the reference to the chiefs being in Oguaa (Cape Coast) to meet the governor firmly places the drama's ending in mid-1874. In 1872 the British government had decided that the protectorate should become a crown colony. Soon after they defeated the Ashanti, "in the teeth of opposition from the educated Africans and the Chiefs on 24th July, 1874," the British finally realized their ambition (GIS, 4). Aidoo's bringing together of the public-political and the private-political in this way underscores the necessity of viewing *Anowa* in its historical specificity, a complex interaction of the issues of gender, economics, and politics within the context of ideological struggle.

Anowa's knowledge of the causes and character of her circumstances deepens in the closing phase of the drama. "You said it right, my child" (111), she declares at the end of scene 3 to the departing girl. Anowa knows that Kofi Ako has betrayed her and himself by relying on the magic of sika-duro, and this awareness makes her rhetorical question and the subsequent exchange with the boy all the more poignant (117). All that remains to be done is for Kofi to admit his guilt publicly; such an admission would, in the eyes of Anowa and the internal and external audience-participants of the drama, act as a purgation, a catharsis for the collective wrong perpetrated by all of us against ourselves and others. But Kofi Ako is too embarrassed, and he threatens to charge Anowa with witchcraft (120). Because he knows that such a false accusation would be the ultimate betrayal, true to his reliance on the material wealth he has acquired, he attempts to bribe Anowa to go away; he promises her a house in Yebi (120–21). Kofi's solution only adds insult to injury, and it forces Anowa, who is now on the verge of hysterical outrage, to be more pointed in her accusations (121–22). As scene 4 ends, Kofi Ako, offstage, puts a bullet through his head. "*Fere ne owuo efenim owuo.*" (If it is a matter of choosing between disgrace and death, then I shall prefer death.) We are left with Anowa, now childlike in her "insanity," talking to the portrait of Queen Victoria and giggling to herself.

Her emotional and ideological sensitivity, an attribute sometimes explained as arising from vanity or supernatural causes, serves to heighten her alienation. Kofi Ako's cupidity, his ideological capitulation to British bourgeois values, and the revelation of his psychosexual dysfunction, lead the two inexorably to a pathetic double suicide, or to Kofi Ako's suicide and Anowa's madness. That is, if we choose to end the drama before the last printed word of text, then the bracket remains open and we are left with insanity and suicide—both of which are unproductive—and we, the audience-readers, are again asked to adjudicate the value of this seemingly wasteful (ir)resolution. If we take the text to the last page, however, then the action of *Anowa* is bracketed by the unresolved arguments of The-Mouth-That-Eats-Salt-and-Pepper and the echo of the wailing atentenben drum and the rhetorical question of the Old Man of the chorus: "Who knows if Anowa would have been a better woman, a better person if we had not been what we are?" (124). For whom does the drum wail and mourn?

In 1970, when this play was published, the Ghanaian audience-reader would not have forgotten that four short years before, many Ghanaians had celebrated in the streets of the capital on the occasion of the military overthrow of the Nkrumah government. Although that coup was rumored to have been backed by the U.S. Central Intelligence Agency, the immediate pretext was that Nkrumah had betrayed the Ghanaian people—"There is surely one thing we know how to do very well. And that is assigning blame when things go wrong" (124). The same Kwame Nkrumah who, on 6 March 1957, 113 years after the signing of the Bond of 1844, had led Gold Coast to political independence had become in 1970, in the eyes of the official Ghanaian press (then under the stewardship of the supposedly democratic government of Dr. Kofi Busia), persona non grata and an exile. For whom does the drum wail and mourn? Unlike Anowa, we do not have to be "like all the beautiful maidens in the tales" (67), for we are not dramatic fictions, but subjects in and of that historical project Aidoo's second drama so frankly presents.

# Back to the Present;
# Or *No Sweetness Here*

Aidoo's short stories, written over the eight years that spanned the crucial period just before and immediately after the 1966 military overthrow of the Kwame Nkrumah government, were collected and published in 1970 by Longman of England as *No Sweetness Here*. The next year, Double-day published the first U.S. edition and in 1972 a second edition with an introduction by the South African writer Ezekiel Mphahlele.[1] It is, perhaps, Mphahlele's introduction that set the tone and focus of subsequent criticism of the collection's eleven stories:

> Ama Ata Aidoo celebrates womanhood in general and motherhood in particular. She stands up for the woman. . . . The men in Miss Aidoo's fiction are mere shadows or voices or just "fillers." Somewhere, quietly, they seem to be manipulating the woman's life or negatively controlling it or simply having a good time. . . . Given this premise the woman, without worrying about her traditional place, simply gets up on her feet and asserts not her importance in relation to the male, but her motherhood.[2]

Although Mphahlele's focus is not misplaced, succeeding criticism has tended to seize upon feminism as the primary or privileged concern of Aidoo's literary project. This criticism often ignores or downplays the possibility that "[these] short stories, like the play [*Anowa*], are simple and direct, *being concerned with the real problems of ordinary people*. . . . Ama Ata writes with transparent honesty: behind it there is the feeling, the same as in the novels of Ayi Kwei Armah, of being near to tears" (italics added).[3] Having examined in her historical drama, *Anowa*, many of the complex social and economic causes of contemporary problems, Aidoo, in this collection of stories, portrays in greater detail the lived consequences of those problems. As in that historical drama, Aidoo delineates the resultant confluence of personal choices and public imperative. She draws attention to the predicament of women's marginalization and oppression; as she stresses both in the short stories and elsewhere, however, these injustices are part of a larger pattern of practices that affront human dignity and self-worth:

> Whatever gender, whatever nationality we belong to: we must also resist any attempts at being persuaded to think that the woman question has to be superseded by the struggle against any local exploitative system, the nationalist struggle or the struggle against imperialism and global monopoly capital. *For what is becoming clear is that in the long run, none of these fronts is either of greater relevance than the rest or even separate from them.*[4] (italics added)

Generally, criticism of Aidoo's works has ignored the cautionary nature of this quotation and so displaced the richness and insight afforded by Aidoo's artistic genius and complex vision of the world. Aidoo's short stories do not simply "depict the conditions and quality of life of traditional and modern African womanhood . . . [nor simply] offer a solution to the dilemma of the modern urban African woman."[5]

*No Sweetness Here* is not a haphazard collection of short stories each complete and entire unto itself. The order in which the stories are presented and their concerns and stylistic characteristics work separately and together toward the dramatic performance of a story-telling event. Indeed, the whole collection may be experienced as a dramatic narrative performance, or *fefewo*,[6] in five acts, or phases. The whole is stage managed by Aidoo's ubiquitous narrator—the Bird of the Wayside.[7] The first phase involves two episodes or stories: "Everything Counts" and "For Whom Things Did Not Change." The second phase consists of "In the Cutting of a Drink." The next, and longest, phase includes "The Message," "Certain Winds from the South," "No Sweetness Here," and "A Gift from Somewhere." The fourth and fifth phases contain two episodes each: "Two Sisters" and "The Late Bud," followed by "Something to Talk About on the Way to the Funeral" and "Other Versions." As Aidoo remarked in an interview with Maxine Lautre-McGregor:

> If I don't have a play around, I will invite people to come to listen to poetry, either in English or in Fanti, or to come to listen to tales, folk-tales or modern stories—entertain them—I mean this is my concept of entertainment. In fact I pride myself on the fact that my stories are written to be heard primarily. . . . We cannot tell our stories maybe with the same expertise as our forefathers. But to me, all the art of the speaking voice could be brought back so easily. We are not that far away from our traditions. (Pieterse and Duerden, 24)

The value of such a fefewo or total narrative performance does not end with the telling of one particular episode or story but goes on to involve the audience-reader in a total aesthetic and ideological critical experience. Thus, as did the deployment of the dilemma tale convention in the earlier dramas, these stories seek to facilitate "interminable palavers" occasioned by their (ir)resolution.

The stories in phase 1 are concerned with the subject-positions of two representative petit bourgeois characters as they attempt to negotiate and understand their place and role within neocolonial Ghanaian society. Both protagonists, Sissie in "Everything Counts" and Kobina in "For Whom Things Did Not Change," grapple with their desires for a genuine trans-formation of this society, even as they seek to explain their guilt about the betrayal of the promises that marked the end of colonial rule. Aidoo's narrator-stage manager, the Bird of the Wayside, expertly shifts the focus of both the characters' and the audience-reader's attention and perspectives through a range of emotional, intellectual, and social registers, effectively keeping us slightly off balance. Sometimes, as with Sissie, our experience of shared guilt is quickly soothed by the evocation of joyful moments of our past: "At other times, when her world was sweet like when she and Fiifi were together, the pictures that came into her mind were not so ter-rible" (1). Yet, for Aidoo, the entertainment value of such moments is *not* in the forgetting of other, more horrifying memories: "Extremists are sure they [wigs] are made from the hairs of dead white folk—this one gave her nightmares, for she had read somewhere, a long time ago, about Germans making lampshades out of Jewish people's skins" (1). The narrator cannot keep the harsh facts of the world from intruding upon Sissie's or our consciousness. In the last instance, economics and ideology—the ownership of the material and means of production, the character of the production relationships, and the assertions of ideology—are the determinate factors in understanding social development.

The first of phase 1's two episodes takes place on a university campus in the South, while the other occurs at a government resthouse in northern Ghana. Such a wide geographical separation of episodes is significant, for the regions have an intimate and complex historical relationship. Its ensuing elaboration in the dramatic narratives of Aidoo's fefewo helps the audience-reader understand the present neocolonial attitudes of the book's protagonists and actors. To outline the nature of that regional relationship:

> Of all the nationalities in the geographical area called Ghana today and the Gold Coast in the past, apart from a few other African migrant minority ethnic groups from neighbouring former French colonies, no single group of nationalities continues to be exploited as the Northern Ghanaian Nationalities. . . . For centuries before the era of the export of agricultural products to Europe, this part of West Africa had become notorious as a source of slaves for the Atlantic Slave Trade. . . . Later when the imperialist powers decided to colonially subjugate the coastal parts of the Gold Coast, the northern nationalities were used as cannon fodder of early colonialism. In 1852, the British decided to raise a local mercenary military force. This force was called the Gold Coast Corps. It was mainly recruited from escaped or redeemed slaves of the Gonja, Dagomba, Wangera and Grunshi tribes [all Northern nationalities]. In the Akan speaking areas of the South, these people were called "Donkorfo" [an old Akan word for slave].[8]

Such a legacy, for a young, idealistic southerner like Kobina, festers like an open sore. The juxtaposition of the first two episodes in phase 1 not only signifies a shift in space, acknowledging the regional relationship, but prevents us from taking refuge in the seemingly autonomous ivory tower of the university campus where "everything counts" and the niceties of economic theory offer elegant solutions to uncomfortably concrete everyday problems (5).

Kobina, the young medical doctor, is on a trip through the North. He meets Zirigu, the caretaker of the government resthouse, and his wife, Setu. His idealism and naïveté, like Sissie's, make him feel awkward about the colonial servant-officer relationship that Zirigu and Setu establish in their dealings with him. The narrative is, in part, about Kobina's education: his acquisition of real knowledge about master-servant relationships, dependency, and rituals; the need to recoup what is useful from the old traditions and to question the uncritical adoption of the new practices of the neocolonial era. Indeed, the urge to be rid of the multiple consequences of Ghana's historical inheritance are first presented when Sissie, as an economics professor, struggles to reconcile her defense of wearing a wig (2) while a student in London, and her abhorrence of the practice when she returns home to teach (4). Similarly, Kobina's attempt to bridge the class and cultural divide between himself as a southern doctor and his northern hosts/servants is epitomized in the tension between his discursive practices (that is, his continual use of standard, or received-pronunciation, English) and the dramatic though somewhat pedestrian orality of Zirigu's (Pidgin English) narrative performances (25–33).

The narrator-stage manager begins the first episode with a series of scenes involving Sissie arguing with other students (male) in London. The choice of London, the capital of the former empire, underscores the British assumption of that city as the world's center during the colonial times. But Sissie sees the larger problems facing Ghana/Africa and argues, at the risk of alienating herself from her colleagues, that "they," other Africans in London, should get their priorities right. Further, she understands that they have been transformed into neocolonial subjects; they are unable to escape the claims of bourgeois ideology, so concentrated at the center of a collapsed empire. The traditional palavers have taken on a different character, and the male students react in new and strange ways: "They looked terrible, their eyes changing, turning red and warning her that if she wasn't careful, they would destroy her. Ah, they frightened her a lot, quite often too. Especially when she thought of what filled them with that kind of hatred" (2). It is, perhaps, a Western turn of mind, a tendency to place things, issues, and people in hierarchical categories, coupled with the privileging of patriarchy and the free dispensing of expert advice that has wrought this change (2–3). Ironically, this same kind of expert continues to give us, neocolonial subjects, "first-class dangerous advice," even after formal independence. It is they who teach us about the "war of the sexes," among other things. Our own familiarity with *Anowa* validates our suspicion that "if there had been any [war of the sexes] at all in the old days . . . [it] could not possibly have been on such a scale" (3). In those days, as now, sexual politics were integral to the struggle against the interconnected oppressions of gender, national or ethnic origin, and class.

The clarity, if not the intensity, of such politics is given a different expression in the second episode. To further accentuate the complex implications of various social situations and communicative acts, the Bird of the Wayside, in the third of four internal monologues, allows Kobina to express, in "his *educated* language," what he sees as Zirigu's problem: "When a black man is with his wife who cooks and chores for him, he is a man. When he is with white folk for whom he cooks and chores, he is a woman. Dear Lord, what then is a black man who cooks and chores for black men?" (20). Despite Kobina's intellectualizing of the concrete problem confronting people like Zirigu, we see that the battle lines of sexual politics become somewhat muddied in the neocolonial swamp. The corollary of this issue is another question: What is the black man who lets other black men cook and chore for him? It is the answer to this question that Kobina's actions and responses in his relationship with Zirigu speak to. To be able to answer both questions and truly address the problematic implications of the subsequent answers, Kobina needs to further educate himself and, more importantly, to communicate with those who have the potential to change things (19). Zirigu, on the other hand, while more or less free from those strictures, has to overcome years of conditioning by another set of discursive behaviors, a legacy of the colonial era (Prah, 28). Kobina has a somewhat idealized view of "the revolution" and those who will play a leading role in the transformation of the neocolonial society (23–25).

Sissie, however, sees herself as in the vanguard, transforming the society to which she has returned. The Bird of the Wayside's narrative traces the emergence of Sissie's realization that one needs more than theoretical knowledge of the material conditions of the society one wants to change. She has a rude awakening when she finds that her compatriots have not only taken to wearing wigs with crude abandon but are also using skin-lightening creams in their desire to be "white." The narrator evokes the nightmare of Frantz Fanon's *Black Skin, White Masks*, transforming and concretizing the abstract formulation that,

> if there is an inferiority complex, it is the outcome of a double process:
> —primarily, economic;
> —subsequently, the internalization—or, better, the epidermalization of this inferiority. (Fanon, 11)

As we share Sissie's frustrations, fears, and anger, we realize that at those very instances of heightened emotional intensity we are as innocent as we are guilty. Like the characters Sissie left behind in London, each of us is acknowledging, on a personal level, our subjection to the dominant European bourgeois ideology, even as we excuse our own weaknesses while attacking the other. We, along with Sissie, should be cautious about feeling superior to, or abrogating to ourselves a leadership role within the specificity of, the neocolonial conditions, described or actual, of Ghana. For, in the seemingly insulated autonomy of our readership, the narrator's tone gently mocks both Sissie and us.

As readers, we tend to refine the text in the bourgeois ways we have learnt; unfortunately, such processing cannot account for the complexities of the neocolonial situation, or the orally grounded depiction of that reality in what was once an outpost on the periphery of the British Empire. In this fefewo, Ghana is no longer peripheral; it is at the heart of the matter. Sissie's spirited desire to correct the ills of neocolonialism during her first semester recalls the naïveté of another been-to—Baako, in Ayi Kwei Armah's *Fragments*. Baako, also a petit bourgeois intellectual, so "cerebralizes" the fact of always and already being a neocolonial *sujet en soi* that he suffers a nervous breakdown. Sissie, in contrast, is moving beyond the highly introspective position of the Baakos of African literature; consequently, she is able to "real-ize" the neocolonial's predicament in vomit and tears.

As Fanon reminds us, "Reality, for once, requires a total understanding.

On the objective level as on the subjective level" (11). Similarly, we must understand the storyteller's narrative on *both* these levels of cognition, just as Sissie has to learn that, although she is correct about the crucial role of economics in nation building, one must also recognize the insidious nature of bourgeois oppression and its ideological claims. For instance, when Sissie sees the young female students in her class, she is struck by their appearance, their aspirations to "look" more "white," more European, and thus supposedly more attractive. She attempts, unconsciously at first, to shift her subject-position, assuming the perspective of a young Ghanaian male. "Loved and respected" for her beauty *and* intelligence, Sissie ironically finds herself possessed by "a jealousy so big, she did not know what to do with it" (5); she thus reveals her interiorization of Western patriarchal ideology. The forces that Sissie thought had influenced her experiences, and that had seemed so intense, so clearly delineated, in London, now reveal themselves to be as powerful in their covert penetration of her consciousness as they are in their overtly self-deprecating expression. Her behavior was like the potentially fatal attraction of the car and the electrical appliances that her relatives craved and assumed that she would supply. Such consumer symbols of the successful been-to were anathema to Sissie, who saw them as "ropes with which we are hanging ourselves" (7)

Sissie's cognizance of her own subjective role in perpetuating the neocolonial arrangements is paralleled by Kobina's recognition that the strategies of his discursive practices handicap his ability to *hear* the dispossessed and marginalized. His social and economic status hinder his real appreciation of the complexities, both objective and subjective, of what is at stake in the genuine fulfillment of the promises made at Independence. Kobina learns that his need to know, to "hear," can only be effected by his willing suspension of so-called normative ways of speaking, reading, and listening. In practice, he must adopt a critical oral aesthetic and ideology. Aidoo's stage manager, the Bird of the Wayside, re-centers that marginalized moment, in the text, through the insistence of the spoken word, of mininarrative performances by characters such as Zirigu and Setu, who are less distant, Aidoo has said, "from our traditions" (Pieterse and Duerden, 24) than ourselves.

The narrator-stage manager shifts our attention to an exchange between Zirigu and Setu about their "strange one. This young master" (9). The conversation is reminiscent of the exchanges between the two women, "your neighbours," in *The Dilemma of a Ghost*, and The-Mouth-That-Eats-Salt-and-Pepper in *Anowa*. The dialogue between husband and wife contextualizes the action that is being narrated by the Bird of the Wayside, thus demonstrating the intimate relationship between narrator-stage manager, characters, text, and the varied levels of audience. Setu and Zirigu, although expressing different ideas about the "strange one" and their own lives, have more in common than the choruses of Aidoo's earlier dramas. Both perceive Kobina to be different and speculate as to why. Zirigu is more perplexed by that difference than his wife, Setu, however, for she has less contact with Kobina. Zirigu, calling on his years of experience as a steward, seeks to explain this difference in terms of Kobina, a southerner, being a "Believer," a Muslim. Unlike the Ghanaian politicians and administrators who followed the European colonial functionaries, Kobina has not brought a woman or concubine with him (10).

Zirigu and Setu's conversation turns to their own economic plight, but only as a point of departure for more "interminable palavers." Just as the wig was the symbol of the insidious nature of oppression in the previous episode, for the indignant Setu, prostitution and concubinage symbolize the complicity of both "big men" and the numerous "fathers and mothers" who benefit from the continued rape of persons and property after the formal end of colonialism (11–15). Her identification of those who must share the guilt for "doing unholy things" (13) is fueled by a vexation that propels her toward a more radical position vis-à-vis injustice and oppression. In many ways she is like Anowa, who acknowledges the need for change, especially if we are to avoid being slaves to our histories. Zirigu, on the other hand, is somewhat like the Old Man, although more pessimistic (13–14). Both are poor northerners, so, despite their perceptiveness and desires, their long history of disadvantage makes it difficult for them to clearly articulate their real yearnings. Beyond the generalized outbursts of rage and frustration, or enigmatic interjections such as "Ah" and "Mmm" (14–15), their resistance to and anger against oppression is hardly heard, let alone effective. Against the anguish of the predicament of these northerners, the so-called war of the sexes and the elevation of wig wearing to the number-one task in pursuit of the revolution by Sissie's southern "been-to" compatriots seem trifling and self-indulgent.

Kobina's education, in keeping with Aidoo's deployment of elements from the orature, begins after an evening meal of "tuo" prepared by Setu and "pito" shared with Zirigu. After the wine, the story telling begins. Kobina's voice diminishes into silence as he *listens* to Zirigu (24–25). The northerner's story opens on a note of remorse and resignation over the passing of a precolonial culture. The tone suggests a lamentation for the fading of an era typified by a gerontocracy that maintained the flexibility of consensus and cooperation (25–26). With the advent of colonialism, nomadic life was introduced into northern society. As Zirigu states, "They used to say that to travel then was the thing" (26). Like the conscripts of the Gold Coast Corps of 1852, Zirigu went into the colonial army and served in "Burma—or some place like that" (26–27). Even after Independence, the cycle of conscripted military service in foreign lands due to the machinations and rivalries of imperialist powers continued. Kobina realizes that he shares a similar experience with Zirigu, for he "went to the Congo with our boys."[9]

This shared background helps Kobina to begin forming a more realistic picture of the lived experiences of the marginalized subject in the neocolonial context. Yet, more often for northerners, what happened after their return from these foreign wars disturbed and insulted their self-esteem (27–33). If the returnees were lucky, they might find employment in the South. As the Ghanaian sociologist Kwesi Prah has noted, the attempts by northern migrants to save a little money was generally frustrated. Added to this they often had to live in overcrowded "slum areas called Zongos. Here men, women and children live in the most unhealthy conditions imaginable" (Prah, 26–28). Since Zirigu and his wife were not completely subject to the degree of social discrimination and economic exploitation that other northerners in the South experienced, we might consider them fortunate. Nevertheless, the rest of the caretaker's narrative only confirms the greater betrayal of the common citizen, the denial of the pledges of Independence, and the ostentation flaunted in the faces of those for whom not much has changed since the era of the Atlantic slave trade. Life has not been easy for the household. Zirigu's meager salary and Setu's income have had to be supplemented by subsistence farming. The economics of the educated, the theoretical formulas about the level of savings and capital accumulation in developing countries, seem fanciful if not insulting to the Zirigus and

Setus of the world (30). But what is more painful than exhortations to save are the unkept promises of development.

For the educated Ghanaian/African audience-reader, like Kobina, such knowledge itches like a mosquito bite. A non-African would overcome the specificity of cultural and historical difference through class or gender experiences or both. Zirigu's story is the unpleasant truth that reveals our callousness toward the well-being of others, so long as we are comfortable and can have the benefits of electricity and a private bathroom where we can evacuate our bowels or vomit. It is the story of the arrogance that leads us to "think all of [them] from the north are Moslems. It is because [we] do not know anything about the north" (31). So, when Zirigu is told that the rest house is to be renovated, his hopes naturally rise. After all, the British colonialists have gone, and it is the new era. But the promises of better amenities were not kept (31–32). After so many promises, after so many betrayals, the powerless are left with nothing but their anger and alcoholism. Zirigu admits, "For a long time, I was drinking. I wanted to go away. I wanted to kill somebody. . . . But Setu talked to me. She said I was behaving like a child. That it is nothing. We should never forget who we are, that's all" (32–33). Setu's advice echoes the comment by the Old Man, at the end of *Anowa*, when he observes that, in spite of all the adversity and betrayals, Anowa was "true to herself." So Zirigu, who does not want "to be like them [civil servants] . . . or like you [Kobina]," deserves our respect and admiration—as does Setu, who, for different reasons, also wishes to be herself.

We can imagine that Zirigu's narrative does not let Kobina "sleep well"; for, yet again, we find the resolution of the story inadequate. The primary narrator, the Bird of the Wayside, has retreated deep within the text, and she lets one "for whom things did not change" have the final say. Letting Zirigu tell us and Kobina his tale brings us closer to the experience of anger and frustration. In our reluctance to confront the consequences of that experience, we might even see it as a cathartic event. In short, Zirigu, by telling his story, purges his own emotions and those of Kobina, his immediate audience. But clearly, the catharsis (if there is one) is not to be confined within the textual story-telling performance. Nor can we believe Zirigu's claim that "now the anger is gone, and I stay here. My young Master, what does Independence mean?" (33). Rather, we dwell on the latter half of the quotation. Like the final utterance of the first episode, "that was the other thing about the revolution" (8), the double-edged sharpness of Zirigu's rhetorical question also leaves the textual protagonist and us *thinking*.

The only episode in phase 2, "In the Cutting of a Drink," is the one narrative that most explicitly enacts the total experience of a fefewo, in miniature. The most permanent Western contribution to Aidoo's art is the *written word,* the text itself. That text's function, in part, is to *fix* the narrative in a particular mode; in addition, Aidoo's use of orature emphasizes the *fluidity of the narrated experience* in the performative acts of her narrators. As Ruth Finnegan has pointed out, "One of the most striking characteristics of much oral literature [is] its flexible and unfixed quality. This applies particularly in the case of prose. In the actual narration of stories . . . there is very often no fixed wording, and the narrator is free to bind together the various episodes, motifs, characters, and forms at his disposal into his own unique creation, suited to the audience, the occasion, or the whim of the moment."[10] As though to underscore this episode's "flexible and unfixed quality," our usual narrator-stage manager, the Bird of the Wayside, is absent, and the whole narrative event is performed by an anonymous narrator. We thus come to experience *his* "unique creation," his stylized "verbal elaboration, [and] the drama of [his] performance" (Finnegan, 319), without a mediating voice. This story is told by a young man, to an audience of his family and assorted villagers, about his experiences in Accra. In this dramatic narrative, the narrator has assumed fully the role of the actor-raconteur. It is interesting that Zirigu, the final narrator of the previous episode, is reticent about acting and fears being cast in the role of a woman, even though the logical implications of his work as a "steward-boy" seem to dictate that he assume the role of feminized subject and raconteur. In this episode, however, the narrator is quite willing to assume various roles for the benefit of his audience; he thus enacts the process of his education and maturation during the course of his narrative performance.

A southerner, like Kobina in the previous story, this "young man" tells us about his quest to the city in search of his sister, Mansa, who had been apprenticed to a seamstress twelve years earlier. The juxtaposition of this phase and the last episode of phase 1 is significant, because it extends and develops the discussion raised previously about the meaning of

"Independence." And, although the geographical context of the action is the South, the locus of both story-telling events—Zirigu's and the un-named young man's—is rural. Aidoo thus underscores the similarities of experiences between North and South rather than the differences, which were a major focus in the previous phase. "In the Cutting of a Drink" focuses on issues of youth and opportunity, especially for women in the urban setting. The presentation of these issues is dramatically narrated be-fore an older audience, with the exception of the narrator's younger sister, while in "For Whom Things Did Not Change" we had the views of an older generation's missed or denied opportunities presented to a young and singular audience, Kobina.

The young narrator of "In the Cutting of a Drink" is accomplished in his art of story telling (Brown, 1981, 101–4), in contrast to Zirigu's rather pedestrian recounting of his experiences. The former's self-interruptions and management of the interjections of his mother (38), his uncles (39), and even his little sister (41) speak of great skill. This contrasts with the narrator's initial innocence and naïveté upon his arrival in the city:

> I say, my uncles, if you are going to Accra and anyone tells you that the best place for you to drop down is at the Circle, then he has done you good, but . . . Hm . . . I even do not know how to describe it. . . . But my elders, I do not want to waste your time. . . . Each time I tried to raise my eyes, I was dizzy from the number of cars which were passing. . . . Then a lorry came along and I beckoned to the driver to stop. Not that it really stopped. . . . Hm . . . I nearly fell down climbing in. As we went round the thing which was like a big bowl on a very huge stump of wood, I had it in mind to have a good look at it, and later Duayaw told me that it shoots water in the air. (35–36)

He meets Duayaw, a relative, in Mamprobi and tells him of his mission. "Duayaw asked me whether it was my intention then to look for my sis-ter in the city. I told him yes. He laughed saying, 'You are funny. Do you think you can find a woman in this place? You do not know where she is staying. You do not even know whether she is married or not. Where can we find her if someone big has married her and she is now living in one of those big bungalows which are some ten miles from the city?'" (37). The urban environment is as unfamiliar to the rural narrator and his familial audience as the North was to Kobina, the doctor, and as Ghana was to Sissie after her return from London. Aidoo's narrator is able to recreate for his audience of mother, younger sister, and uncles that feeling of unfamiliarity, primarily through his authority as first-person narrator-actor: "Do you cry 'My Lord,' mother? You are surprised about what I said about the marriage? Do not be. I was surprised too, when we talked that way. I too cried 'My lord.' . . . Yes, I too did, mother. But you and I have forgotten that Mansa was born a girl and girls do not take much time to grow. We are thinking of her as we last saw her when she was ten years old. But mother, that is twelve years ago" (37).

What Mansa's brother has learned in the city, and what his family has to recognize is that "In the urban areas of contemporary Ghana, prostitution and child labor is common. Many 10 to 13 year old itinerant hawkers in the urban areas of the country, in fact combine hawking with prostitution" (Prah, 29). The internal audience of the text must understand that, in the neocolonial society of urban Ghana, many traditional customs and practices do not apply, for good or ill. In this context of a changed social order, in which the values and morals of a quasi-traditional rural community are continually undermined, the central concern of opportunity, especially for women, gains greater significance. The traditionally exalted status of motherhood is scoffed at in the urban setting, as the narrator admits: "I asked him whether he knew where she was, and if he knew whether she had any children—'Children?' he cried, and he started laughing, a certain laugh" (37). Women eat with the men (38), they drink beer (39), and they dance with strangers in bars (41). All these actions are surprising or shocking to the various members of the internal (textual) audience; more importantly, for us, the external audience-reader, they reveal the limitations of the rural society's ability to adjust to the new dispensation. They also evidence the conservative disposition of the rural society with regard to the range of possible behaviors open to women. For the rural community, the behavior of the modern Ghanaian urbanites reveals the extent of ideological overdetermination by Western cultural practices. Such overdetermination is manifest not only in the concrete actions of dancing, drinking, and eating but also at the linguistic level, which perhaps speaks of a more insidious and pervasive dominance. Only when one of the three "bad women of the city" (42) speaks Fante, which the narrator understands, do they dance. This introduction eventually leads him to ask one of the other "bad women" for a dance; as it happens, she turns out to be his sister, Mansa. The narrator's stereotypical labeling of the women as "bad women of the city" arises, in part, from the conservative rural ethic. This reaction is also complicated by the narrator's unacknowledged sexual attraction for the women (Brown, 1981, 103–4) and his ignorance of the sanctions that limit women's choices in neocolonial urban society (43). The narrator is genuinely shocked and hurt by his sister's response to the arrogant tone of his question: "Young woman, is this the work you do?" (42). Like Zirigu's admonition in response to Kobina's assumption that all northerners are Moslems (31), Mansa's retort is humbling: "And who are you to ask me such questions? I say, who are you? Let me tell you that any kind of work is work. You villager, you villager, who are you?" (43). From the narrator's position of ignorant superiority, all women of the city are either "bad" or "married to a big man and all is well" (42). Mansa's laughter, which follows the narrator's question, "Do you not know me?" speaks not of a physical hunger or recognition but of a deeper, masked need for true companionship arising from her visceral awareness of the commodification of her body and her being—her reduction to *sujet-pour-l'autre*. Like "the air-stewardesses to the grade-three typists in the offices" (4), Mansa's companion, the one who first danced with her brother, "was as black as you and I, but her hair was very long and fell on her shoulders like that of a white woman. I did not touch it but I saw it was very soft. Her lips with that red paint looked like a fresh wound. There was no space between her skin and her dress" (42). Yet the suggestion of violence and sexual excitement vanishes, for "after I [the narrator] had danced, I was colder than before" (42). The abrupt return to the coldness of reality parallels the epiphanic experiences of Sissie after a beauty contest (7) and, we can assume, of Kobina after listening to Zirigu's story.

Mansa's brother, who was "sent to find a lost child," found a woman. Only after his immature arrogance has been deflated by his sister's reprimand, laughter, and enigmatic "I think you are my brother . . . Hm" (43) does he begin to comprehend what his sister's city life signifies. He might weep inwardly with the rest of the family in the village; the bitter tone implied in his last words does not, however, tell the whole story: "Cut me a drink. . . . Any kind of work is work. . . . This is what Mansa told me with a mouth that looked like clotted blood. Any kind of work is work . . . so do not weep. She will come home this Christmas. My brother, cut me another drink. Any form of work is work . . . is work . . . is work!" (43).

He has learned that, in this modern age, the old values that held the community together, tainted as they might be by alien philosophies, are the very ones that in the end may keep our bodies and souls together and dry our tears. "What [indeed] is there to weep about?" If we recall all our sisters and brothers, acknowledge the dispossessed and marginalized as part of our family, then we are true to ourselves. The whole narrative performance seems to insist that there must be something redemptive in that act. "So do not weep. She will come home this Christmas," asserts the young but wiser narrator. This hope of reunion, even in an age of alienation, exploitation, and ignorance, is the supportive idea that runs throughout these phases of the African neocolonial experience.

The third phase opens with another story set in the South, and, like the preceding phase, involves a journey from a village to a city, Cape Coast. "The Message," told by the Bird of the Wayside, continues the tenuous optimism evidenced in the closing scene of the previous performance; this story, however, concerns the trials of a grandmother, Maami Esi Amfoa, over the mistaken assumption that her granddaughter, Esi Amfoa, has died in labor. Actually, the granddaughter had a cesarean section. The Bird of the Wayside plays all the parts in this performance, and so the typical third-person narrative voice of Western prose stories is as elusive from the text as the many missing quotation marks. At least half of these passages are obviously meant to be spoken utterances (46); therefore, it becomes difficult to attribute the unmarked passages to what one usually terms stream-of-consciousness narrative. It might be more useful to see these passages as indicative of the fluidity of oral performance. In the final scene of the dramatic act, there is a shift in the register of the narrative voice toward the usual received standard English, but the tone is closer to the other voices heard in the main body of the presentation.

If the consequences of Mansa's brother's ignorance and naïveté were arrogance and patriarchal myopia in "In the Cutting of a Drink," the ignorance of the villagers in "The Message" produces an opposite effect. The village community sympathizes with Maami Amfoa's perceived loss and immediately rallies to help her on the trip to Cape Coast, where Esi Amfoa, her granddaughter, was admitted to hospital. Like the two previous episodes, this is presented in a rural context; since the Bird of the Wayside is the actor-raconteur in her own right, however, it is a far more dramatic narrative.

The story-performance can be divided into three parts or scenes. The first scene occurs in the village. It concerns the reception of the news about young Esi Amfoa's cesarean and its immediate effects upon the villagers in general, and Esi Amfoa's grandmother in particular (45–46). In the dramatic performance of this narrative, we can imagine the Bird of the Wayside giving Maami Amfoa's unmarked muttering or thoughts as asides, directly to the audience: "My little bundle, come. . . . These people on the coast do not know how to do a thing and I am not going to have anybody mishandling my child's body. I hope they give it to me. Horrible things I have heard done to people's bodies. Cutting them up and using them for instructions. Whereas even murderers still have decent burials" (46). The new dispensation, represented here by the hospital and its administrators, determines the fate not only of the living but also of the dead. Part of Maami Amfoa's anguish is caused by the knowledge that the colonial government had already taken her only son, "Kojo Amisa who went to sodja and fell in the great war, overseas" (47). This reference to the second imperialist war, recalling similar allusions in the opening phases of this fefewo, underscores the pervasive power of the former colonial authority, a power that does not discriminate in terms of who, northerner or southerner, will live and die in its service. Maami Amfoa's knowledge is compounded by the fear that the inheritors of that old order now seem to have claimed her only granddaughter.

Scene 2 concerns Maami Amfoa's journey to Cape Coast. Part of this scene is centered on the repartee between the passengers and the bus driver, "Draba" Anan, whose manner is a mixture of respect for traditional values and a worldly-wise chauvinistic profanity (48–49). The rest of the scene focuses on Maami Amfoa's fretful thoughts about what she will meet in Cape Coast (50). Once she arrives, the signs of age and worry begin to tell. The bus driver's respect for age and his concern about the old woman's obvious discomfiture prompt him to accompany her on the last leg of what seems to be a journey to a funeral. Maami Amfoa's pessimistic attitude contrasts sharply with the naive optimism of Mansa's brother, who had also gone to the city to find a "lost child" but found a girl turned into a woman.

The third and final scene enacts Maami Amfoa's reception at the hospital and her joy at seeing her granddaughter—"the only child of my only son" (52). This scene, however, begins on a discouraging note. Maami Amfoa's granddaughter, in order to be admitted to hospital, has had to give her European name, Mary Koomson, a name with which her grandmother is unfamiliar. The situation is further evidence of the disruptiveness of the long arm of colonialism. To aggravate matters, "Draba" Anan and Maami Amfoa meet a nurse, Jessy Treeson, a "scrappy nurse-in-training" (54). She is not only arrogant, but she has only hackneyed images of "these villagers," which arise from her ignorance and false sense of superiority (52). Finally, after the aggravation and suspense, Maami Amfoa is taken to see her grand-daughter and her newly born twins. In contrast to the somewhat bitter and restrained closure of "In the Cutting of a Drink," the Bird of the Wayside's emotionally intense performance finds the old woman giving unrestrained expression to all her pent-up feelings (54).

"Certain Winds from the South," the next episode, returns to the neo-colonial conditions delineated in phase 2. The question of what prompts Issa and M'ma Asana's husband to go south might seem as elusive as those winds, but in this subdued dramatic narrative it is as powerful as "this ten-gram thing" that propelled Maami Amfoa to take an equally traumatic jour-ney in search of her only granddaughter. The vivacious ending of Maami Amfoa's saga contrasts with "the chill in the air" that permeates this record of women left alone to look after their families and homes. Meanwhile, their men are seduced by dubious promises and search not for lost girls or granddaughters but for work and a little capital. Lest the Bird of the Wayside's audience become too complacent after the happy resolution of the previous story, the raconteur's story reminds us that, "within the class structure of neocolonial Ghana today, . . . the northern nationalities pre-dominate in the ranks of the oppressed classes" (Prah, 29). Just as "For Whom Things Did Not Change" focused mainly on the devastating impact of colonialism and neocolonialism on the male, "Certain Winds from the South" directs our attention to the fate of those left behind—the mothers, the wives, and the children.

In Ghana, the South functions in a manner similar to the global pull exerted by the West. The South is a socioeconomic magnet for northern Third World labor and resources. Even "in 1956, . . . ninety-eight percent of all workers in the payroll of the Accra Town Council, thirty-six percent of the workers of the Accra Public Works Department, and seventy-five percent of the proletarianized and semiproletarianized labor on the cocoa farms came from the north" (Prah, 28–29). Today's statistics differ only marginally. Behind these percentages are human beings whose lives have been permanently altered by those "certain winds from the south." For the mothers and wives left to look after families on the meager incomes derived from petty trading or subsistence farming, life seems to be a series of never-ending calamities, a daily burden of pain and death (55). Such pain and futility is poetically expressed by M'ma Asana: "Show me a fresh corpse my sister, so I can weep you old tears" (56). Her tears are bitter, unlike the joyous weeping of Maami Amfoa over the body of her *living* granddaughter. For Maami Amfoa, the South, the hospital at Cape Coast, represents a miracle. In contrast, the South and southerners represent the new colonizers for M'ma Asana, the expropriators of not only the natural resources of the North, symbolized by the duicker, but also the human resources—the young men like Issa, and M'ma Asana's husband. Like Zirigu, M'ma Asana laments the passing of the old days; and, like him, she has learned to acquiesce to this new way of life.

Issa, the father of the newly born Fuseni, grandson of M'ma Asana, comes to visit his mother-in-law late one evening. His arrival brings back the memories of M'ma's permanently absent husband. Issa leads her outside the compound to break the news about his resolve to go south (57). It is not an easy task for Issa. He struggles over the moral and social implications of his decision to go in search of work. To leave Hawa, his wife and the mother of Fuseni, is to abdicate his role as a responsible father. To stay and watch them slowly starve because of the lack of economic opportunity is equally irresponsible. The complex nature of his dilemma, acknowledged by both Brown (1981, 108–10) and Nicholson (126–31) in their critical works, enriches M'ma's story and advice to her daughter, Hawa. Aidoo, however, does not show "hostility towards the male" (Brown, 108); as in the previous stories, and especially in *Anowa*, she reveals the historical and ideological causal links to the contemporary situation this episode delineates.

Unlike Mansa's brother, M'ma understands that the problems facing Issa and her daughter differ radically from those that faced her, some twenty years earlier, when her husband left out of vanity to be a soldier in the colonial army (61). In spite of her recognition that "any kind of work is work," she rightly points to the alienating nature of such work as cutting grass (58–59). The consequences of becoming involved in the capitalist economy of the South and its cities are devastating for all the participants. For the female university students or the beauty contestants, it means wigs, hot combs, and bleaching creams; for women like Mansa, it means prostitution; for a man like Setu's hot-tempered brother, it means prison; and for men like Kojo Amisa and M'ma's husband, it means death in a foreign land for an alien cause (63–64).

When M'ma tells her daughter, Hawa, about Issa's departure (61), we learn of its impact indirectly. Hawa's reactions are implied by the responses of her mother; the narrative flow is not interrupted. The use of this narrative strategy emphasizes our role as eavesdroppers. While we are *listening* to this highly personal testimony of the consequences of neocolonialism in the lives of these northern women, we, as audience-reader, realize the extent of our *exclusion from* the narrated experience. Such knowledge can only be gained indirectly. M'ma's tale demonstrates her stubborn faith and desire to salvage something of significance from that life: "Even if it takes all the money, I hope to get us some smoked fish, the biggest I can find, to make us a real good sauce" (64). This affirmation of meaningful production contrasts with the Bird of the Wayside, who, in Aidoo's *Dilemma of a Ghost*, portrayed herself as "an asthmatic old hag / Eternally breaking the nuts / Whose soup, alas / Nourished a bundle of whitened bones" (7). Despite the apparent lack of sweetness in their lives, M'ma Asana will make "a real good sauce" for the nourishment of her daughter and grandchild, just as the whole fefewo educates and, in some measure, comforts and sustains us, the eavesdroppers.

The next episode, "No Sweetness Here," brutally modifies our expectations, coming as it does in a phase that has expressed a creeping optimism about individual, if not collective, resistance to the negative forces of neocolonialism. Although a Fanti by birth, the narrator is an outsider in the village of Bamso: "I was a teacher, and I went the white man's way," she admits (67). As an outsider, she can neither impartially adjudicate the conflicts and issues nor accurately define the villagers' interpretations of the events, about which she is our informant. Her actions are dominated by the clock (86); but, as her narrative demonstrates, she does not seem to comprehend time's significance in the events that she describes. This use of an outside narrator develops the concept of eavesdropping established in "Certain Winds from the South" one step further. The narrator, like us, can only sympathize with Maami Ama and the tragedy that befalls her. Once again, education and social status hinder the narrator's ability to truly empathize with the subjects of her dramatic narrative (83).

"No Sweetness Here" is the story of Maami Ama, her ten-year-old son, Kwesi, his untimely death due to a snakebite, and her divorce. Throughout the story, the narrator, Chicha, emphasizes her close ties with Maami Ama and Kwesi, one of her promising students (84). Yet, during her exposition, Chicha adopts a slightly detached style reminiscent of the Nigerian novelist, Chinua Achebe.[11] In a particularly important retelling of a conversation with Maami Ama we learn that

"Tomorrow is Ahobaa. Even if one does not feel happy, one must have some yam for old Ahor."

"Yes. So I understand. The old saviour deserves it. After all it is not often that a man offers himself a sacrifice to the gods to save his people from a pestilence."

"No, Chicha, we Fantis were so lucky." (69)

Maami Ama's divorce proceedings are to take place on the very day that celebrates the sacrifice of one individual for the welfare of the larger community. We also learn that Maami Ama is a Methodist, and that she had baptized her son to protect him from the machinations of Kodjo Fi, her husband, and his family (70). Maami Ama's deep religious faith and the scheduling of the divorce proceedings to take place during Ahobaada help to explain why, in the final analysis, she does not contest the divorce, despite her status, according to the customary matrilineal law, as the wronged party (72–73).

The events of "No Sweetness Here" take place over the course of three days. The feast of Ahor, the day on which the tragic events occur (81–82), recalls the sacrifice of Jesus Christ. Ironically, the Christian Messiah was killed by the jealousy and envy of others, and a similar cause is suggested for Kwesi's death. Maami Ama's deep sense of Christian commitment and faith is reflected in our final image of her: "She was kneeling, and like one drowning who catches at a straw, she was clutching Kwesi's books and school uniform to her breast. 'Maami Ama, Maami Ama,' I called out to her. She did not move" (85). The loud lamentations of those who, only hours before, had bartered over his body seem insincere compared to the silence of the kneeling figure, who truly "loved her son; and this is a statement silly, as silly as saying Maami Ama is a woman" (66). Suggestively, the narrator informs us that, at the funeral, she "had let the children sing 'Saviour Blessed Saviour'" (85).

Are we then to interpret the events as an unfortunate accident, since "we do not understand it. Life is not sweet" (82)? Or, should we believe that "perhaps the village has displeased the gods in some unknown way and that is why they have taken away this boy" (83)? Is it not linked to Aho-baada and the crucifixion of Christ? That is, through the sacrifice of the individual we are reminded of the need to correct the social wrongs and, it is hoped, to be participants in a rebirth, possibly a resurrection reflective of the title of the next mini-drama: "A Gift from Somewhere"?

Chicha makes no attempt to adjudicate between the contending interpretations of the events she has been party to and recalled for us. The complex ideology is revealed with minimal commentary. Where she does comment, the narrator makes it clear that such observations are based on her own limited ideological perspective as a Westernized outsider. Thus the textual narrator, like her oral counterpart, the Bird of the Wayside, leaves the adjudication and interminable palavers up to us. Further, the introduction of the mystical element is not fortuitous. It helps to define the temperament and resistance of women and men like Maami Ama, Maami Amfoa, and Setu and Zirigu. Maami Ama, despite her personal loss, does not, cannot, abdicate in the face of oppressive forces apparently beyond her control. She comforts herself by humming a religious lyric: "We are fighting / We are fighting / We are fighting for Canaan, the Heavenly Kingdom above" (69). That spirit of resistance sustains her; it cannot be neatly explained by the educated narrator, for its origin cannot be quantified in economic or other scientific terms.

The final episode in phase 3, "A Gift from Somewhere," holds up to critical scrutiny the metaphysical speculations implied in the preceding episode, and the unmistakably self-centered motivations of ordinary people. This is achieved by the use of two narrators, the Bird of the Wayside and Mami Fanti, who tell the same story from their own perspectives. An itinerant northern medicine man, the Mallam of the Bound Mouth, enters the compound of Mami Fanti, who is holding her dying son in her arms.[12] The Mallam's arrival can be interpreted in a number of ways, and the structure of the narrative suggests ambiguity. During the opening scene (87–94) of this story, the Bird of the Wayside explicitly details the thoughts of the principal characters, thereby casting doubt on a simple or metaphysical explanation of the events in "A Gift from Somewhere." Mami Fanti, like Badua in *Anowa*, seems condemned to give birth to children who die during infancy (93–94). The mood of resignation is even more intense than in "No Sweetness Here," and the lingering odor of death seems to be permanent (87).

The Mallam's acquaintance with death (93–94), his reliance on the goodwill of the inhabitants of the villages through which he passes (87), and his doubts about the efficacy of his "powers" prompt him to make a hasty retreat after ritualistically assuring Mami Fanti that her son will live (90–93). The Bird of the Wayside's presentation of the Mallam recalls a long tradition of notable false prophets, from Wole Soyinka's covetous Brother Jero to Sembene Ousmane's thieving Mahmoud Fall and Andrée Chedid's reactionary Hadj Osman.[13] Mami Fanti's own succession of infant deaths does not predispose her to believe in the Mallam or in his assurances that her sick child will live (88).

Unlike Chicha or Maami Ama, the unfortunate Mami Fanti cannot go "the white man's way," or trust in the divine providence of a Christian God (88). Without that external and alien cultural crutch, what does a poor peasant woman have to protect her sick son? She can draw on no quietly bubbling spring of faith and hope as Maami Ama does in the silence of "the inner chamber" (85). In contrast, what we hear is a desperate plea for the power of tradition to heal and reestablish a productive order.

Mami Fanti's "possessed" ravings and anguish complement the Mallam's "bewilderment" and seeming helplessness (89–90). In actuality, he has an advantage, since, despite his self-doubt and fear that "this baby is dead," his role as the Mallam of the Bound Mouth empowers him. It is a reciprocal product of the politics of divination and the associated activities of a Kramo (Mendonsa, 24–25). As one going through the motions, without conviction, the Mallam symbolically spits on the child and massages its frail body. He gives the distraught mother the rules of the taboo she must keep if the boy is to live and departs as silently as he appeared (93).

This introduction, dramatic though the action might be, is retold with restraint and detachment. It is as though the narrator-raconteur has been stylistically influenced by the outsider's tone of Chicha in "No Sweetness Here." In fact, Aidoo's structuring of the tale and the tone of the introductory phase makes the story's style closer to that of "For Whom Things Did Not Change" and "Certain Winds from the South." The latter two story-dramas and "A Gift from Somewhere" are introduced by the somewhat detached, omniscient Bird of the Wayside—the narrator-actor who then defers to one of the narrator-characters. This narrative strategy is used particularly when the narrator-character is a peasant. In "A Gift from Somewhere" the transition between the Bird of the Wayside and the narrator-character, in this case Mami Fanti, is marked by a typographical gap in the text. This lacuna is not followed by any direct indication that a new narrator is about to begin her story. In addition, the start of the narrator-character's tale is not indented in the text, the usual signifier of a new paragraph. The graphic lacuna and the absence of indentation suggest that the Bird of the Wayside narrator of the introduction is, indeed, an actor; one who, after a brief pause (signified by the lacuna), assumes the role and voice of the new narrator-character, Mami Fanti.

Like Zirigu and M'ma, Mami Fanti recounts the significant incidents in her life, particularly those that have occurred since the visit of the Mallam. Without the Bird of the Wayside's omniscient view, Mami Fanti's story is more personal and gives us an insider's perspective of the events narrated, *objectively,* in the introductory phase. This insider perspective raises many of the same issues left unresolved in "No Sweetness Here." Namely, to what agency or power can we attribute our fortunes, good or bad? Indeed, does anything, outside ourselves, look out for us in our daily lives? And ultimately, does it matter if we do or do not *know,* for certain, where those messages, winds, or gifts come from?

Within the context of these philosophical speculations, which open and frame Mami Fanti's reminiscence (94–99), is an elaborate variation of the domestic situation faced by Maami Ama in "No Sweetness Here." Because Kweku Nyamekye is the first of Mami Fanti's children to live beyond infancy, she treats him especially well, even spoils him. Mami Fanti, like Maami Ama and Chicha, sees her son as a scholar, for education offers a way beyond the physical confines of the village and the cultural and psychological constraints of the taboo. The similarities between the two episodes become even more apparent as we learn that Mami Fanti's husband is very much like Kojo Fi and cannot understand the simple fact that his first wife "loved her son: and this is a statement silly, as silly as saying [Mami Fanti] is a woman" (66). But unlike Maami Ama, Mami Fanti is first emotionally hurt and later physically abused by her jealous and bullying husband (Nicholson, 137–43). Like Kofi Ako in *Anowa,* Mami Fanti's husband conveniently forgets the problems that marked their early life together.

In the same way that the Bird of the Wayside introduced Mami Fanti's story, we have a return to that detached opening and personalized closing of the brackets (99). The first-person viewpoint of the final scene of "A Gift from Somewhere" limits the audience-reader's knowledge; we are confined to the kernel space of the narrator, assuming the subjective, nonprivileged perspective of Mami Fanti. So limited, we can thank "all" the messages, the winds, and the gifts, for abstract speculations cannot be more *real* than "this scar," a reminder of the imperfections of this material world (99). Despite the limits of our knowledge, the improbable can happen, and we do survive—even if, and especially when, we are so oppressed that there seems no hope of deliverance.

Such a positivistic philosophy may be fitting for a peasant mother whose blessing is a child who has survived his tenth birthday and fetches her "a few little prawns" (98) because it is a Friday, after all, only a harmless indulgence. But in the hustle and bustle of contemporary urban Ghana, can such indulgence be justified? "Two Sisters," the first episode in phase 4 of Aidoo's fefewo, explores this problem and its attendant ramifications. The narrator, the Bird of the Wayside, returns to the city to enact a few days in the lives of Connie and Mercy. Connie, the elder sister, is trapped in an unhappy marriage to James—her irresponsible husband. Mercy, unmarried, is James's female counterpart, who jumps from the bed of one "bigshot" to another in search of the material comforts of the bourgeoisie (Nicholson, 171–74).

Lloyd Brown is quite correct in describing this story as "intensely satiric" of the middle-class neocolonial elite of Ghana. Further, he is most astute in his observation that

> the plot is pointedly hackneyed, for the ultimate irony of the sisters' lives is the essentially déjà vu quality of their borrowed middle-class aspirations. As Aidoo's personified Gulf of Guinea muses, people are worms whose lives are repetitions of old patterns. . . . This kind of deliberately inconclusive conclusion is further proof of Aidoo's frank realism, and of her refusal to treat her women on the basis of some idealistic wish fulfillment. The satire of Connie's hackneyed dreams amounts to a rejection of the popular literary clichés about an idealized womanhood. (96, 119–20)

However, Brown's praise of Aidoo's style as displaying "frank realism," of holding up a mirror to life, and his suggestion that her fefewo is primarily concerned with the responses of a variety of Ghanaian women to their oppression, run the risk of valorizing victimhood. He asserts that Aidoo's combination of form and content

> *allows the reader to experience the central issue which links all of these diverse women. This is the sense of vulnerability and of limitations which inspires a proud self-assertiveness* in the old women of "Certain Winds from the South" and "The Message," which encourages a covert subversiveness in "A Gift from Somewhere," or which explains that "bitchy" tearfulness which the male derides in "Two Sisters." . . . the sense of established sexual patterns is formally—that is, structurally—reinforced by the manner in which the narrative as a whole becomes an extension of that individual's consciousness. On this basis, Aidoo's stories are . . . carefully executed designs which blend with theme and character. (Brown, 1981, 120–21, italics added)

Although the valorization of victimhood is oblique, it runs counter to the "carefully executed designs" of Aidoo's dramatic narratives. Further,

Brown's analysis does not fully account for the "blend[ing of] theme and character" in those episodes in which the principal characters or narrators are men who attempt to actively resist the dominant ideologies of patriarchy and the bourgeois order of the neocolonial state.

To understand those "carefully executed designs," we must look beyond the suggestions of a "rejection of" vapid bourgeois romances with their implicit male-privileging denouements—especially if, after reading a story like "Two Sisters," we come away with the sense that Connie's and Mercy's "lives have obviously settled into an unresolved repetition of old patterns." Indeed, we should be careful not to think that our ever-changing, ever-constant narrator is asking us merely to see Mercy as a woman whose "prospects [at the end of the tale] are no more favorable than before"; or that Connie is satirized just because she epitomizes "the popular literary clichés about an idealized womanhood" (Brown, 1981, 120). Certainly, something more is being asked of us as audience-readers.

In Aidoo's second drama, *Anowa*, through the words and actions of Badua and the Old Woman, we see how the ideological demands that proscribed the lives of women during the nascent colonial era were often supported by the victims themselves. So too in "Two Sisters," Aidoo or the Bird of the Wayside narrator explores this complex ideological underpinning of patriarchal oppression in a neocolonial urban setting. The lives of Connie and Mercy, at least from a distance, epitomize the desires of those, like Zirigu and Setu, who are constantly excluded from the promise of Independence. On closer examination, however, the two sisters are more like Badua and the Old Woman who actively participate in their own oppression and marginalization. Connie follows the advice of Maami Ama's mother "that in marriage, a woman must sometimes be a fool" (71). But Connie's limited understanding of herself, her husband, and her society prevents her from realizing that she has "been a fool for far too long a time" (71), that she, in fact, continually "cringes to a man" who is as cynical and self-seeking as her sister, Mercy. Mercy is not as worldly-wise as Mansa, who understands the price of the ticket in the urban wasteland of a neocolony. This lack of knowledge shows in Mercy's fantasies and bed hopping with rich old lecherous men like Mensar-Arthur and Captain Ashey.

Connie, James, and Mercy are caught in the neocolonial illusions peddled as the "good life." Each tries to consummate those dreams; however, the need to associate with the "powerful," as a means to affirm oneself and to acquire material wealth, only leads to the perpetuation of "nothing new" (115), as James cynically asserts after the coup. But Connie is an adult, an expectant mother, who wants to be seen as epitomizing the bourgeois stereotypes of the *good wife and mother*. James is a coward and an opportunist who wishes that he was a *real man*. Mercy is an example of arrested maturity, an unreformed adult Yaaba, the protagonist in "The Late Bud." She remains a child, lacking a sense of responsibility. For her, life remains a game with luxurious prizes for the winning players. The shoes, like the wig in "Everything Counts" and the sewing machine motor that Mensar-Arthur buys on his trip to London, symbolize those prizes. Mercy is not totally oblivious to the consequences of her games, however; the "uncertainty" (104) in her voice indicates that she recognizes, perhaps only vaguely, the moral dubiousness of her behavior and the cost of such prizes. This often unvoiced and unacknowledged culpability distinguishes Mercy from the pitiful naïveté of Wanjiru (alias Beatrice) in Ngugi wa Thiong'o's "Minutes of Glory," or the defiantly angry Mansa in "In the Cutting of a Drink."[14]

The drive for self-validation is given an extra twist in "The Late Bud," the other episode in this phase. Given the lamentably sordid pettiness of the action in "Two Sisters," we might see Yaaba's desperate need to hear her mother, Benyiwa, call her "my child" (121) as a similar desire for self-affirmation through the "other," to be sujet-pour-l'autre. Were Yaaba not only ten years old, we might be justified in drawing such a conclusion. But Yaaba enjoys playing rather than being at home to run errands and being "good" (120–21). She can see no relevance for herself in the proverb that introduces the episode: "The good child who willingly goes on errands eats the food of peace" (119). She tries to convince herself that the world of adult obligations does not concern her. Yet she is disturbed more by her mother's refusal to call her "my child" than by the abuse and criticism her mother continually hurls at her (121). By privileging us with this information, the Bird of the Wayside also introduces the more controversial issue of child socialization in a neocolonial context. On one level "The Late Bud" is akin to a traditional folktale. It is meant for the instruction of children, warning against laziness and approving of responsibility (125–26). On another level, the whole narrative reveals the limitations of a gerontocracy that inhibits the honest exchange of information between adult and child. Such psychological ill-treatment leads Yaaba to doubt her own status in the household. "Is this woman my mother?" she asks herself (126).

Having secretly overheard her mother complaining about Yaaba's behavior (122–23), Yaaba asks her playmates, Panyin and Kakra, to wake her early the next morning so that they can all go to the "red-earth pit" to get the clay for her mother. It is the day before Christmas Sunday when Yaaba resolves to prove to all that she can be as responsible as her sister Adwoa. What particularly annoys her mother is that she is ten years old. Old enough, in Ghanaian terms, to begin assuming the responsibilities of adulthood, more so because she is a girl. In an impulsive act of atonement, Yaaba decides to go for the clay in the middle of the night. This decision leads to her near-fatal accident, which occurs, ironically, in the early hours of Christmas Sunday. The agitated concern of the villagers recalls a similar response by the villagers in "A Gift from Somewhere."

As the village Kramo, the medicine man, ministers to Yaaba's injuries, "the cock had crowed once, when they laid her down" (128). Yaaba's father and the other wives question Benyiwa about the events surrounding the child's accident; she can neither explain the accident itself nor the hoe in Yaaba's hand. The Bird of the Wayside pointedly informs us that this palaver continued while Yaaba slept, and "the second cock-crow came. The church bell soon did its Christmas reveille. In the distance, they heard the songs of the dawn procession. Quite near in the doorway, the regular pat, pat of the twins' footsteps drew nearer towards the elderly group by the hearth. Both parties were surprised at the encounter" (129). On this Christmas Sunday we realize that "the world is a strange place" (130). We are reminded of the events in "No Sweetness Here" and the feast of Ahobaada, which taught us some unpleasant truths about ourselves. The pride of the elders prevents them from losing face in front of Panyin and Kakra, but that same pride nearly cost Benyiwa her daughter's life. Her tears are evidence enough of her genuine love for "my child Yaaba" (130). The link between this episode and "No Sweetness Here" is obvious: from the particularity of the day on which the two events took place to the fact that, in both dramatic narratives, the future of a ten-year-old child is in the hands of elders who should behave with more sensitivity and forethought.

In "Two Sisters" we also note that the adults do not behave appropriately. By means of dialogue (first between the sisters, then between Mercy and Mensar-Arthur, and finally, between Connie and James) and the effective use of narrative intrusions we begin to see just how the characters behave inappropriately, and how they take part in the complex process of their own undoing. The tone of the Bird of the Wayside's commentary clearly indicates her critical view of the compromises these characters make. Further, the narrator strongly suggests that it is, at best, childish for the audience-reader to believe that "the arrival of the new baby has magically waved away the difficulties between James and Connie" (115). The reason for their seemingly remarkable transformation is much more likely that "he is that kind of a man, and she is that kind of a woman." Both James and Connie continually play games of self-deception, even as each comments on the shortcomings of their lives and Mercy's butterfly behavior. The two sisters accuse each other of undermining the position of women, without realizing that they are "a pair of women, your neighbours / chattering their lives away" (*The Dilemma*, 33).

Behind the superficiality of their lives is the sadness of an estranged existence we are to confront in the life of Marija, the German woman who befriends Sissie in Aidoo's first novel, *Our Sister Killjoy*. It is also a world of fragments in which none of the characters has a view of the whole. It is mundane and petty, like the life of the man and his wife in Ayi Kwei Armah's *The Beautyful Ones Are Not Yet Born*. Mercy, like the politician in Armah's novel, does not mind crawling through the excrement to make her escape to a better life (114). Connie, however, like the famed Chichidodo of Armah's novel, likes the worms (that is, the material benefits of capitalism and patriarchal hegemony) that live and grow fat in the feces, but she cannot abide the excreta that nourishes those worms. After some obligatory protestations, Connie accepts the sewing machine motor and all that her consent implies, despite herself (114–15). Unlike Zirigu and Setu or M'ma Asana, who rely on their own convictions and inner strength, Connie is ever at the mercy of external forces and events.

James, on the other hand, realizes the precarious nature of his opportunism; he "never got his car." His disappointment tempers his arrogance, and, though he remains cynical, his relationship with his wife after the coup might be characterized as one of benign hostility. He prefers life as a "responsible" husband with his "respectable" wife and baby to the vulnerability of engaging in the politics of opportunism. This explains his seemingly magical change after the coup. The arrival of the baby is only an apparent cause for the emergence of the new James. Both Connie and James have learned to be satisfied with each other, rather than to seek the notoriety that accrues to Mercy, who actively uses herself and, ultimately, keeps "all of us down" (117–18). The conduct of James and Connie is as self-deceiving as Mercy's exploitation of her own "vulnerability" and "victimhood" is ultimately self-destructive. We may be tempted to see Yaaba's misdirected attempts to gain acceptance from her mother and elders as another version of the actions of Connie and Mercy; however, both episodes in this phase emphasize the need to see the interrelatedness of the whole.

In this context, "The Late Bud" concerns the education of the truly late, as in old, buds. In the village as well as in the city, our elders—from the Mensar-Arthurs to the Captain Asheys—are doing our nation a disservice. When they—our fathers and mothers—are too prideful or insensitive; and our brothers and husbands are either bullies or opportunists; and our sisters and wives "keep us all down," we cannot expect to break away from the old routines. We should not have to wait until another almost-fatal calamity, another coup or funeral, before we recognize the oppressed as deserving of being treated as "my child." In the main, the Bird of the Wayside seems to suggest that human actions are devoid of value viewed apart from their histories or contexts. In order to evaluate particular actions we must appreciate their peculiar histories; and, although they may be superficially similar, we cannot assume that their consequences will be the same.

The final phase of Aidoo's fefewo ends with a recapitulation that accentuates her formal innovations and thematic concerns; and yet, as we have come to expect, she leaves us with her typical inconclusive conclusions. The first episode of this phase, "Something to Talk About on the Way to the Funeral," is a stylistic return to the dramatic effectiveness that typified the performance of Mansa's brother in "In the Cutting of a Drink." This performance is for a single individual, "Adwoa my sister," however, and is given by a nameless narrator, a citizen of the village of Ofuntumase. Again, we are placed in the position of eavesdroppers. These two sisters gossip about Auntie Araba, the old woman, whose funeral they are on their way to. Adwoa, who lives with her civil servant husband in the gold-mining town of Tarkwa, has been away from the village for some time. The walk to the funeral affords Adwoa the opportunity to catch up on the latest news and gossip from her sister, the Bird of the Wayside's new guise.

"Other Versions," the last episode in the collection, is both a repetition and an elaboration of the formal and thematic concerns broached in the opening episode of the fefewo, "Everything Counts," and addressed in "No Sweetness Here" and "The Late Bud." Ostensibly, in a structural sense, we have a closure of the bracket that introduced this fefewo. This episode concerns a young man, Kofi, who has left Ghana to study in the United States. The narrative is told mainly from the perspective of this student, a candidate for the role of a been-to. Unlike Sissie's, however, his awakening occurs away from home, in a hostile culture; and yet, rather than producing a sense of rupture, it gives rise to a firm sense of connectedness. The narrative, although ending on an optimistic note, does not suggest an easy future for Kofi, or for the African-American woman he meets on the subway, who reminds him of his mother and those left behind in the neocolony. In fact, we sense that Kofi is still maturing. He must work through the feelings of guilt associated with his status as a privileged scholar. (In this respect, he is like Kobina, the young doctor in "For Whom Things Did Not Change.") Only then can he understand the implications of the neocolonial arrangements that have propelled him into the clutches of the inheritors of the former colonial empire.

We do not have to travel to the United States to appreciate the consequences of the legacy of colonialism. The Bird of the Wayside, in "Something to Talk About," in the tradition of the accomplished storyteller, takes Adwoa and her audience-reader to "bird-town" (138); we hear about the fortunes, good and bad, of Auntie Araba, her son Ato, and Mansa, her daughter-in-law. We learn of deception, selfishness, insensitivity, and disappointment. We find one good man and many who are not so good. In short, we are told the history of Auntie Araba. It is also a history of a society in transition. The narrative progresses as a dialogue, with Adwoa punctuating the flow of this chronicle with her impatient questions. Yet the Bird of the Wayside will not be hurried in this reconstruction. She focuses our attention on the behaviors of men and women, in rural and urban situations, as they act and respond to the forces of oppression and the conflicting mores of tradition and the neocolonial order.

Auntie Araba was a beautiful and popular woman in the community.

Her voice, "like good honey, was rough and heavy, its sweetness within itself" (134) emblematic of her character. Her abilities as a baker, her sound business sense and compassion won her many friends and enemies. Seduced in her youth, when she was apprenticed to some well-to-do relatives, by "that lawyer-or-doctor-or-something-like-that who was the lady's husband" (135), Auntie Araba returns home "looking like a ram from the north. Big, beautiful and strong" (135). Her life seems charmed, and she will survive, unlike other animals from the North (56) that are sacrificed to satisfy "those sweet-toothed Southerners." Her mother knows that her pregnancy is not her fault; therefore, the young Araba receives nurturing support rather than insults or condemnation. This is in contrast to the reaction of Mansa's father, when he learns that Auntie Araba's son, Ato, is responsible for his daughter's unplanned pregnancy (140). In fact, it seems that we cannot break out of the "same routine," for Ato, "the big scholar we hear of" (135), having ruined the young girl's chances of going to college or even getting a secondary education, refuses to turn up on the day he is supposed to marry her (144). His cowardice is reminiscent of his namesake, Ato (Yawson), in *The Dilemma*.

Scandal seems to stalk Auntie Araba all her life; yet, in spite of the outrages against her, we know "a good woman does not rot" (137). Her son's irresponsible behavior is not due to some fault in her, since "they say that before he was six years old, he was fighting her" (138). Unlike the respectful Nyamekye in "A Gift from Somewhere," Ato has a vicious streak. Auntie Araba's strength and perseverance enable her to survive not only the pain of having an unappreciative son but also the rumors maligning her character and marriage to Egya Nyaako (137). These suppositions remind us of the reactions evoked by Anowa's decision to marry and help Kofi Ako "do something with his life" (*The Dilemma*, 78). The major difference between the sets of marriage partners, apart from their obvious separation in time, is that Auntie Araba and Egya Nyaako shared similar economic and social outlooks and were economically secure *before* they married. Although Anowa and Kofi did become economically secure, their fundamental disagreement over the issues of domestic slavery and *sikaduro* almost guaranteed Anowa's sense of disaffection, madness, and subsequent death. And although they share a comparable historical moment with the characters of "Something to Talk About," the black-skinned white-masked bourgeois aspirations of Connie and James, like those of the neocolony in which they live, are doomed to failure without economic independence.

Auntie Araba's capacity for hard work is matched by her maternal devotion toward Mansa, who grows more like her (145), and toward her grandchild. Auntie Araba becomes a matriarchal figure, in the eyes of the narrator, Sister Adwoa, and most of the village. Even though the worthless Ato is her only child, she is surrounded figuratively by an extended and loving family. Her centrality as matriarch is evidenced by the throng of people who attend her lavishly prepared funeral. In this sense, she realizes Anowa's vision of herself as the archetypal mother figure from whose orifices "poured men, women and children" (*The Dilemma*, 106) who are seized and torn apart by boiled lobsters (Europeans). Despite her knowledge that the best work should be socially worthwhile and should not conflate one's labor and biology, she is unable to prevent her son's antisocial activities, or his opportunistic manipulation of his gender status for economic gain (144).

We should not be convinced, however, that this history of the life and times of Auntie Araba, which ends with echoes from the disquietingly pensive central episode, "No Sweetness Here," and the mutely optimistic "In the Cutting of a Drink," signifies the futility or death of resistance to patriarchy and other exploitative practices. One of the important lessons we gain from overhearing this tale is that biological affinity does not insure domestic peace. In addition, we have to acknowledge that a character's gender does not automatically define that character's nature. Kofi's experiences in the United States and his growing maturity highlight these conclusions. His tale starts on an intimate note, inviting the audience-reader to listen carefully to how "the whole thing . . . started" (147).

Throughout the performance Kofi recounts the significant role of his mother and of other mothers in his early maturation. Kofi's first steps toward independence start in a room that was "like a coffin" (148), which he shares with his friend Bekoe. The two young men's inauspicious entry into the capitalist job market as "sorting hands" situates issues that link this with other tales in this fefewo, in particular, with "Something to Talk About." First, Kofi's character is the opposite of that of the irresponsible Ato, who had the advantage of an economically secure mother. Second, the dilemmas of a matrilineal society's ideology subsumed by a system of patriarchal privilege and compounded by neocolonialism's abuse are dramatically expressed in the anger and resentment Kofi feels when his mother insists that he give four pounds of his first and subsequent paychecks to his father (151–52).

Kofi's mother's economic situation, like M'ma Asana, Maami Ama, and Mami Fanti, leaves a lot to be desired. It becomes easy for us to agree with the narrator's view that his mother rightly deserves the token "four pounds" for her years of labor and sacrifice (Nicholson, 149–53). Also, like Kofi, we may be perplexed by his mother's attitude, which resembles that of Maami Ama, and by his suspicion that her reluctance to accept her son's freely given money is what "keep[s] all of us down" (Aidoo, "Two Sisters," 105); however, we must understand the complexity of social etiquette created by the confluence of traditional and colonial ideologies in neocolonial Ghana (Aidoo, "Other Versions," 150–52). The consequences of such a confluence, internalized and accepted as "normal," inhibit his mother's ability to accept the fruits of her labor. As Aidoo has said, because "of the colonial experience we still, unfortunately, are very much lacking in confidence in ourselves and what belongs to us. It is beautiful to have independence, but it's what has happened to our minds that is to me the most frightening thing about the colonial experience" (Pieterse and Duerden, 26). But the colonial experience, with its overt manipulation of the colonized subject, has assumed other, more covert guises in contemporary Ghana. The neocolonial subject is still at the mercy of the subtle machinations of imperialist economic interests; and even Kofi's presence in the United States is not accidental. He is the recipient of a business syndicate's scholarship, a syndicate that had been "looking out for [an] especially bright . . . African" (Aidoo, "Other Versions," 152–53).

Kofi only begins to understand the reasons for his mother's refusal to accept his money when, after a dinner in which "the main course for the evening was me" (153), at the Merrows' "high and mighty hut" he meets the cook, Mrs. Hye. In this racist situation he makes the link between the "invisible" cook, other African-American mothers who toil without recognition, and his own mother back home in Ghana. A few days after the fateful meeting with Mrs. Hye, Kofi meets another "mother" on the subway. He feels compelled, "like one goaded with a fire-brand," to acknowledge what she symbolizes by giving her "twelve dollars" (155–56). Politely, she refuses his gift. As he emerges from underground, Kofi realizes not only that "all good mothers" (Nicholson, 153) are selfless; but that the act of paying his "mother" reduces what she does to a soulless monetary transaction—which is not to say that women do not want just compensation for their labor, or that they wish to be used and abused. More importantly, Kofi realizes that the greatest gift that he can give to his mother is to be true to himself, like Anowa. By eschewing the irresponsible, exploitative, and opportunistic route of the Atos and Kodjo Fis of this world, Kofi eloquently plays out the possibility of "other versions" of this reality that so strongly tries to insist there is "no sweetness here."

# For Lovers and Others, Not Just Another Version

*Our Sister Killjoy*, like Aidoo's short stories, deals
with so many problems. Once again, its success
depends largely on the ability of the author to lend
all the problems equal spikes. In that regard Ngugi
and Sembene come to mind—writers who are fully
aware in their works that a campaign for social justice
is meaningful only when all disadvantaged people in
human society receive undiscriminating attention.
It is that same principle which makes Aidoo's works
feminist literature with a difference.
—Chimalum Nwankwo

The epigraph to this chapter clearly places Aidoo in the company of Africa's
foremost writers. The comparison with Ngugi wa Thiong'o and Ousmane
is even more appropriate in the light of recent works by the two writers. In
Ngugi's critical work, *Writing Against Neocolonialism*, he points out that the
1970s saw an "awakening to the realities of imperialism."[1] This growing
discernment of the complex nature and ramifications of the neocolonialist
enterprise was reflected in the political and economic arenas, as well as in

the literary and ideological ones, in a growing number of African countries. The progressive writer of the seventies "was beginning to take sides
with the people in the class struggle" (15). In short, the progressive writer
began to champion an alternative to the neocolonial vision. This confrontation and unmasking of the ideological and economic operations of the
neocolonial state, which informed *No Sweetness Here*, is given sharper focus
in *Our Sister Killjoy: Or, Reflections from a Black-Eyed Squint*.

Aidoo's works have always been original and challenging, especially in
her insistence on mingling the formal elements and aesthetics of orature
and the concerns of contemporary Ghana, Africa, and its diaspora with
the impact of Western imperialism. In this regard, her authorial project is
akin to that of Sembene Ousmane's *The Last of the Empire*. In making this
comparison with the Senegalese writer and filmmaker, I am not suggesting
that either is indebted to the other. It stands to reason that ideologically
*committed* (in Ngugi's sense of the word) African writers have been influenced by each other, and by the shape of events taking place within their
respective countries and the continent as a whole. It is, however, interesting that *Our Sister Killjoy* and Ousmane's *The Last of the Empire* were
originally published within two years of each other, Aidoo's first. In aid-
ing those unfamiliar with the synthesis of certain conventions of African
orature and Western forms, specifically in Ousmane's work, a number of
issues should be noted since they help illuminate Aidoo's work.

The dialectic between the narrative structure and content is elaborated
and extended in *The Last of the Empire* so as to actively engage the audience in a polylectic examination of the contradictions of this neocolonial
age. Ousmane's point of departure is overtly challenging to the reader's
unexamined cultural and ideological presuppositions. From the author's
foreword to Doyen Cheikh Tidiane's (also known as Doyen Sall) decision
as to the title of his memories on the "last" page, the text continually calls
attention to its fictionalized content and its covert authorial overdetermination. In effect, the total text docs the work of literary-ideological criticism; it reveals its own subtext even as its realistic mode seemingly displaces
that ideological subtext. The aesthetic and ideological achievement of *The
Last of the Empire* is further illustrated by its synthesis of other conventions
of African oral tradition (seen in part by the parenthetical interjections
of the griot, or raconteur), and the selective manipulation of elements of

the received Western codes of the novel. To appreciate this novel, Ous-mane's latest, one must *experience* the text as *performance*. Everything that is printed (or not) should be likened to a gesture or utterance from a *speaker;* thus, when we note that it is subtitled "A Senegalese Novel" and that after the dedication there is an author's foreword, we should be alert. It is this foreword that functions as the key *and* lock to understanding this very "Senegalese novel":

> This book is not to be taken for anything other than a work of imagi-nation.
>     . . . These men and women of our dear SUNUGAL—Senegal are far superior to the mediocre types portrayed in this book. I will (never) forgive any reader who makes any comparison, any connection even covert between these "fictional characters" and our valiant fellow citi-zens, devoted unto death (however it may strike) to building our future. I will not hesitate to have recourse to our laws (which are fair and just).
>
> Sembene<br>Galle Ceddo<br>August 1976–January 1981 [2]

Unlike the authors of Western novels, particularly early ones, whose fore-words attempt to convince the reader of the verisimilitude of the fictions their novels actually are, Ousmane forces the audience-readers to acknowl-edge the elaborate mediation of their imagination in the production of the text or performance. This prefatory warning and disclaimer subverts the expectations of Ousmane's casual Western-educated audience-reader.

Although sharing similar cultural ground with Aidoo, it may be argued that Efua Sutherland occupies a slightly different ideological space; never-theless, they both use conventions of Ghanaian orature for comparable purposes. In the foreword to the 1987 edition of her plays, Sutherland, who describes her type of drama as the Anansesem (literally, Ananse stories, and the story telling itself), observed that "[it is] a community art. All the people present are performers in one way or another, either actively or potentially. . . . People come to a session prepared to be, in story-telling parlance, 'hoaxed.' . . . Of the many problems . . . the most tricky has been how to invest it [the drama] with some capacity for invoking this element of community participation."[3] Both Aidoo and Ousmane, it seems, have taken this "community art" one step further. Aidoo's innovative aesthetics and ideological attitude, like Ousmane's and Ngugi's, contribute toward the realization of a truly *African* literature.[4] With these writers, authentic African novels emerge from the womb of neocolonialism.

As the title of this chapter suggests, *Our Sister Killjoy* is not just another version of a contemporary fefewo. Many critics have described it as a novel, for lack of a better term, because of the complexity involved in distinguishing the character of the narrative voice(s), the fusion of prose and poetry, and the epistolary "Love Letter" that concludes the work. Almost all criticism of *Our Sister Killjoy* has commented on these aspects of Aidoo's style.[5] For instance, the sleeve notes of the Nok edition attribute "the speaking voice . . . [to] Sissie"; it would be a mistake, however, albeit an understandable one, to attribute the narrative voice in the first three sections to Sissie. First, the Bird of the Wayside, the omniscient narrator, knows the inner thoughts of her characters; second, Sissie, the protagonist, is always referred to in these three sections in the third person singular; and, third, the narrator's insight, wit, sarcasm, and empathy show a deeper awareness and commitment to the struggles of the oppressed than Sissie at first evidences. Structurally, *Our Sister Killjoy* adopts the same strategy of narrative-performance, or episodes, as "For Whom Things Did Not Change" and "A Gift from Somewhere" in Aidoo's fefewo *No Sweetness Here*. The Bird of the Wayside is the narrator of the first part of the work; then one of the characters (Sissie) in that first part has the final word. During the course of the *nutinyawo* (a collection of prose-poetry narratives) Sissie, like her literary predecessor, Anowa, is shown to be "a young woman who grows up" (*The Dilemma*, 56).[6] As a sign acknowledging Sissie's maturation, the Bird of the Wayside withdraws as narrator and allows Sissie to write (speak) in her own style (voice)—hence, "A Love Letter."

*Our Sister Killjoy* is a Ghanaian novel in the same sense that Ousmane's *The Last of the Empire* is a Senegalese novel or Ngugi's *Matigari* a Kenyan one. *Our Sister Killjoy* begins with the author's dedication and libation to the ancestors:

> For You
> Nanabanyin Tandoh,

> who knows how to build;
> people
> structures
>
> lives. . . .
> (lines 1–6, n.p.) [7]

and the memory of those, particularly "Roger Genoud / the son of Marcel Genoud," whose work was committed to building and explaining attempts toward more *human* and *humane* societies—"people / structures / lives." [8] In alluding to both Nanabanyin Tandoh and the Genouds, Aidoo is extending recognition to both Ghanaian/African and French/European ancestors whose struggles were significant in nationalist terms, and from an internationalist perspective. Thus the nutinyawo are placed within a large geopolitical frame. What is important are the "people" and their "lives," rather than the "structures," which are meaningful only within the parameters of the "people" and their "lives." Within those limits, we sympathize with the poet's claim that

> there was no cloth
> strong enough to
> hold my spilling intestines in.
> (lines 14–16, n.p.)

Despite the striking image of disembowelment, an apt response to the daily horrors faced by the oppressed, the author's sympathy for and solidarity with them is economically evoked in this poem. The libation affirms Aidoo's desire to explain that which many others seem incapable of doing.

Her dedication completed, Aidoo's voice retreats, allowing the Bird of the Wayside to take us "Into a Bad Dream"—the opening *nutinya*. We are then left with the rest of page one and the whole of page two as blank paper, and page two has no pagination. We are tricked, quite literally, into "the blank of whiteness"; or perhaps we are invited to take a journey opposite to Marlow's trip into *The Heart of Darkness*. The reversal of Conrad's central metaphor for the exploration of the imperial project marks Aidoo's overt departure from the aesthetic-ideological paradigm that supports that other journey. The Bird of the Wayside knows that, despite the psychological damage wrought by that blank whiteness in our history, there are people whose resistance, whose work, will take us out of a "bad dream" toward those "dazzling conclusions" (3–5). To refocus our attention on the nature of some of these ideological "ticky-tackies" (5), the Bird of the Wayside slows down the pace on the next page by continuing the narrative in prose, rather than poetry.

This introductory nutinya affords the narrator a chance to clear the ideological ground before beginning the narrative of Sissie's trip, as a member of an international volunteer organization, INVOLU, to work in a pine nursery in a Bavarian village. The Bird of the Wayside's attack is uncompromising. Both the "nigger who is 'moderate'" and his "academic-pseudo-intellectual version" are roundly condemned for their shallowness and duplicity, their subservience to their "bosses," and the patronizing attitude they display toward their own people. The passions the Bird of the Wayside feels toward these Africans is nicely conveyed by the Akan proverb *Otorofo na ose, me dansefo wo Aburo Byri*, which loosely translated means "the one with the slippery-tongue says, 'my witness is in Europe'" (74). In order to better ponder the horrific implications of the behavior of those whose witnesses are in Europe, and who daily betray their own people by mindlessly repeating the bourgeois universalist cant, we are left with more blank whiteness (the rest of page six and most of page seven).

When the Bird of the Wayside returns to continue the nutinya, it is as though a member of the audience, shocked by the narrator's vehemence, has made an interjection to which the narrator replies,

> Yes, my brother,
> The worst of them
> these days supply local
> statistics for those population studies, and
> toy with
> genocidal formulations.
> That's where the latest crumbs
> are being thrown!
>
> (7)

After this aside, the narrator sketches how Sissie was chosen by the German government, through its embassy, as part of "a people's efforts / 'to make good again.'" The narrator's ironic "black-eyed squint" notices that "they had come to the campus looking for her in a black Mercedes-Benz, its flag furled," and that the power of the former colonialist nation extends far enough to pull "strings for her to obtain her passport in a week instead of three months" (8). Sissie's most memorable encounter with those who "pulled strings," like Kofi's with the Merrows, is during a dinner at which she is "the main course for the evening" (*No Sweetness Here*, 153). At the dinner, she meets Sammy, a young Ghanaian who "laughed all the time: even when there was nothing to laugh at" (9). He epitomizes the stereotypical happy and servile colonial subject, and his manner upsets Sissie. This rather uncomfortable meeting with Sammy, one of many she is to meet on her journey into the blank whiteness, is only the beginning of her education and maturation.

Even her flight to Germany is complicated by larger political factors, which further expand the context and contradictions of Sissie's journey. She has to catch a connecting flight from Johannesburg in Lagos. Once on board, she is politely shown to the back of the plane, in order not to upset the racist sensibilities of the white South African passengers. The Bird of the Wayside's ironic comment, "Ma-a-ma, ain't no one can laugh at hisself like us," recalls the idiomatic phrasing of African-American English and further confirms that the narrator is more traveled than Sissie. The inclusion of this idiomatic statement, like a blues lyric, also establishes the connection between the discrimination and racism faced by Africans in "the pit that is South Africa" and the Jim Crowism of the United States (10). But once in Germany, things are no better for the unsophisticated Sissie. At the railway station in Frankfurt, her innocence is shattered: "'Ja, das Schwartze Madchen,'" (12) a mother politely tells her daughter, indicating the bewildered Sissie. Her journey and education having begun in earnest. The Bird of the Wayside moves the narrative into the clipped economy of poetry, leaving us to ponder this new realization:

> What she also came to know was that someone somewhere would
> always see in any kind of difference, an excuse to be mean.
>> A way to get land, land, more . . .
>> . . . Clothes to cover skins,
>> Jewels to adorn,
>> Houses for shelter, to lie down and sleep.

A harsher edge to a voice.
A sharper ring to commands.
Power, Child, Power.
For this is all anything is about.
Power to decide
Who is to live,
Who is to die.

(13)

And in the blank whiteness that follows, we *do* think about who has "power to decide / Who is to live, / Who is to die, / . . . Where, / . . . When, / . . . How" (13–16).[9]

The next nutinya, "The Plums," is the longest of the Bird of the Wayside's nutinyawo. It explores the implications of the "power to decide" and the knowledge "that someone somewhere would always see in any kind of difference, an excuse to be mean" as it affects Sissie in her journey through the blank whiteness of Europe. Because of her habit of standing in a round sentry post overlooking the town and surrounding countryside, she meets Marija Sommer, the young German mother of Adolf (the second), the son of an absent father (23). Marija often walks past this sentry post as she pushes her baby in a pram. As the nutinya proceeds, the Bird of the Wayside's omniscient commentaries are rendered as verse, more often than not, and carry the ironic tones of someone who has traveled much and seen deep into the blank of whiteness. The Bird of the Wayside's first poetic utterance in this section establishes, in the minds of the audience-reader, the historical (feudal) roots of patriarchal abuse and oppression in Germany (19), as well as a thematic link of betrayal witnessed by "those forts" (*The Dilemma*, 66). Like the Bavarian castle whose walls have witnessed many crimes, "those forts" in Ghana have been turned into police barracks, prisons, and even a government building—their infamous histories forgotten, or repressed.

Central to this nutinya is the relationship between the two women and what each learns from that experience. Marija's ignorance of other peoples is painfully obvious as she asks Sissie if she is Indian (19). The Bird of the Wayside's scathing sarcasm finds free reign as she comments on the ignorance of "a young / Hausfrau" who thinks that Ghana is near Canada (24). Her most biting sarcasm, however, is reserved for her comments about the legacy left by Christian missionaries who went to Africa to save the hea-thens (25–27). Though Marija cannot understand why Sissie should have been called Mary in school, the Bird of the Wayside leaves us in no doubt about the whys and wherefores. Lest the audience-reader think that the Bird of the Wayside only wishes to catalogue the sins of various oppressors, the vitriolic intensity of her "reflections from a black-eyed squint" gradu-ally turn to the evolving relationship between Marija and Sissie, our sister. Their association, founded on a mutual sense of isolation, becomes the talk of the small town.

At first, they are content with their walks, and Marija learns a great deal about the outside world from her friendship with "the African Miss" (46). After each visit, Marija gives Sissie a brown bag of plums to take back to the castle where "our sister" stays with her roommates, who "were such infants" (41). Yet Sissie is unaware of the undercurrents that feed Marija's need for her friendship. The Bird of the Wayside explains Marija's emo-tional cravings by placing them in a larger context. First, it is clear that Marija, despite her cozy little house and her adoration of Little Adolf, is sujet-en-soi. Her life, like Connie's in "Two Sisters," is a lonely delusion. The arrival of Sissie, the exotic other, seems to be a good opportunity to escape "the deserted looking chamber or its simple funereal elegance. . . . A love-nest in an attic that seems to be only a nest now, with love gone into mortgage and holiday hopes" (63–64). It is the bourgeois dream that haunts and perverts the lives of people as culturally and geographically distant as Connie in "Two Sisters" or "an Indian / in Gottengen or There-abouts" (29). When economic imperatives take the love out of the love nest, Marija is left alone with her child. Big Adolf works overtime in order to pay the mortgage, not with the love that Marija puts into baking a plum cake or into picking the choicest plums from the one tree in her garden, not because "work is love made visible" (41), but because Big Adolf is "a factory hand" (43) who lives a "lower-middle class" (64) life. The Sommers live in a world that has decayed "into a Bad Dream," where "the thinned-out-end of the old aristocracy and those traditional lickers of aristocratic arse, the pastor, the burgomaster and the schoolteacher, . . . Joined by the latest newly-arrived" (44) look on disapprovingly and enviously at Marija's friendship with Sissie.

The affair's slow development uncovers much that had been hidden from Sissie's awareness, and she has a chance to ponder its implications and learn about the world beyond the castle walls. This process begins in earnest when her relationship with Marija crosses the line from the fantasy of puppy love to the reality of lesbianism, for "she was only an unconscious African schoolgirl" (46) who viewed their relationship as a game in which she was the "man" (61–62). But their relationship had crossed an unmarked boundary, and Sissie's reaction to Marija's curious look contrasts with the previous occasions when their eyes met and they just smiled (40). Her predicament, the result of a discarding of the "ticky-tackies [she has] saddled and surrounded [herself] with" (5), is alleviated by her movement toward the "dazzling conclusions" (4) about relationships, lesbian or heterosexual; about why she, an African woman, is in Bavaria; about how economic, cultural, and other forms of exploitation are all connected.

After a strangely Freudian and surrealistic entry into Marija's bedroom, as if "down into some primeval cave" (62), Sissie first begins to realize the corrupting magnitude of systematic exploitation. She experiences the power it affords a person to inflict pain on others and, eventually, to feel "like a bastard. Not a bitch. A bastard" (75). When, at the eleventh hour, she tells Marija that she will be unable to have lunch with the Bavarian hausfrau, Big Adolf, and Little Adolf because she is going away, Sissie senses the confusion and vulnerability of the other (75–76). Like her fantasies, Sissie's nascent lesbian relationship had begun to assume the power dynamics of a sexist heterosexual one. It was a perversion as horrifying as the stories she had heard, in which she imagined herself as "one of these black boys in one of these involvements with white girls in Europe" (61). The ending of such involvements, like that between Modin and Aimée in Ayi Kwei Armah's *Why Are We So Blest?*, is for "these black boys" to have "their penises cut" (62).[10] Ultimately, despite their succulent appeal, the plums of the *nutinya's* title are about the nature and abuse of power in a world that seems to prevent and overdetermine the realization of meaningful human relationships.

Despite the "inner joys" that arose from their unpretentious acceptance of each other's company, both Sissie and Marija are made "too aware of the sad ways of man" (48). "Knowledge gained since" (67) her friendship and embrace with Marija stimulates Sissie's understanding of the repercussions of colonialism and neocolonialism and the shared, though barely repressed, sense of guilt (65–66). For Marija, the aborted intimacy of another woman's love is not enough to help her break out of the bourgeois prison of a little town in Bavaria. Sissie leaves Marija, but not the memories, on a train that "was determined to return Our Sister to her origins" (82). The irony of this claim becomes apparent in the Bird of the Wayside's third nutinya, "From Our Sister Killjoy." Her experience in Germany has given the once naive Sissie a more sagacious perspective on life. She has begun to mature and is well on her way to becoming, in some eyes, a "Killjoy."

The third nutinya is more complex than the two previous ones, because the Bird of the Wayside allows us greater access to the thoughts of the increasingly articulate and maturing Sissie. Her experiences in this phase lead Sissie to a more committed and critical outlook. Away from the surveillance and chaperonage of INVOLU's proxies—"the Bavarian dames" (36)—Sissie visits London. The narrator frames Our Sister's visit to London, "her colonial home," by evoking our recollections of others who have willingly or involuntarily left Ghana or other Third World countries to work or study elsewhere (22–23). Sissie is shocked to find on the streets of London "so many Black people" (85). Indeed, her compassion and sympathy for other people's suffering, apparent in the conflicting emotions of her relationship with Marija, are unrestrained as she views the wretched masses. Like her, they have rushed "to the imperial seat because that is where they know all salvation comes from" (87).

Sissie's stay in London is much longer than the one month (73) she had intended; consequently, she has missed at least a term's work at her university back home in Ghana. But this does not really matter, for her "education" still continues. While in London, she learns more, ironically, about herself and the psychological and economic effects of colonialism and neocolonialism than she would have listening to a lecture from her namesake in "Everything Counts." Many of the personal reasons for the postponement of her return are explained, in Sissie's own words, in "A Love Letter." But more importantly, her delay is motivated by a genuine desire to understand why those Africans she sees on the crowded streets stay in London, where nothing is "sacred," and "no spot is holy" (79). "From Our Sister Killjoy" is a nutinya that charts the crucial transformation from naive Sissie to mature Sister Killjoy, and we are confidants in this process.

Sissie's curiosity is not satisfied by the excuses her fellow Africans give for their self-exile, since she now knows "that in a cold land, poverty shows as nowhere else" (89). Beneath their masquerade as perennial students lies the shabby reality of being recipients of the leftovers of imperial handouts (85–86). Attracted to the "Imperial seat," like northerners to the urban centers in southern Ghana,

> they work hard for the
> Doctorates—
> They work too hard,
> Giving away
> Not only themselves, but
> All of us—
>
> The price is high,
> My brother!
>
> (87)

Shortchanged, these migrants can only clothe themselves in the ridiculous "cheap plastic versions of the latest middle-class fashions" (79). Their dreams shattered, they cannot admit the truth behind the illusions that insist that "things are only what they seemed" (79). Ultimately, Our Sister is not convinced by the denials of these other versions of Sammy and his European bourgeois originals, by their intellectual acrobatics, or by their claims that the world is free (89) or a happy place embodying "universal truth, universal art, universal literature"(6).

During her extended visit, Sissie meets and talks with African "student" groups and Europeans who wish "to make good again" (8), yet they only regurgitate so many variations on this universalist theme. Through these meetings and conversations "things are working out . . . towards their dazzling conclusions," and Sissie has begun to understand how, ideologically and economically speaking, things are not what they seem. In this regard, Our Sister appreciates the full meaning of the Akan proverb *Wudi Buroni ade a, woko aprem ano;* that is, when you eat the white man's pay, you fight at the cannon's mouth. In short, the display of power exhibited by the neo-colonial bourgeoisie and its allies, the intelligentsia, is not real power. The Bird of the Wayside describes these betrayers of the wretched of the earth in Nigerian pidgin:

Who no sabe book
Sabe noting' for e contrey
no fit hear notin' self.

Oga, 'this big Africa man go sit down te-e-ey, look at this Oniyibo
man wey e talk, wey e mout-go ya, ya, ya,' . . .

beautiful,
no?

(94–95)

Our Sister's growing consciousness, colored by her "black-eyed squint," reaches an epiphany when she meets her "very considerate friend" (90) and fellow victim's relative, Kunle. Kunle is just one of the "many, many Sammys" (9) that "time" has brought into Sissie's life. In London seven years, he is not concerned about the civil war in his homeland, Nigeria. What absorbs his every waking and, perhaps, dreaming moment is the news that a South African, Dr. Christiaan Barnard, has performed the first successful human heart transplant. The horrifying subtext of this "triumph" is lost to the narrow, self-denigrating Kunle, who, unlike Sissie and her "very considerate friend," naively thinks that "things were only what they seemed." He sees the transplant as not only a triumph of science but as "the type of development that can solve the question of apartheid" (96). Memories of another Adolf and his final solution echo in Kunle's proclamation of this "most wonderful piece of news," and Our Sister is left speechless. Though Sissie's friend goes on questioning his relative about this triumph of science, Kunle's insistence that Dr. Barnard used the hearts of cats and dogs before he ever dared to use human ones finally leaves his relative as speechless as Sissie. Fortunately, that capacity for laughter in the face of our sorrows, which makes "life somewhat possible" (68), saves Sissie from apoplexy and a complete loss of hope (98–99).

The inappropriateness of Kunle's fearful defense of "the Christian Doctor" is sadly apparent, for while he mouths these inanities, in his relative's "dingy but rather respectable penny-economy hotel room" (90), his mother and family are suffering the consequences of the greed of African leaders (103–6). The concluding irony of the whole pitiful performance is that Kunle, "like so many of us, wished he had had the courage to be a coward enough to stay forever in England" (107); but he returns, only to die as a consequence of his prideful display of a pauper's power. The Bird of the Wayside's sardonic narration of his end is leavened by the same compassion we have seen "from Our Sister Killjoy" as she matures "from knowledge gained since" her experiences in the blank of whiteness. For Kunle, and other "migrant birds," there will be no escape once they have entered "Into a Bad Dream."

This version is not just a variation on the theme of one person's education in the geopolitical expanse called the United States of America, another area of the blank of whiteness, where an epiphanic meeting allows Kofi to understand the meaning of the sacrifices of his mother. This version is a potential geopsychic nightmare for lovers and others, because:

> Here under the sun,
> Being a woman
> Has not
> Is not
> Cannot
> Never will be a
> Child's game.
>                    (51)

The game plan for this version is global. It affects "migrant birds" everywhere, male and female, young and old. So, if it takes a "black-eyed squint" to see what lies beneath the surface of "THOSE LETTERS FROM HOME" (104) and the values that insist that though "the world is rough, it's still fine to get paid to have an orgasm" (35), then Our Sister must find a way to tell it like it is. As the Akan proverb states, Knowledge gained is not gold dust to be put in a bag and hidden away.

"A Love Letter" is Sissie's sorting out of her disparate experiences, her way of understanding herself as both sujet-en-soi and, one hopes, the articulate and "doing" sujet-pour-soi. The Bird of the Wayside frames Our Sister Killjoy's *nyakpakpa* (meditation) with a portion of a conversation overheard, fittingly enough, "on a University Campus" (*The Dilemma*, 35), and an account of Our Sister's return to Africa. Such framing, as we have seen throughout Aidoo's works, is the hallmark of a gifted griot or narrator-actor. This prefatory eavesdropping that the Bird of the Wayside makes us privy to concentrates our attention on an issue that addresses a long history of racism and its confluence with other streams of exploitation, the awareness of which supplies the headwaters from which "A Love Letter" emerges.

Sissie's missive, written on the flight back to Africa, is ostensibly meant for her "Precious Something," who, despite Sissie's obvious affection and love, turns out to be just another "moderate" with "courage enough to stay forever in England" (107, 117). The opening statement of her letter returns us to the basic problem touched on by the Bird of the Wayside (28–29): "First of all, there is this language. This language" (112). It is important that the first problem is that of language. Without language, the ability to communicate effectively, one finds it difficult, if not impossible, to express one's love or hate. Without language, how can Sissie (or we) describe the world (or text) both as it seems and, more urgently, as it *is*? Finally, language will enable Sissie to do something about what her "Precious Something" characterizes as her "negativism," and which he conveniently and patronizingly restricts to Sissie's political views (112)—both public and private.

Her maturing character and her experiences, her "righteous anger" (121) and "mouth" (122), cannot allow her, as a human being, as an African, and as a woman (this order is arbitrary) to stay quiet—Sissie knows too much. Despite her regard for her "Beloved," despite her grudging acknowledgment of "Uncle's" much-needed presence in "London Town" (124–26), despite all those working for "the relatives" back home—despite all the excuses for staying abroad, Our Sister must insist on speaking her mind, in her own terms. The things that Our Sister Killjoy has learnt are not flattering universalist platitudes, for along with the "pseudo-scientific junk" (114), the "modern versions of ancient cruelties," and the geopolitical machinations of the so-called advanced countries (116) Sissie learns what it means to be "a Little / Black / Woman" (48) who "was groping for a way to tell him what was in my mind. Of life being relevantly lived. Of the intangible realities. Such stuff. Yet I didn't want to get caught up in a lot of metaphysical crap. When an atmosphere is as inert as Africa today, the worst thing you can do to anyone is to sell him your dreams . . . I needn't have worried because the famous doctor was off on his own tangent again"

(129). Even her "Precious Something" will not listen, since he does not see in his treatment of Sissie a replication of the sexist dichotomies and paternalism that obviated any meaningful relationship between Sissie and Marija and that figuratively characterize the relationship between the oppressed and the oppressor under colonialism and neocolonialism (117–18).

Although Sissie's honesty leads her to find fault even with her own behavior, this candor does not leave her a victim who glories in her own victimhood. She has seen too much, experienced too many things, to allow herself to slip into that existential cul-de-sac. As she admits, after her fruitless exhortations to her fellow Africans to return home, "something was threatening to collapse in me" (130). Sissie cannot become an apostate. To choose that path would utterly condemn her to being sujet-en-soi, without any possibility of escaping from the blank of whiteness. She would be like all the rest who stayed, those "migrant birds" who "die / Senselessly" (108). With her letter unfinished, Sissie drifts into sleep. When she wakes up, over the continent of Africa, the Bird of the Wayside has resumed her narrational authority. After reading over what she has written, Sissie decides that there is no need to post the letter, and "Sissie wondered whether she had spoken aloud to herself" (133).

Even though Sissie does not send the letter, although her need to communicate was "so great," it does not matter. What we are left with—and this is implied in the substance and purpose of Our Sister's "Love Letter," is how (without becoming "superior monkeys") we are to find a language, an effective means to compassionately communicate something *relevant* to those who have not yet been seduced and compromised by those succulent "plums"—"the leftovers of imperial handouts" (86); or "gone, gone, gone" (121) irrevocably into the blank of whiteness of a bad dream—so that we will have a collective vision to inform our *actions*. Through the penetrating linguistic brilliance of the Bird of the Wayside, we have been taken not only "Into a Bad Dream," but through that nightmare. We have witnessed Our Sister Killjoy's education and maturation in this *Ghanaian novel*, this *fefewo aloo nutinyawo kple eme nyakpakpa,* that is, a collection of prose-poetry narrative performances and a meditation for the audience-reader's contemplation. Just as we have been expertly guided through the raging torrents of "a terribly confused social stream" (118) that is part of the historical confluence of forces that mark this neocolonial reality, we have participated in our own educational development. In "lend[ing] all the problems [of neocolonial life] equal spikes" (Nwankwo, 155) in the manner she does, Aidoo is able to avoid both the "metaphysical crap" and a restrictive binary opposition in the ideological subtext of this elaborate fefewo. Unlike Ngugi's Kenyan novel, *Matigari*, which invites the audience-readers to participate in their own development, the decolonization of their minds, but leaves them trapped like a shuttle in a Manichaean crypt, *Our Sister Killjoy* suggests a more complex and contradictory trajectory to genuine emancipation and the transformation of "Africa . . . with its unavoidable warmth and even after these thousands of years, its uncertainties" (133). This closure might be described as "pessoptimistic," since its declaration of a positive restructuring of society is tempered by a realistic acknowledgment of doubt.[11]

# Poetic Interlude—Retrospect and Prospect

*Someone Talking to Sometime* is the title of Aidoo's first collection of poetry. Its appearance in 1985 was a long-delayed and welcomed event.[1] Aidoo's poetic talents, although much in evidence in *Our Sister Killjoy* and, to a lesser degree, in her other works, have been undervalued, mainly because most of Aidoo's poetry has been presented orally to small audiences, principally in Ghana, and particularly at the University of Cape Coast during the 1970s. The few published poems are scattered in various journals (most of which are difficult to come by) and anthologies.[2] In addition to the general dearth of serious, first-rate criticism of modern African poetry, it was most inauspicious that a voluminous work on West African poetry by Robert Fraser should mention Aidoo only twice: first, in association with the unique contributions of Efua Sutherland and Joe DeGraft to Ghanaian dramaturgy at the Institute of African Studies, Legon; and, second, in her capacity as a short story writer.[3] This neglect is particularly disturbing in an ambitious work by someone who was Aidoo's colleague at the University of Cape Coast during the early seventies.

These poems constitute an intermission, a retrospective and prospective contemplation, of Aidoo's literary project to date. The end of the previous chapter suggested that Sissie and the audience-readers, "who have not yet 'gone, gone, gone,'" are left with the problem of finding a language, an effective medium for communicating something *relevant,* in regard to the struggles of the wretched of Africa and, by extension, of the world. These poems, appropriately titled *Someone Talking to Sometime,* are an artistic "revisioning" of the ideological and economic realities that have over-determined the lives of countless men, women, and children in *this* era of neocolonialism. Further, they embody Aidoo's primary aesthetic and ideological concern—active human beings (the generic "someone")—from the publication of her first play, *The Dilemma of a Ghost,* through *No Sweetness Here* to *Our Sister Killjoy,* communicating *in history* ("sometime").

The radical "pessoptimism" evidenced in the closing movement of Aidoo's Ghanaian novel signals (and this is foregrounded in the full title) a period of *reflection* and rededication to the struggle for genuine equality and mutual respect between men and women, between "black" and "white" people; and real ideological and economic freedom, as opposed to the alienating mystifications of the ideological and economic varieties of capitalist hegemony. The successful resolution of such a struggle would lead (pessoptimistically speaking) to a new era of relevant global development and reciprocity among all of humanity's suffering "migrant birds." But such dreams must invariably start at home. For Aidoo's primary audience, the struggle begins in Ghana, "in Africa. And that [feels] like fresh wild honey on the tongue: a mixture of complete sweetness and smoky roughage . . . home with its unavoidable warmth and even after these thousands of years, its uncertainties" (*Our Sister Killjoy,* 133).

In the same way that the eleven nyakpakpawo or episodes in *No Sweetness Here* are not haphazardly put together, neither are Aidoo's poems. Like those short dramatic narratives, the poems must be seen as forming one organic whole. More than a bringing together of all her published and unpublished poems, it is a meticulously detailed itinerary, not into the blank of whiteness but into the "sweetness and smoky roughage" of Africa's blackness and beyond.

The volume consists of forty-five poems divided into two major parts. Eleven poems in part 1 are grouped under the title "Of Love and Commitment," the title of the second poem in the collection; another section of seven poems is titled "New Orleans Mid-1970s." Part 2, "Someone Talking to Sometime," has six major sections: "Routine Drugs" (six poems), "Reply to Fontamara" (five), "Legacies" (six), "Someone Really Talking to

Sometime This Time" (five), "Kwadwom from a Stillborn Creole Kingdom" (three), and "Tomorrow's Song" (one long poem). The full impact
and significance of the poems emerge only in their individual and collective
articulation. In the first instance, we may appreciate them as constituents
of a section; in the second, as sections in relation to other sections and in
terms of the juxtaposition of the two major parts.

*Someone Talking to Sometime* begins, as does *Our Sister Killjoy*, with an
opening dedication or libation to the ancestors. These ancestors are all
Ghanaian, however—Fanti, to be specific. Thus the concern and major
focus of the poems is established from the outset. These poems are for and
about Ghana, Ghanaians, Africans on the continent, and "migrant birds"
abroad. This invocation and dedication to the ancestors signals another
characteristic of these poems; namely, the increasing usage of Fanti as an
integral part of Aidoo's new "language" for the communication of something *relevant:*

> Nananom:
> Yefre hom aa,
> Yennfre hom gyan
> Yefre hom
>   Gye nkwa
>   Gye ahoodzen
>   Gye ahotor
>   Gye atseyi
>   Gye akokodur aa wodze ko gye oman si fam' pi!
>
>
> We call on you
> for life
> for strength
> for peace of mind and
> the courage with which
> to fight
> to redeem, keep and maintain
> our land and her
> people.
>
> (118)[4]

Consistent with Aidoo's object of developing and educating her audience-reader, she provides notes that explain the meaning of the Fanti used in the libation and other poems in the text, as in the translation supplied here. These notes are not primarily for a Western audience. The very real problems that arise from the multiplicity of Africa's numerous languages make translations vital in order that *other Africans* can understand that this is "someone really talking to sometime this time."[5]

In these discussions of Aidoo's poems I will continue the convention of referring to the poetic "I" or narrator, which is sometimes rendered as the third person "she" or "he" in some poems, as the Bird of the Wayside. Such a protean narrator often occurs in traditional oral poetry and lends depth and contrast to the perspectives presented by the poet. This flexible outlook, met with in *No Sweetness Here* and *Our Sister Killjoy*, is in evidence in traditional dirges where the personal (individual) and public (extended family) voices may merge to express the particular poet's private sorrow and the societal anguish over the loss of a fellow human being.[6] In this regard, Aidoo's poetry differs in emphasis from that of the Ewe oral poet-singer Henoga Domegbe, who "sings only of the sadness, the emptiness of life, *his own life*. His songs may record something of the anguish of his society, but they must be seen first as a creative expression of *the agony of an individual soul*" (italics added). In fact, Aidoo's and Kofi Anyidoho's poetry, *Earthchild* and *A Harvest of Our Dreams*, share a similar pessoptimism, even though the latter, especially in style, evokes the memory of Domegbe and other Ewe poet-singers.[7]

The first poem in Aidoo's collection, "Crisis," which prefaces the title poem of part 1, establishes the personal and public concerns of the poet's persona—the Bird of the Wayside—picking up the thematic concern of the libation. As the poem begins, she is left alone amid the trappings of economics and religion, "counting cowries / clutching crosses," while she questions if she can summon the "faith" that will enable her to survive the "private sorrows and / public despair" of this neocolonial age. Feelings of isolation, doubt, and foreboding permeate the poem, yet the Bird of the Wayside recognizes that, despite the anxiety and frustration of being "on the brink of fulfillment," the situation is not terminal. As she looks at a Ghana (Africa) that "even after these thousands of years, [still presents us with] its uncertainties" (*Our Sister Killjoy*, 133), she speculates if, in a different set of historical and social conditions, in some other next "sometime," she will ever

> know
>
> joy
> when it comes again
> the next time round?
> (n.p.)

For now, at least, the question is left unanswered, for these are not auspicious times for philosophical musings. The narrator-guide takes us back to share "a bit of yesterday's happiness" and, in the next poem, to talk "Of Love and Commitment."

In "Of Love and Commitment" the poet-narrator remembers her first real love, in which she was "Dido / of the latter days," and her "Aeneas" teased her often. But the poem is not a sentimental pining over the bliss of "doing / things I had never done before," despite the lyrical quality that captures the fond memories of first love against the background of crisis. The poem is a dirge to lost love, both private and public, out of which she discovers an ironic blessing:

> Oh my dear
> how shall I thank you for
> fathering
> the mother in
> me.
> (11)

The poem-dirge is framed by the Bird of the Wayside's remembrance of her "Aeneas" and the love they once had. Within this frame are the public or political losses and the additional recollection of the death of "Kwame Ata," her twin brother, whose "soul" she must "carry / . . . / doubly restless" (12). The overthrow of Ghana's first president and the subsequent rumors about his origins, Malcolm X's revolutionary ideas and his assassination, Stokely Carmichael, and the violence of the U.S. police (11–12) are the public-political memories that haunt the poet. These recollections come as the poet-narrator helps her lover pack, and the contradictory emotions of the inevitable parting are poignantly expressed:

Yes, a new world was being
born with the new day,
when we shoved the last item into the cab.

But the packing took a long time.

Or the talking did.

(12)

Recalling the uncertain ending of "Crisis," the poem's closing stanzas return to the personal response of the Bird of the Wayside in the delirious series of repetitions and questions:

Perhaps the wind blows out his clothes?
Leave the rest of my hair unplaited, sister,
Leave the threads hanging loose.

I must hurry to my love's room.
I must hurry to shut his window.
I must hurry to my true love's room,
before the rain gets in, sister,
before the rain gets in.

(13)

The use of variable-repetition, elaboration, and improvization on words, phrases, and lines produces a musical effect akin to traditional incantatory or ritualistic verse. Such variable-repetition, used extensively in these poems, not only adds a resonance that recalls and echoes the words and phrases within a particular poem or between poems but also helps produce a complex interweaving of thematic concerns. The oral nature of Aidoo's poems, and "Of Love and Commitment" in particular, can be seen in the references to the poet-narrator's audience. In "Of Love and Commitment" this is achieved by way of dramatic gaps between lines or stanzas and by direct questions to the audience-reader, such as the "How did I know?" of the opening line. The immediate audience of the poem is identified later as "sister," a woman who is weaving the poet-narrator's hair (13).

In the next poem, "Yours Faithfully. . . . . ." (13–15), the Bird of the Wayside returns from the emotional agitation "of love and commitment" to the legacy that has left us "counting cowries / clutching crosses" in "Crisis."

She questions the legacy of colonialism, especially its admixture of religious salvation and political "message of peace and goodwill." Whatever infatuation or responsibility we had seems to have been lost in our fascination with "this cassock of / doubtful whiteness" (13). The poem briefly highlights our "capitulation" under the imperial onslaught of nineteenth-century European nations. She ends this succinct poem with a bitingly sarcastic assertion: "We too have done well / by one another . . . I insist" (14). The poems in this section trace a zigzag between that colonial past and the present, even as they are personalized by the Bird of the Wayside's "black-eyed squint," and evoke the precolonial soul of orature tempered by neocolonial literary practices.

In "Cornfields in Accra," the next poem, she tells us of what we have inherited in the blighted urban landscape of the neocolony. The tension between form and content is maintained by the use of a choral refrain: "They told us / our mothers told us / they told us" (15). Although the contemporary Ghanaian citizen, it seems, has turned a deaf ear to the wisdom of the ancestors in favor of "a pot-pourri of fragrant words" ("Yours Faithfully," 14), there is some hope in our tenacity for life. Despite our status as a debtor nation, the pollution of our urban environment, "we planted our corn. / Not whole seeds from / last year's harvests" (15) but rather the neocolonial titbits rumored to have come from "Russia" or some third country (16). Amid the pollution of so-called development, the corn grew and we reaped a harvest,

> gleaned and threshed
> our corn, and
> roasted it aromatic—
> that is,
> after office hours
> on Saturdays and throughout the whole of Sunday.
> (17)

The poem concludes with a question or two for the naysayers:

> Then
> we shall ask to see
> him.

Who says
we
shall not survive among these turbines.

Who
says
we shall not survive among the turbines?

(17–18)

In "Greetings from London," the poet-narrator is speaking to Sissie as she takes us to where those "turbines" were produced. As in *Anowa*, we return to the latter half of the nineteenth century. This time, the Bird of the Wayside spreads her wings even further, climbing to give us an overview of the whole Western enterprise, from "grandfather [who] severed a leg in / 1867 / climbing palm trees" (18) to get the oil to keep the Manchester textile mills running; to the opening up of Cherokee country; and then through time and space to southern Africa and back to Texas in the mid-twentieth century (18–19). Our return to southern Africa centers on Rhodesia and Ian Smith's Unilateral Declaration of Independence. The poet-narrator, as self-critical neocolonial sujet-pour-soi, reveals her own susceptibility to the ideological claims of the blank of whiteness. "Meanwhile, / I hold a sherry in my hand / eating shit" (19) in London, where she has an equal chance of being killed accidentally or, in her worst nightmare, being someone's meal:

gather
up
my brain
for
a christmas pudding to
Texas.

(19)

This view of the West as cannibalistic recalls the description of Kofi's meal with the Merrows in "Other Versions" (*No Sweetness Here*) and Sissie's farewell dinner at the embassy in *Our Sister Killjoy*.

In the same unwavering self-critical voice, the Bird of the Wayside asks a number of crucial questions in the next poem, "For Kinna I," which, like the nyakpakpa "The Late Bud," seems to be advice to a child but contains more wisdom for adults. These questions and the memories of childhood innocence are recollected in the context of a mother placating a child whose finger has been cut. The tenderness is punctuated by the realization that we adults are as hurt and despondent about the "bleeding" in our own neo-colonial lives as Kinna is over her injured finger. This mood of despondency gives rise to the bitternes that permeates the remaining poems in this section. "Three Poems for Atta"—"1. Ghana Funerals"; "2. Nation-Building"; and "3. A Salute to African Universities" (22–28)—assess Africa's rhetoric of revolution, her petit bourgeois intellectuals and leaders who actively encourage the continued exploitation of the continent's natural and human resources:

> Busy as we are
> Building in earnest,
> Firm, solid, foundations for
> Our Zombie dynasties.
> (*Our Sister Killjoy*, 31)

The poet-narrator draws the connections between our role—"we are to blame" ("2. Nation-Building," 24)—in the rise of colonialism, its evolution into neocolonialism, and the continued assaults on other people's culture and knowledge by Europeans:

> My Brother,
> let's just have
> —another cup of tea—
>
> And if
> this is
> the
> neo-colonial crime
> ask for
> whose art it was
>
> Before the British
> stole
>         it.
>
> Ain't nothing new here yet.
> (25)

The caustic emotions directed against the national politicians, the intelligentsia, and the global arrangements that leave "Africa, / Earth's Bonded Whore" (28) bubble just under the surface. Finally, the Bird of the Wayside's barely controlled anger explodes in the closing movement of "3. A Salute to African Universities"—whose colonial origins are nothing about which we can rejoice (25).

In a measured though no less intense tone, the next poem, "For Steve Hymer—A Propos 1966," shows the hypocrisy of "this / latter-day Babylon" (29). The title's date would have special meaning for Africans in general, and Ghanaians in particular, because it was the year that marked the military coup (liberally assisted by the Central Intelligence Agency) that overthrew the Kwame Nkrumah government. The poet-narrator warns the oppressed not to kowtow to the sentiments and values of the oppressor "because / death visits us in more ways / than one" (30). Apart from this need to escape the many faces of death, the poet-narrator asserts, through the imagery of germinating grain seeds, that the idealism that motivates such people as herself will lead and is leading to the growth of hardier, more committed, and more persistent fighters against oppression. The "Of Love and Commitment" section of part 1 ends with two companion poems, "As the Dust Begins to Settle—A Long Story" and "Regrets," both touching rebuttals to the naysayers, betrayers, and doubters of the previous poems—"Three Poems for Atta" and "For Steve Hymer—A Propos 1966."

These two companion poems come under the title "Two for Kojo." The first concerns the recollections of a poet-narrator who goes to prison, hoping to meet her loved one, a political prisoner, presumably the Kojo of the title. There is a wistfulness in the remembrances, which are both an expression of her love and affection for Kojo and a means to maintain an optimistic equilibrium as she waits patiently to find out if she will be allowed to see the prisoner (32–33). As she anticipates some positive word, the poet-narrator contemplates the sad reality of imprisonment in a neocolonial state such as Ghana, with its bureaucratic and statistical absurdities (34). Unfortunately, just as "some questions are / too heavy to ask" (34), so, as the "genial warders" know, some requests must be left unanswered (35). The poet-narrator returns, having neither seen Kojo nor even learned if her fears and doubts about his well-being have any basis in fact, rather than "myth" and "legend." The poem ends in the bitterly ironic indictment of her associates, petit bourgeois intellectual "revolutionaries":

And I
trace my steps
carefully, back to the
comrades
who,
        between
birthday parties
       and
wedding receptions, are
busy
so very busy,
debating
the depth of
the clarity of
your
revolutionary commitment.
        (35)

"Regrets," the Bird of the Wayside's other "long story," narrates the feelings of a mother whose son is also "in bondage to the state" (34). This mother, like the poet-narrator in the companion poem, hopes against doubt to see her son, who is incarcerated because of his beliefs and commitment. The poem recalls Nana Kwame Adu, mentioned in the libation/dedication to the ancestors:

    —my father's father
who was tortured to death in a colonial prison for
being "an insolent African".
        (n.p.)

The despair and anguish that the mother feels reminds the poet-narrator of another woman, Anowa, who, because of the powerful effect of colonialism and its impact upon her personal life literally drowned in her own regrets and tears as a form of atonement for the social ills she found so abhorrent,

    as she, like
some other lost version of herself
pants in from the river

where she had
tried to wash the
old years away.
(36)

The poet-narrator establishes the bond with that historical moment by re-
interpreting the cliché "Silence is golden," extending the conceit to describe
the mechanism of the capitalist market (36–37), so as to unequivocally
ground the mother's despair in its neocolonial context. As we empathize
with the mother's anguish, the Bird of the Wayside, through a number of
well-chosen words and phrases, echoes the narratives of other characters
with whom we have sympathized, such as Yaaba and her mother in "The
Late Bud"; Mami Fanti in "A Gift from Somewhere"; Maami Ama and
the death of her son Kwesi in "No Sweetness Here"; M'ma Asana and her
daughter Hawa, both of whom lost their men to "the plums" of colonialism
and neocolonialism in "Certain Winds from the South"; and even Zirigu
and Setu, for whom the promise of independence meant little change in
their lives:

Desperately
she brought in red earth
to polish the floor;
the better, in good times,
to reflect
such glorious visage
as he carried.

She would always
listen for his footsteps.

And
since dreams can take
time to die,
she prayed
he not only lived
but even in all that gloom,
he could forgive
himself, and her,
for mistakes made

out of so much desire

to please.

(37–38)

Even the reference to "red earth / to polish the floor" echoes the wisdom expressed in the earlier poem in this section, "Cornfields in Accra." Such verbal echoes and inter- and intra-textual cross-referencing help to create a homogeneous stylistic and thematic matrix, despite the variety of situations, that corresponds to the environment shared by traditional oral artists and their audience. Kofi Anyidoho, who relies on a judicious use of the Ewe dirge form in his poetry, and Atukwei Okai, whose acute sense of the dramatic and complete immersion in contemporary and traditional Ga culture are the hallmark of his macaronic verse, both achieve an overall effect similar to Aidoo's compactly braided poems.[8]

The poet-narrator's "black-eyed squint" revealed that beneath the tenderness "of love and commitment" lay the potentially destructive crisis of doubt, anger, and betrayal that typified the nine years following Ghana's so-called independence. In the same way, "New Orleans: Mid-1970s / . . . some tropics are cold" confirms the belief that the existential situation facing African-Americans is no less crisis-ridden and fraught with contradictions than that of Ghanaians and other Africans. This section consists of seven poems that parallel the dominant tone of the poems in "Of Love and Commitment" and evoke the mood that taints Our Sister's journey into the blank of whiteness in *Our Sister Killjoy*. Like that Ghanaian novel, the first poem of this section, "The City—An Apology to Patricia," reveals an impartial poet-narrator viewing, with a characteristically perceptive eye and ear for the manners and cadences of the people's speech, the ironies and contradictions of the old Louisiana port city:

> Flowing water
> still water
> is clear
> is muddy
>
> Hellow traveller, your destiny
> within this city was parleyed depuis
> longtemps.

(41)

Indeed, the history that "was parleyed depuis / longtemps" becomes the focus of the poems in this section of part 1. The Bird of the Wayside explores the "flowing water / still water," the contradictory currents of the Mississippi that symbolize both the history of the United States and the fate of Africa's daughters and sons, whose pain, sweat, tears, and lives built this nation.

"Mardi Gras," with its references to "such / strange and / sudden fruits," (43) echoes Billie Holiday's powerfully moving indictment of a nation that, in practice, counted her as three-fifths of a person. As she maps these racist incongruities, our poet-guide does not lose her capacity to see the humor in this sad state of a union:

> Since in
> this land of
> sharp descriptions, and
> determined name-calling,
> no one seems to have a
> name for either the
> kinky-haired
> thick-lipped
> honkies,
>
> or
>
> the straight-nosed
> blue-eyed
> spooks.
>
> (44)

Just as bloodlines are mixed and confused, so the endemic racism of the United States is not confined to the South. It is not possible for the Bird of the Wayside or Africa's children, who eat "lunch at Dooky's" (44–46), to really "call / Boston home" (45). The problem seems similar to the isolation Sissie experienced in Bavaria:

> Marija,
> There is nowhere in the
> Western world is a
> Must—

No city is sacred,
No spot is holy.

. . . . . . . . . .

It is a pity, Marija,

But
Humans
Not places,
Make memories.
(*Our Sister Killjoy*, 79–81)

Since it is people who make our fondest memories, it is fitting that the next poem should be titled "Carolyn." This poem, like "For Kinna I" in the first section of this part, is one of comfort; and it establishes the bond between two people, between women across the vastness of the Atlantic Ocean and the separation of a history of slavery, colonialism, and neocolonialism (46–49). Like the lessons Sissie learns from her journey into the blank of whiteness, the Bird of the Wayside advises Carolyn and other sisters to maintain an all-embracing perspective on the issues of interpersonal relationships, despite and in spite of the failings of the "brothers" and a general weariness (48).

Whether it is "For a Zulu in the Bayous" (49–51) or "Lorisnrudi" (51–53), these poems recollect the joy of "migrant birds" meeting and finding some connection with each other, only to endure the sorrow of parting too soon: "I shall / miss you / miss you / miss you" (53). The final poem of this section and of part 1, "Acknowledgements—With an Apology to Roland" (53–56), stresses, without apology, the need to keep our feet on the ground of history and in this reality. The poet-guide acknowledges our tendency to valorize those fleeting relationships that enable us to survive the stresses and fevers of this life (56); but we must also see that such comfort tempts us to set ourselves outside of time, outside of an economic and ideological stream that has its wellspring in history, rather than in some autonomous idealistic realm.

The modern history of first contact with Europe: slavery, racism, and colonialism; the birth of the nation-state of Ghana in 1957; the U.S. civil rights movement of the sixties; the 1966 coup that overthrew the Nkrumah government; the assassinations of Malcom X and Martin Luther King,

Jr.; the long hot summers symbolized by the riots in Watts and Newark; and the oil crisis of the early seventies ("For a Zulu in the Bayous," 49) are the realities from which the poems in part 1 gain their force and relevance. In relation to Aidoo's other works, these poems act as multiple voices in counterpoint, commenting on and amplifying the themes that those earlier works addressed. In terms of Ghana's history, we are taken past the coup that continued the same old routine of complicity that characterized "Two Sisters" in *No Sweetness Here*. We are past the first period of military rule and the unproductive civilian interlude that followed it. The Bird of the Wayside has guided us into Ghana's second period of military caretaking, and we are ready to begin part 2, "Someone Talking to Sometime."

The poems in part 2 address the problems of the seventies and eighties and finally look to the future in "Tomorrow's Song." The poet-narrator assumes the voice of "someone," or the voices of particular characters talking to us in a specific "sometime," a unique moment in Ghana's and Africa's history. This insistence on the historical specificity of the poetic communications obviates both narrow formalist criticism and valorization of the poet-narrator as expressing the cultural schizophrenia that has characterized the work of many African and Third World artists and intellectuals. These petit bourgeois artists and intellectuals reveal, in their works, a value system that defends Western bourgeois privilege by celebrating the supposed transcendental status of the artist while simultaneously, through the inclusion of wholesale appeals to traditional values and practices, assumes mystical proof of their rather suspect "Authenegraficanity".[9]

The poems in part 2 have their center in Ghana and concern the daily lives of the women, men, and children who struggle for the necessities of life. As we have seen, however, even if the focus is the waiting-room of a prison in Ghana or "lunch at Dooky's," our poet-guide carefully draws the global and individual connections for us. She is an active participant in the action she describes, and her reluctance to exonerate herself accentuates our own involvement in the situations presented to us. In the opening section, "Routine Drugs," we witness the struggles of those, especially women, who suffer an unrelenting incorporation into the urban working class (Prah, 28–29) without the network of social support once provided by the extended family. The struggle for a more than tolerable life becomes congruently difficult. Against the stark actualities of such an existence, the petit bourgeois intellectual response is to "'learn to / laugh and / live'"(61).

This callous advice is exposed for the opiate that it is. "Routine Drugs II," the second poem in this section, in which the "routine drugs" become the antithesis of their use in "Routine Drugs I," describes the plight of that worker-mother who has broken her arm. The narcotic stupor of Ghanaian/ African intellectuals and their senior partners, the political leaders, results in the misappropriation of resources; consequently, the worker-mother suffers unattended in a hospital, worrying about the fate of her children at home. The impact of such gross negligence on the part of Africa's rulers leads to unwarranted domestic strife for the worker-mother and her spouse. The husband, in frustration and anger, lashes out at her, a fellow victim, rather than at their real enemies—the supporters of the status quo who, because of their complaisance about the dictates of international capitalism, allow such horrors to continue (63).

The concern with marginalized and oppressed women, integral to Aidoo's multiple aesthetic-ideological focus as a writer, is again taken up in the gynaecologically ironic exploration of woman's position(s) in "Gynae One." The poem opens with a popular children's song whose sexual connotations become more overt in the third stanza:

> Trolley out,
> Trolley in.
> Trolley out,
> Trolley in.
> (64)

The poet-narrator then goes to the heart or, more correctly, the womb of the matter:

> Getting scraped
> lying in
> 'vestigating only.
> Post-partum complications:
> Tying it up
> Throwing one out.
> Removing it all.
>
> Dying for it
> Dying with it
> Dying from it.

Or
just
dying
dying
dying
dying.
(64)

If it is not enough to struggle through life without the benefit of "routine drugs" as necessary medication while the rulers and intellectuals stupefy themselves with other "routine drugs," then women must open themselves to "routine" invasions of their bodies. It is, as the poet-guide states, "all agony, / no / ecstasy" (65). The structure of these three lines allows two contradictory meanings to emerge, heightening the irony of woman's position in a male-dominated society. The poem closes by ironically undercutting the conventional wisdom of the claim that all women know is that God "is a man" (65).

Section 2 opens, like "Routine Drugs," with two poems that have the same title as the whole section: "Reply to Fontamara (I and II)" (75–77). These poems, Aidoo indicates in her notes, are "a reaction against an earlier personal response to 'Love Letter,' a poem by Fadrin of Haiti" (118). The complete Fadrin poem is included in Aidoo's notes and is particularly significant in respect to *Our Sister Killjoy* and the "Reply to Fontamara" poems. It is a plea to a lover who has gone to "that strange country, at the other end of the world when / December arrives with its fog, snow and hail" (118). The lover should not hesitate to return to Fontamara, for the poet knows that such a climate, and such people, who live "at the other end of the world," can be depressingly cold and inhospitable. Both "Reply to Fontamara" poems are dirges of the kind we have come to expect from Aidoo and continue the mood of the final poem in the last section— "Wondering about Him Who Said No to the Glare of the Open Day: In Memory of My Twin-Brother Whom I Never Knew Because He Had Been Still-Born" (68–72). Unlike Fadrin's poem, which presents Fontamara as a tropical Eden, the antithesis of "that strange country," the Bird of the Wayside refuses to create such an easy binary opposition, since she knows that "some tropics are cold." The second "Fontamara" poem mourns the pain and loss African-Americans have suffered, even as it celebrates their resilience and proud resistance to "the roar of the / chain-saw" (76) of oppression.

"Now That the Weather Man Has Gone Crazy" (77) is a short poem that addresses, without deceptions, the numbing of our sensitivity to the variations and transformations in our environment. These continuities and discontinuities erode hope, leading us to forget that nothing is as it seems and everything is subject to change in time. Such blindness is a result of our ignorance of the causes of the disparities in our lives; the world as it appears, as it is depicted by the dominant bourgeois ideology, thus seems absurd, even nihilistic. The poem shows just how crazy the acceptance of this perspective is. "Heavy Traffic" (78) and "From the Only Speech That Was Not Delivered at the Rally" (79–80), which end this section, adopt the more overtly political highlife song styles much in evidence in 1977 and 1978, when economic mismanagement and the political corruption of the National Redemption Council/Supreme Military Council of Acheampong/Akuffo was most intense.[10]

The poet-narrator's light-hearted tone contrasts with the ideological messages of the two poems. The references to imported consumer goods, like "corned beef," that end the poem "Heavy Traffic" invoke memories of colonial cultural and economic control, since access to these items were part of that regime's method of social domination. More importantly, the items became status symbols that were often prominently displayed in the homes of the emergent national bourgeoisie. Consequently, these commodities have been used alternately as symbols of status and power, or dependence and alienation. "From the Only Speech" is even more ironic in its rendition of a speech (though more like a confession) of a typical opportunistic political candidate of the type that surfaced on the Ghanaian sociopolitical scene during the bogus Union Government period of General Acheampong's moribund military regime.[11]

In "Legacies," section 3 of part 2, Aidoo's poet-narrator adopts a number of voices ranging from a concerned doctor, a mother, and a wife to the female mourner-singer characteristic of Ghanaian dirges. Unlike the mourner-singers in the traditional context of the dirge, the Bird of the Wayside does not just bemoan the loss of a lover (Ghana) snatched away by death (neocolonial hegemony); she asserts a more revolutionary attitude, which, paradoxically, finds its source in precolonial gnomic lore. By this strategy the textual and authorial ideologies coincide on the ground of theory and praxis elaborated by Amilcar Cabral in *Return to the Source*. The last poem of this section, "Totems," recalls, in a more direct manner, the dilemmas of the neocolonial subject that was the focus of Aidoo's first drama. Our poet-guide comes "upon an / owl at the / crossroads blinking with / confusion greater than / mine" (92), rather than a ghost. It is also in order that the owl, a predatory nocturnal bird, should exhibit such confusion in "the glare of the open day," just as the ghost properly belongs, in traditional stories, to the hours of darkness. Although these neocolonial times may have all the characteristics of these stories, they are by no means traditional.

Aidoo's poet-narrator further emphasizes the changed character of the present by alluding to the marriage of Anowa and Kofi Ako in Aidoo's second drama, *Anowa*:

> They-of-the-Crow
> cannot
> carve out
> destinies through
> marriage.
>
> Whoever can?
>
> He does
> too well by her.
> (92)

By means of such intertextual variable-repetitions and echoes, "Totems" admonishes the naive cultural nationalists in the dirge-singer's audience who wish her song to reflect the ahistorical ideology of negritude or "authenegraficanity":

> Perch where you can, and
> tell your story. They make
> us believe that all roofs
> cover homes from the rain.

Akua my sister,
No one chooses to stand
under a tree in a storm.

. . . . . . . . . .

Itu kwan
ma
Adze sa wo aa
na
Adze asa wo!!!

(93)

The proverb that ends the poem means "Inescapable reality can only be coped with"; there is no possibility of a fantastic flight into some prelapsarian pristine Africa. We have no choice but to listen to the Bird of the Wayside and face the music.

It is therefore crucial that, as the title of section 4 states, we realize that "someone [is] really talking to sometime this time." This need to confront Ghana's and Africa's present predicament is underscored by the starkness of the epigraph that prefaces the first poem in this section, "1977":

There was a reported natural disaster every 6½ days in 1977. In most of them [no] fewer than 100 died. The average death toll was 263. . . .
. . . disasters are necessary to keep populations in check.

*People* Vol. 5, no. 2, 1978. (96)

The poems that follow insist that we, as audience and participants in the present neocolonial social reality, which is more like a nightmare, wake up before it is too late to do anything but atrophy.

There can be no doubt that, despite the economic catastrophes that plagued Ghana from the mid-1970s, many intellectuals and artists and their class allies in business and government enjoyed a standard of living significantly better than the below-poverty-line existence of the majority of Ghanaian peasants and workers. So, in "Issues I," we are included in an unflattering portrait of indulgent and unscrupulous behavior that insults the very people our researches and poetry profess to help and celebrate:

WE met
them
daily in the
queues:
the mother and the children
for whom she'd got
the best recipes for
cooking
stones.

(101)

As a social class, we are an abomination of nature, like the manchild in Aboliga the Frog's book of freaks and oddities in Ayi Kwei Armah's *The Beautyful Ones Are Not Yet Born*. It is a wonder that, as a class, we have survived to inflict our petty wants on so many for so long.

The fifth section, "Kwadwom from a Stillborn Creole Kingdom," is the poet-guide's lamentation for Ghana/Africa and its diaspora (*kwadwom* is a solo keening). The use of the word *Creole* discreetly implies sociopolitical as well as genetic hybridization and, therefore, refers to Ghana/Africa in the sense that, as a neocolonial state/continent, it is a product of European (Western) and indigenous influences. In its more common usage, "Creole" recalls the last two stanzas of "Mardi Gras" in part 1, section 2, in which the Bird of the Wayside wonders what to call participants in the Mardi Gras festival (44). The first of the three poems in this section, "Egyeifi's Farewell" (107), is a solo performance lamenting the death of Aidoo's aunt. In the notes, however, Aidoo informs us that "'Egyeifi' is a praise name for Nkroma (Nkrumah) the ninth-born child [though her aunt was only named after a ninth-born child]. . . . Of course, I can't stop folks from associating the poem with Kwame Nkrumah or any other Nkroma/Nkrumah if they want to" (120). One suspects that Aidoo would not be mortally offended if her readers did associate the poem with Kwame Nkrumah. Despite it's being a dirge, the poem has a somewhat lively mood to it, as the singer recalls the aspersions cast by the aunt on the ability of the poet-mourner to take care of her own daughter.

Part 1 and the five sections of part 2 of this collection of poems take us on a detailed journey across the terrain of the modern world, particularly as it is revealed in the ideological and economic topography of neocolonial Ghana/Africa and the North American sector of the African diaspora. This guided tour into the "sweetness and smoky roughage" of Ghana/Africa's "blackness" has not been flattering or indeed optimistic in the sense of a whitewash of negritude. The Bird of the Wayside has told it like it is: the bad, the ugly and, invariably, some of the good. By means of the poetic strategies outlined here, she creates a complex textual matrix that encompasses her works to date. In addition, the contexture of the poems, the polylectical character of their form, content, and ideology, their various stylistic and ideational configurations, enter, explore, and emerge from the specificity of the Ghanaian (and "black") experiences they describe to arrive squarely in the present phase of our neocolonial history. December 1981 saw the second coming of Flt. Lt. J. J. Rawlings onto Ghana's political stage, when "the rank and file of Ghana's military forces deposed the current regime of President Hilla Limann and his People's National Party (PNP) and abolished the parliamentary system. Since then the country has been embroiled in an intensifying class struggle which could seriously threaten the structures and relations of neocolonialism."[12] It is highly significant that Ama Ata Aidoo was subsequently appointed to and accepted the post of secretary for education, a position she held from 1982 until late 1983, when the alignment of political forces shifted yet again. Aidoo's revolutionary attempts at a complete and thorough restructuring of Ghana's educational system were delayed by those who felt threatened by such changes.

It is against this intensification of the people's struggle in Ghana, which still continues, though not quite as intensely as in 1982–83, that we must read the last poem of part 2—"Tomorrow's Song." From this viewpoint we may better appreciate the degree of love and commitment that the Bird of the Wayside reveals in her attachment to the continuing struggles of the marginalized—female or male, in Ghana or elsewhere. The "song" is prefaced by a short verse in which the poet-guide affirms the courage of the oppressed:

> We
> no more
> fear

these images of
hell.
    (112)

This newfound feeling of power that the Bird of the Wayside expresses has its roots in the labors of the subjugated. Thus she defiantly and ironically begins her song of hope and struggle:

WANTED URGENTLY FOR IMMEDIATE EMPLOYMENT:

Prophets to
update our notions of
doom.

The when of it
the how.

Or perhaps, we need
only ask

any
Torturer on a Monthly Salary?
                        (113)

Despite the hopes, raised by the December intervention, of destroying the various departments of the repressive state apparatus, glaring contradictions persisted. In her critique of the aftermath of the ousting of the PNP government, the poet-guide pointedly remarks that "good intentions" (114) do not a revolution make.

The "song" then develops the metaphor of Ghana as a child whose parents, through a mistaken sense of love and a belief in the philosophy that expects a child "to sink or to swim" (114), have abdicated their role as responsible guardians. The poet-guide, as mother, asks for pardon not just because she left the child to her own devices but because the medications for the sick child, "consoling / infusions" (114), were inadequate placebos at best (in the political sense—reformist) and, at worst, (ideologically) lethal (114–15). The father's vapid defense of his actions, "So child / you know I

meant no harm" (115), is exposed in its condescension and bankruptcy by
the child's steady reply:

> Father,
> No one
> ever
> means
> any
> harm
>
>             And of course,
>     neither did you
>     when you let me
>     play with the knife around my infant face.
>                             (115)

By allowing the child (Ghana's oppressed masses) to speak for herself, the
poet-guide avoids the condescension of the father *and* stresses that the oppressed need to articulate the problems and issues that most concretely
affect them. As perceptive as they are incriminating, the child's words also
convey the possibility of transforming the structures and neocolonial relations that have blinded her:

> Yet
> who knows
> now,
>             that
> though my sockets
> are
> empty,
> a father's
>             AND
> a mother's
> love
> illuminate
> my way?

In the end
you would only have given the best you had
        or
thought
you had.

(116)

The last movement of "Tomorrow's Song" reverts to the poet-guide's voice. She examines how uncomfortable the dominant bourgeois ideology of neocolonial Ghana is and compares the acceptance of that ideology to wearing ill-fitting clothes. The point she is making is not based on a narrowly conceived national chauvinism; rather, she warns against the importation of alien socioeconomic practices without regard for the concrete realities of the context into which they are brought. Such indiscriminate mimicry leads to mounting antagonistic contradictions, increasing the intensity of exploitation and leading to a paralytic loss of hope. But things are never what they seem, and we must say "No" to "the fury of a heatwave in mid-winter or / a tropical snowstorm," since we do not know if some child, some woman, or some man not yet born will stir us to action. Our poet-guide can only ask:

Who knows,
but in some thicket where time has counted itself out,
some unsane souls are searching for the
roots
        which
shall drag
out
the sneeze

that . . .

(117)

The hegemonic presence, in Ghana and elsewhere, of bourgeois ideology and capitalism is a historically conditioned fact; however, in spite of the nay-sayers and the masters of illusions, one can deny neither the aspirations of the oppressed nor the courage of those who are willing to look for ways and means to bring about the necessary revolutionary transformation of Ghanaian and African neocolonial society. Consistent with this belief and the Bird of the Wayside's usual practice, *Someone Talking to Sometime* ends with an ellipsis. When we are rid of the effluvia, or, at least, of most of it, the Bird of the Wayside or some other poet-guide will preserve that chapter of our struggle.

# A New Tail
# to an Old Tale

Aidoo's second African novel, *Changes—A Love Story*, represents the re-sumption of her *developing art*, after the contemplative poetic interlude, to renew that literary-ideological journey and struggle that started in the early 1960s with the production and publication of *The Dilemma of a Ghost*. This Ghanaian novel returns from the hopes of "Tomorrow's Song" to take another look at "these images of / hell" (*Someone Talking to Sometime*, 112) and to taste that very Ghanaian "mixture of complete sweetness and smoky roughage" (*Our Sister Killjoy*, 133). The novel should be described as a *fefewo aloo nutinyawo kple eme nyakpakpawo*.[1] It is divided into three parts, which recount the trials and tribulations in the life and loves of Esi Sekyi, a young, educated, career woman caught at another kind of crossroads from that which confronted her male precursor, Ato Yawson, in *The Dilemma of a Ghost*. Esi is an ambitious civil servant in the Department of Urban Statistics who falls in love with Ali Kondey, a northerner for whom things seem to have changed. As the story begins, she is living in Accra with her first husband, Oko, and their only daughter, Ogyaanowa.

In part 1 the narrator, the Bird of the Wayside, introduces us to the principal characters in this *nutinya*, which partly focuses on the evolution of Esi's love for Ali and the decay of her marriages. We learn about the histories of these characters who are members of the Ghanaian neocolonial elite, "the more deserving members of society. Like the users of hotel lobbies. Like Mrs. Esi Sekyi and her friend, Mrs. Opokuya Dakwa" (43).[2] Aidoo's examination of the personal problems, the political, social, and cultural knots that have tied up the minds and energies of the emergent neocolonial elites, should not be taken as an abandonment of the "ranks of the wretched." Rather, we should see this fictional analysis as a humble admission on Aidoo's part that, although she may speak and write about them, and about the contradictions of our collective experiences, she cannot and must not speak *for them*. The answers to life's problems are not always easy, as Esi's grandmother knows only too well (109). In addition, Aidoo has stated, in relation to her experience as Ghana's minister for education, that such voice-overs are "a kind of arrogance."[3]

Throughout this introduction, we note that the insightful observations and biting wit of the familiar narrator have not been tempered by the connotations usually associated with love stories. In fact, we, like Esi, are warned that "love is not safe, my Lady Silk, love is dangerous. It is deceitfully sweet like the wine from a fresh palm tree at dawn. But when we need to count on human strength, and when we have to count the pennies for food for our stomachs and clothes for our backs, love is nothing" (42). By suggesting that this is *only* a love story, Aidoo has set us up for a rather rude awakening, designed to disabuse us of our often dearly held pre(mis)conceptions about love and marriage. Such a hoax is initiated in Aidoo's so-called confession to her readers and to "the critic, an apology," which preface the start of this extended story-telling session.[4] The novel seeks to develop our understanding of the real problems that arise in personal relationships always-and-already subject to the political and ideological pressures of a particular historical moment. This new tail to an old tale pivots on the issue of what is "proper," given our neocolonial state, in actualizing an environment in which people can more fully and justly develop their human and humane potential.[5] The implicit questions *Changes* asks its primary Ghanaian audience-reader are personalized in a love story that acknowledges that we have been both subjected to changes and are capable of effecting changes. How have we coped, and how will we cope with the problems that daily confront an educated and not-so-educated person in "a neo-colonial African city that barely managed to drag itself through one more weekday" (33)? The answers to such questions are suggested by both the narrator and characters of this so-called love story.

It is ultimately left to us, however, to adjudicate between the possible solutions presented in the "interminable palavers" that this complex narrative is designed to initiate, partly through its incorporation of elements from African orature. Thus we betray ourselves in thinking that "while the story possesses all the ingredients for a riveting read, this is hindered by Aidoo's rather ponderous and cumbersome style that prevents it from realising its full potential," as Bola Makanjuola writes. It is precisely *we* who are meant to realize its fullest potential by going beyond the private satisfaction of "a riveting read." Makanjuola is right in observing that Esi "feels suffocated and trapped" when she is unable to effectively communicate her feelings to Oko, her first husband. Yet Makanjuola seems to have forgotten that the narrative is also about Ali Kondey, the man with whom Esi falls in love, and whom she later agrees to marry, becoming his second wife. As a consequence of the latter decision, the novel's thematic interior comes into sharper focus. As Makanjuola puts it, "What Aidoo does tackle particularly well is the complexity and potential danger in trying to fuse modern ideas with traditional methods."[6] Makanjuola rightly directs our attention to important elements in the narrative's thematic nucleus; it may be a reaction to the relatively high level of awareness of "feminist" concerns that leads him to offset the usual male-oriented leaning in literary criticism, by ignoring the implications of Aidoo's delineation of her leading male character. Aidoo remarked, "'I always wanted to write about a man like Ali. Ghana is a nation of different peoples,' [and she was] glad of a chance of redressing in some way the southern bias in much of Ghanaian literature" ("Profile," 593).

Such a desire on Aidoo's part is not new, as anyone familiar with the fefewo *No Sweetness Here* would quickly realize. What is new is Aidoo's ability to create a work that brings her major concerns together in such a sustained and thought-provoking manner. Echoes of her other works reverberate through these pages and in her characters' words and actions, so that we are almost taken in by the Bird of the Wayside's performance. As was "For Whom Things Have Not Changed," this story of Esi, Ali, and those whom their lives touch is presented with detachment and sympathy. We are allowed to forget neither the personal in the political nor the political in the personal decisions of each of the characters. As Aidoo has admitted, "I've grown to see that life is not just politics or the liberation struggle, or even economics: love *is* political, and everything is intertwined."[7]

The tactic of giving us the personal histories of each of the principal characters not only places those characters in a credible narrative context but prevents us from indulging our prejudices in the process of interpretation. The Bird of the Wayside discloses both the clear and clouded motivations behind the actions of her characters. We know their private thoughts, the hopes and fears that haunt them, as they race or blunder toward their individual and collective fates. Esi's first husband is rather pedestrian, a typical man who, if he had the inclination, would have agreed with his relatives' desire to get him a "proper wife" (39). Oko actually loves Esi, in his own way, but has adopted uncritically many petty and chauvinistic social attitudes (7). Unlike Ali, he is insensitive. He is unable to understand either Esi's needs or the implications of his own actions until it is too late. In this way, his attitude and behavior are similar to those of Ato Yawson, the protagonist of Aidoo's first drama, *The Dilemma*.

Like Ato's failure to become Eulalie Rush's "Moses" (*The Dilemma*, 47), Oko fails as a husband because, despite his declarations of love, he sees Esi as an adjunct to his ego, a crutch to bolster his image in the eyes of his coworkers and himself. So, even though Esi may have cherished the illusion that "what had attracted him most about me was my air of independence," her friend Opokuya knows that men "who claim they like intelligent and active women are also interested in having such women permanently in their beds and in their kitchens" (45). What contributes to Oko's ultimate deflation and marginalization is his genuine confusion as to how he could "fight with [his] woman's career for her attention" (70). This situation is something his education and experience have not prepared him for. He cannot even conceive of alternate ways to address the predicament in which he found himself after "*That Morning*" (69; italics added).

Paradoxically, Oko's need to be a "Moses" and his limited understanding of the extent and nature of the decay that had infected his marriage prompted his last desperate attempt "to give this relationship another chance" (7). His ideas about the "proper" behavior of men and husbands in relationships of the heart come from his peers, "one of his friends from boarding school days" (7). He is overly reliant on others, his "friends," for self-validation. "You don't care what my friends think of me," he whines to Esi just before he rapes her (9). In addition, Oko is inept when it comes to relating to women, even his sisters and mother. He has been pampered and made the center of attention. As Esi explains to Ali before he goes to her family to ask permission to marry her, Oko is "the kind of man who brings out all of a woman's mothering instincts" (88).

Oko's experiences do not bring him greater understanding or lead him to appreciate the worth of what his myopia has destroyed. He remains comparatively immature and has a hard time accepting that his marriage with Esi is over (71), a problem graphically exemplified by his altercation with Ali (121–22). Yet the Bird of the Wayside does not allow us to condemn him out of hand: "In any case, everyone knows that a man's relationship with women other than his wife, however innocent, can always help ruin a marriage. And that includes his love for his own mother" (44). So when his mother "deposited a breathing parcel on his doorstep, in the form of a very beautiful and very young girl" (71), to be Esi's replacement, he is extremely flattered. His female relatives continually feed his ego, saying that Esi was "a semi-barren witch and . . . [that Oko] was well rid of her, thank God" (70). By so doing, they perpetuate the self-deprecating attitudes evidenced in the behavior of Badua and the Old Woman in *Anowa*, and Connie and Mercy in "Two Sisters."

Oko's female relatives, like their literary precursors, are sujets-en-soi and actively contribute to "keeping all of us down" (*No Sweetness Here*, 117–18). Oko's assault on his wife is a measure not only of his insensitivity but also of the level of his love, which is purely physical (6). Indeed, he is too prideful even to apologize: "In the meantime, Oko was collecting his thoughts together. He was already feeling like telling Esi he was sorry. But he was also convinced that he mustn't. He got out of bed, taking the entire sleeping cloth with him. . . . [It was] trailing behind Oko who looked like some arrogant king" (10). This incident is seized upon by Esi as her reason for leaving Oko. Through the Bird of the Wayside's relatively brief disclosure of Esi's thoughts on the matter, we appear to be encouraged to devalue the issue of marital rape in the neocolonial African context. In fact, we might even be persuaded that "Aidoo tentatively raises the issue of marital rape . . . but never really dwells on the subject. It is as if both Esi and the author realize, that in African society there could not possibly be an 'indigenous word or phrase for it'" (Makanjuola, 474).

Yet we cannot be convinced by such sophistry. There are ways to describe such violations of women, married or single, even if, as Aidoo says, "'I had to be realistic. In terms of our African background, marital rape isn't one of the hottest topics.' In African society, she explains, sex in marriage is the man's prerogative and a woman is considered lucky if her husband should take such aggressive interest in her" ("Profile," 593). For the Bird of the Wayside and her primary audience-reader, this is *not* the most pertinent issue. The rape is important, but it should not be confused with the narrative's central concerns; it is a symptom of much more fundamental personal, social, and political dislocations. The problems of Esi's polygamous marriage to Ali are another, as Aidoo explained in an interview: "The resulting difficulties . . . highlight the 'contemporary malaise in relationships between men and women. The factors which made polygamous marriages work have been broken down in the urban environment,' Ata Aidoo [*sic*] says we do not pay attention to the rules that *both sexes* [italics mine] had to abide by in the past" ("Profile," 593).

In short, these nutinyawo resituate the issues of African sexual and marital relationships in a "proper" perspective, disclosing the deception behind the claim that "polygamy is an / African Disease" (*Someone Talking to Sometime*, 42) as it prompts us to ask some "big questions . . . of [neocolonial] life" (166). In contrast to Oko's female relatives, Aba and Ama, the women who begin part 2 of *Changes*, reflect both the work's debt to the drama of orature and its origins as a "radio play which never materialized."[8] Like the conversations of the two women, "your neighbours," in *The Dilemma*, this "gossip" creates the contextual frame that emphasizes the issues of a woman's place and her relationship to another man or men by placing them within the larger network of neocolonial connections, while tracing their colonial and precolonial antecedents. In this part, the Bird of the Wayside narrates the consequences of Esi and Ali's decision to enter into their modern polygamous marriage. We are clearly shown how the personal choices made "within this city [were] parleyed depuis / longtemps" (*Someone Talking to Sometime*, 41) by the confrontation between traditional Africa and imperial Europe.

The character whose history most explicitly fills in the outline of that confrontation is Ali Kondey, a northerner and representative of the new internationalized West African citizen. We are introduced to Ali's father, Musa Musa, and grandfather, Musa Kondey, both of whom became substantial men in their community. The young Musa Musa had run away from home because he slept while a lion had attacked and eaten one of the sheep he was supposed to guard. Like Anowa, he made his fortune on the road as a trader. We learn that Musa Musa, or Ali Baba, as he was called after the birth of his son, kept his money under his mattress, since he did not trust the colonial administrators or their banks (26). Eventually, to validate the wealth he had acquired, Musa Musa procured wives "in each of his eight favourite stops on his trade routes. . . . [In fact,] Ali's father preferred his women young and tender. They had to be virgins, of course" (23). We discover that one of these wives, Ali's mother, Fatimatu, died in childbirth (22–23). As a result, Ali was brought up by Mma Danjuma, Musa Musa's sister, for the first eight years of his life in Bamako (23), although he often traveled with his father. Ali was a gifted child who excelled in Koranic school, and, when he was a little older, he was sent to French school, then to the lycée and on to teacher training college at Atebubu, in Ghana.

At the training college, Ali Kondey and Fusena, who would become his first wife, were classmates and close friends. Their relationship was as innocent as it was mutually respectful and satisfying. Neither would have admitted that one day they would be married. After graduating, they found that they were both teaching in Tamale. The relationship matured until there was no longer any possibility of denying the fact that they would get married (57–61). The Bird of the Wayside's detailed descriptions of the developing relationship between Ali and Fusena establishes a necessary intimacy between audience-reader and the two characters, especially with Fusena. This bond helps us appreciate more fully the complexity of the emotional turmoil they are to experience. "Later still he [Ali] gave up teaching and got himself to England, where he acquired both a Bachelor's and Master's degree in Sociology and Economics" (30). Fusena and their first child join him in London, where she not only comes face to face with the "blank of whiteness" but realizes "that by marrying Ali, she had exchanged a friend for a husband" (66).

The attraction of the "plums," which drew Ali to London for *his* further education, is to have unforeseen effects on the marriage. On their return to Ghana, Ali the been-to, armed with "knowledge gained since" (*Our Sister Killjoy*, 67), puts his degrees to practical use. He establishes the Linga Hideaway travel and tourist agency (22) and refuses to let Fusena teach on the grounds that "there should be a more lucrative job you [Fusena] could do and still have time to look after the children" (67). The Bird of the Wayside claims that "the only way in which Ali was not like his father, and did not seem to care, was in the area of women. Ali liked his women mature, and he had no special use for virginity, especially in very young girls" (24); nevertheless, Musa Musa's general attitude, his socialization, affects his son. Although Ali feels deeply committed to Fusena, he "liked the company of interesting women" (57). Further, he believed, more or less, in the traditional role of men as the head of the household. His denial of Fusena's desire to educationally advance herself while they are in London or to teach, on their return, puts extreme pressures on the young woman (67). Fusena has had to sacrifice *her* ambitions in the kitchen and bedroom of their marriage.

Yet, to all appearances, Fusena is the ideal wife and mother. As we know, such fictions as this are deceptive, cruel hoaxes in which the bystanders are often convinced that "things are only what they seem" (*Our Sister Killjoy*, 79). It is not surprising, therefore, that "when she [Fusena] heard they were saying that she made more money from the kiosk than the largest supermarket in town, she only smiled to herself" (67). For Fusena, material wealth is no substitute for a fulfilling life. Even though she knows that Ali would never intentionally hurt her (78), the life of a modern African woman or wife can become desperate at times. Such a time occurs when Ali does not consult her about his desire to make Esi his second wife. "Like all 'modern Western-educated Africans,' Ali couldn't help it if he regularly bruised traditions and hurt people. But at least he was one of the few really sensitive ones" (133). His actions in respect to his wife and the elders, inadvertent though they may be, are further proof of the situation we find our neocolonial selves in

> now that
> taboos
> unmoistened

chase one another down
our willing
throats

with

greasy ease.
(*Someone Talking to Sometime*, 109)

In such times as these, it is less a question of determining blame than of commitment, as Esi's grandmother observes: "Life on this earth need not always be some humans being gods and others being sacrificial animals. Indeed, that can be changed. But it would take so much. No, not time. There has always been enough time for anything anyone ever really wanted to do. What it would take is a lot of thinking and a great deal of doing. But one wonders whether we are prepared to tire our minds and our bodies that much" (111). In the meantime, people cope as best they can, given their circumstances.

Fortunately, Fusena is a strong woman who quickly learns, as Esi must later learn, to

keep cool, my sister
keep cool . . .
—in spite of dangerous men—

A tight body and a
strong mind can
weather
storms.
(*Someone Talking to Sometime*, 48)

Like Eulalie Rush before her, Fusena finds some strength in tradition, in a community of other women who have experienced that shock of recognition upon becoming a first, or second, or fifth wife (107). But even the lucky ones share the experience of less fortunate sisters, as the Bird of the Wayside reminds us:

The combination of forces against [them] . . . had been too overwhelming—
    traditional shyness and contempt for the biology of women;

Islamic suppressive ideas about women;

English Victorian prudery and French hypocrisy imported by the
colonisers . . .

All these had variously and together wreaked havoc on the mind
of the modern African woman: especially about herself. As far as Ali
could tell, he told himself, most women behaved as if the world was
full of awful things—beginning with their bodies. His wife Fusena,
a good woman if ever there was one, was no exception. (75)

The devastating personal impact of such a confluence of ideological and
political forces is clear in Fusena's acquiescence to Ali's taking Esi as his
second wife (107). Esi also experiences the emotional push and pull of
becoming a second wife, a well-kept mistress—a role for which she is
ill-prepared, her desire to have everything her way notwithstanding (49).
Though she may think that "monogamy is so stifling" (98), she will realize that in this meantime, as her friend Opokuya points out, "[she] means
marriage" (98).

In part 3, the closing section of this nutinya, the Bird of the Wayside
shows us, in a rapid sequence of events, the penultimate "images of / hell"
that this love story has become. As though we are eavesdroppers,[9] we hear
the one-sided conversation between Ali and Esi, after one of his numerous
trips. The year-old second marriage has settled into the same old routine of
excuses and evasions. The narrator presents this opening replay as though it
were a drama or film script: "Fade in the end-of-day sounds of the city and
its traffic: yes, do fade them in: especially when you are in doubt" (137).
Esi is aware that Ali's visits are less frequent, and she has heard rumors that
he has been paying a great deal of attention to his new secretary (139). Yet
she also finds the rhythm of her daily life satisfying; she is able to devote
time to her job. Though she sometimes misses her daughter, Ogyaanowa,
it is easier to see her than to be with Ali when she feels his absence (138–
39). It is her friend, the discerning Opokuya, who notices that "there was
something slightly lost in Esi's eyes" (140).

Mrs. Opokuya Dakwa, Esi's old secondary school friend, is married to
Kubi Dakwa, who started out as an assistant surveyor. She has been a mid-
wife for over fifteen years and worked in Kumasi Central Hospital when
Esi and Oko were first married. She is perceptive, especially when it comes

to her friend Esi. She is plump, and rather self-conscious about her weight being a health problem (15). Like the other women in this Ghanaian novel, she has a strong character. She met her husband, Kubi, when she was a student nurse, and they were married after she graduated. Two of her four children are in secondary boarding school, while the other two are in primary school (16). Although she seems happily married, a member of the "SWI—Satisfied Wives International"—as Esi puts it (46), she is not. There are the usual problems of coping with the daily hassles of her job, of running a home, of jealous moments, of "Kubi's chronic lateness" (55), which boil under the tranquil surface of her marriage. But her "everlasting *wahala*" (93) was over the issue of getting a second car (17). Over the years of their marriage, however, she and her husband have developed a way of arguing about this issue that, although it comes close to dislocating the calm exterior of their marriage, does not go over the line as Esi and Oko's does (55–56); yet she envies "Esi's freedom of movement" (56).

By the end of the second year of marriage to Ali, Esi is driven to see a doctor for tranquilizers (144). After taking them, she finally falls asleep. Some ten hours later, she is awakened by the noise of a car horn outside the gate to her house. She finally realizes that it is Ali in an unfamiliar car. As it turns out, it is a New Year's present for her (146). But Esi has learned a great deal after a disastrous monogamous marriage and the no-win situation of this modern polygamous one. The gift of the new car surprises her, yet "she secretly admitted that she had known even before Ali actually said the words—that he had brought the car for her, and she understood the gesture as a bribe. A very special bribe. But a bribe all the same—like all the other things he had been giving her. They were all meant to be substitutes for his presence" (147). Ironically, this substantial gift, the very materiality of the car, becomes the catalyst that opens Esi's mind to her marriage as "a complete dead end" (149).

Esi goes to the only one she can call a friend, Opokuya. But her friend's reaction to the information that the car is a present from Ali surprises Esi (153). Like those who see Fusena's kiosk as a sign of her good fortune, Opokuya reacts to Esi's new car from the depths of her own dissatisfaction with "marriage" in these neocolonial times. She asks to buy Esi's old car, scrap though it is, and "Esi looked at her friend as if Opokuya was someone she was meeting for the first time ever" (154). Esi decides to get the

car reconditioned before selling it for a nominal amount to her friend and
fellow traveler. Six months later, the two meet to complete the transaction,
but each is too preoccupied with her own emotions and recent memories
to be at ease. After Opokuya leaves in her "new" car, Esi retreats into her
bedroom; "then to her own surprise, she started to weep. Nothing violent:
just two tears rolling quietly down her cheeks" (161). Esi's "two tears" contrast with Marija's "tear . . . coming out of the left eye only" (*Our Sister
Killjoy*, 65). The distinction underscores the Bird of the Wayside's view that
"loneliness" in the social context of contemporary Europe is both physically and emotionally isolating, while in a neocolonial state like Ghana,
loneliness, like marriage itself, is ultimately a communal affair—isolation is
almost impossible.

Opokuya, enjoying the freedom of owning her own car, treats herself
to the exhilaration of a long night drive. It is now her husband's turn to
worry about her "lateness." Esi, feeling the burden of her "desolation"
and the need for human companionship, has an unexpected visitor, Kubi
(162–63). Kubi feels awkward, and his actions have the hallmark of the
inexperienced:

> How then does one
> Comfort her
> Who weeps for
> A collective loss?
> (*Our Sister Killjoy*, 67)

He attempts to comfort his wife's friend, and Kubi and Esi find themselves
on the verge of a sexual encounter, but each shrinks from the act before it
can be consummated (164). Kubi, at least in this regard, does the "proper"
thing. As with the experience of Sissie and Marija, this embrace is certainly
not one "to talk of . . . to just anyone" (*Our Sister Killjoy*, 65). In fact, as Esi
knows, "there are some tales you don't tell even to yourself" (164).

Although it may be argued that all the major characters—Esi, Ali, Opokuya, Kubi, and Oko—are victims and participants in their own fates,
predicated by their peculiar insertion into this neocolonial phase of the
historical continuum, Fusena, it seems, endures the most; yet her quiet suffering is somewhat mollified by Ali's loyalty to her as his first wife (119).
For all the married women, it seems that Mma Danjuma's thoughts on the

coincidence of the talk of marriage and funerals (61) echo the pathos of the
Bird of the Wayside's poetic declaration:

> They still
> marry us in our
> shrouds, and
> bury us in the fineries of
> the wedding day.
> (*Someone Talking to Sometime*, 71)

Esi, like Opokuya and Fusena before her, eventually learns that

> Here under the sun,
> Being a woman
> Has not
> Is not
> Cannot
> Never will be a
> Child's game
>
> From knowledge gained since—
>
> So why wish a curse on your child
> Desiring her to be female
> ?
> Besides, my sister,
> The ranks of the wretched are
> Full,
> Are full.
> (*Our Sister Killjoy*, 51)

Perhaps the most important character and victim of this love story is the
one from whom we hear the least—Esi's daughter, Ogyaanowa. We might
begin our "interminable palavers" by asking, are these nutinyawo about the
consequences of trying to develop meaningful relationships in a milieu that
daily advertises the futility of such associations? Then, "from knowledge
gained since" our experience of this engaging tale, what kind of world are
we leaving for those unable to articulate, in "a more grown-up language"
(5), their concerns, when we so often and so blatantly refuse to consult

them? For a more mature second wife, there is the comfort "that maybe her bone-blood-flesh self, not her unseen soul, would get answers to some of the big questions she was asking of life" (166). But what about the children who swell the "ranks of the wretched"? Perhaps we can provide the answers in our actions; "maybe, 'one day, one day,'" as the Bird of the Wayside, in her typically elliptical manner, suggests at the end of her new tail to an old tale. . . .

# NOTES

## Introduction

Epigraph: Edgar Wright, "Introduction," in *The Critical Evaluation of African Literature*, ed. Edgar Wright (1973; reprint, London: Heinemann, 1982), ix.

1. Chinua Achebe, *Morning Yet on Creation Day* (London: Heinemann, 1975), 6.

2. Mineke Schipper, "Mother Africa on a Pedestal: The Male Heritage in African Literature and Criticism," in *Women in African Literature Today, No. 15*, ed. Eldred Durosimi Jones, Eustace Palmer, and Marjorie Jones (Trenton, N.J.: Africa World Press, 1987), 47–48.

3. Extended criticism of single-authored texts by African women has been restricted to master's theses and Ph.D. dissertations. With particular reference to the work of Ama Ata Aidoo, two master's theses have come to my attention: Sergius E. K. Essel, "The Philosophy, Ideas, and Outlook of Ama Ata Aidoo: A Critical Analysis of Miss Aidoo's *The Dilemma of a Ghost, Anowa, No Sweetness Here*, and *Our Sister Killjoy*" (master's thesis, University of Cape Coast, Ghana, 1979); and Mary Naana Nicholson, "The Affirmation of African Womanhood in the Works of Ama Ata Aidoo" (master's thesis, University of Florida, 1983). The present work draws upon these two but is based primarily on my own dissertation, "The Developing Art of Ama Ata Aidoo" (State University of New York at Stony Brook, 1988).

4. Kofi Owusu, "Interpreting Interpreting: African Roots, Black Fruits, and the Colored Tree (of 'Knowledge')," *Black Literature Forum* 23, 4 (Winter 1989): 739–65.

5. See Georg M. Gugelberger, ed., *Marxism and African Literature* (Trenton, N.J.: Africa World Press, 1986). His introduction seems to discount Marxism as a viable literary theory for the investigation of African literature. Kofi Owusu's article (note 4) reveals the problems of Gugelberger's argument as they are manifest in an interrogation of African literature as a whole, without specifically addressing Gugelberger's omission of issues of gender.

6. Henry Louis Gates, Jr., "Significant Others," *Contemporary Literature* 29, 4 (Winter 1988): 617.

7. Molara Ogundipe-Leslie, "The Female Writer and Her Commitment," in *Women in African Literature Today, No. 15,* ed. Eldred Durosimi Jones, Eustace Palmer, and Marjorie Jones (Trenton, N.J.: Africa World Press, 1987), 5–13.

8. S. P. Mohanty, "Us and Them: On the Philosophical Bases of Political Criticism," *Yale Journal of Criticism* 2, 2 (1989): 1–31.

9. The use of the word *polylectic* serves, in part, as a verbal reminder that we need to conceptualize this dynamic relationship in terms that prevent the more vulgar reductionist and mechanical conceptions of the traditional "dialectic." This phrasing, however, does not displace the materialist or historical basis of a Marxist analysis. Such an analysis must recognize that the Other and her practices are knowable. Further, a meaningful dialogue with the Other's practices and her products (which are produced in purposeful, mediated activity) is possible. This dialogue, in this case with Aidoo's literary texts, becomes more productive, since a polylectic criticism admits that these *not-wholly-Western* artworks, as products of a human agency, constitute "complex historical phenomen[a], available to us only through a process of hermeneutical comparison and specification" (Mohanty, 23).

10. Ngugi wa Thiong'o, *Writing against Neocolonialism* (Wembley, Middlesex, Eng.: Vita, 1986), 1.

11. In writing "us," I wish to include not only my fellow African petit bourgeois intellectuals but also that reading public who may not—restrictively speaking— belong to the petit or national bourgeoisie but who have internalized many Western bourgeois and colonial prejudices toward the literary/cultural products *we are learning to read against.*

12. Ama Ata Aidoo, *Our Sister Killjoy: Or, Reflections from a Black-Eyed Squint* (1977; reprint, Harlow, U.K.: Longman, 1988), 3–5.

13. Ama Ata Aidoo, "Tomorrow's Song," in *Someone Talking to Sometime* (Harare, Zimbabwe: College Press, 1985), 112.

14. By "primary audience," I am suggesting that Aidoo initially targets a broad spectrum of Ghana's elite (the petit, national, and comprador bourgeoisie) *and* the literate working and peasant classes. That others outside of these groups may find themselves emotionally disturbed, implicated, or engaged in and by Aidoo's works speaks to the power of her "art" to "defamiliarize" or "alienate"—in the Russian formalist or Brechtian senses of that activity.

15. The importance of "an active and critical 'reading'" is underscored by the independent work of other critics, particularly Cynthia Ward, "What They Told Buchi Emecheta: Oral Subjectivity and the Joys of 'Otherhood,'" *PLMA* 105,1 (January 1990): 83–97. She argues for "a fidelity to the oral, [so that] these texts can instead be 'heard' to declare the precedence of 'real' human—therefore essen-

tially untextualizable—voices and meanings over the putative political and histori-cal hegemony of the word" (89). Our "reading," which challenges the assumed primacy of the *word* as *scripture,* always-and-already recognizes that necessary to performance is the *utterance,* which is made possible by human beings (human agency) in ideological-material activity: struggling as historically constituted and constituting subjects consciously living, reproducing, and dying.

16. For another example of the polylectical criticism attempted here, see my essay "Re-Viewing Gloria Naylor," *African Perspectives on African-American Writers,* ed. Femi Ojo-Ade (Westport, Conn.: Greenwood Press, forthcoming).

17. For a more detailed discussion of the evolution of the European presence in what is now Ghana, see chapter 3.

18. Ama Ata Aidoo's introduction to Ayi Kwei Armah, *The Beautyful Ones Are Not Yet Born* (New York: Collier, 1969), x.

19. Efua Sutherland is noted for her instrumental role in the development of con-temporary drama in Ghana. Her influence on Aidoo's work may be more correctly acknowledged in terms of the "psychological space" created by Sutherland's advo-cacy of the creative use of the rich Ghanaian orature in the contemporary context. See, among many articles on her work, Adetokunbo Pearce, "The Didactic Essence of Efua Sutherland's Plays," in *Women in African Literature Today, No. 15*, Chik-wenye Okonjo Ogunyemi, "Efua Theodora Sutherland, *Twentieth-Century Carib-bean and Black African Writers,* ed. Bernth Lindfors and Reinhard Sander (Detroit: Gale, 1992), 284–90. Lloyd W. Brown, *Women Writers in Black Africa* (Westport, Conn.: Greenwood, 1981); and my bio-bibliography in *Fifty African and Caribbean Women Writers,* ed. Anne Adams (Westport, Conn.: Greenwood, forthcoming).

20. Selected works that deal with this period of Ghana's history are included in the bibliography; however, despite its hyperbole, C. L. R. James, *Nkrumah and the Ghana Revolution* (Westport, Conn.: Lawrence Hill, 1977), summed up the emo-tional and intellectual fervor of the time when he described Accra, Ghana, as "the center of the world revolutionary struggle" (164).

21. See Camara Laye, *The African Child* (New York: Farrar, Straus & Giroux, 1954), and Leopold Sedar Senghor, *Prose and Poetry,* trans. John Reed and Clive Wake (London: Oxford University Press, 1965).

22. One is always cautious about collapsing the varied "ethnicities" that actually occupy the geographical area now known as Ghana into one seemingly homoge-neous unit; however, it is arguable that Aidoo's authorial project, while celebrating the particularity of her Fanti origin, also proposes the acknowledgment, if not the realization, of a larger whole that accepts and accommodates those "ethnicities."

## 1. A Bird of the Wayside Sings

1. C. J. Rea, "The Culture Line: A Note on *The Dilemma of a Ghost*," *African Forum* 1, 1 (1966): 111–13.

2. Karen C. Chapman, "Introduction, *The Dilemma of a Ghost*," in *Sturdy Black Bridges: Visions of Black Women in Literature*, ed. Roseann P. Bell, Bettye J. Parker, and Beverly Guy-Sheftall (New York: Doubleday, 1979), 29.

3. These more open-minded critics, led by Eldred D. Jones, "Notes," *Bulletin of the Association for African Literature in English* 2 (1965): 33–34, were willing to engage Aidoo's first drama more or less on its own terms. Both Oyin Ogunba, "Modern Drama in West Africa," in *Perspectives on African Literature*, ed. Christopher Heywood (New York: Africana, 1971), 81–105, and John Nagenda, "Generations of Conflict: Ama Ata Aidoo, J. C. de Graft, and R. Sharif Easmon," in *Protest and Conflict in African Literature*, ed. Cosmo Pieterse and Ian Munro (New York: Africana, 1970), 101–8, comment favorably on Aidoo's "technical and verbal mastery" (Ogunba, 102) which is "so immediate and accurate" (Nagenda, 106). Mildred A. Hill-Lubin, in "The Relationship of African-Americans and Africans: A Recurring Theme in the Works of Ama Ata Aidoo," while pointing out the anachronisms in Aidoo's recreation of African-American speech patterns, stresses that Aidoo's "willingness to treat such a topic (the marriage between an African-American and an African) illustrates her curiosity, originality, individualism and perceptivity, qualities which characterize all her writings" *Présence Africaine* 124, 4th quarter (1982): 190–201.

4. Merun Nasser, "Achebe and His Women: A Social Science Perspective," *Africa Today*, 3d quarter (1980): 21–28.

5. For a particularly enlightening discussion of this and problems related to the study of African women-authored texts, see Femi Ojo-Ade, "Female Writers, Male Critics," *African Literature Today, No. 10*, ed. Eldred Durosimi Jones (London: Heinemann, 1979), 158–79.

6. Ama Ata Aidoo in *African Writers Talking*, ed. Cosmo Pieterse and Dennis Duerden (New York: Africana, 1972), 26.

7. Biodun Jeyifo, *The Truthful Lie: Essays in a Sociology of African Drama* (London: New Beacon, 1985), 47.

8. William R. Bascom, *African Dilemma Tale* (The Hague: Mouton, 1975), 1–3.

9. Sembene Ousmane, *Tribal Scars* (Portsmouth, N.H.: Heinemann, 1974).

10. See Leroy Vail and Landeg White, *Power and the Praise Poem* (Charlottesville, Va.: University Press of Virginia, 1991). Vail and White demonstrate how oral poetry is quite often used as a political tool to criticize perceived injustices against the people by their rulers.

11. Terry Eagleton, *Criticism and Ideology* (London: Verso, 1980), 96–97.

12. oMolara Ogundipe-Leslie, "The Function of Radical Criticism in African Literature Today." Lecture at the Annual Ibadan African Literature Conference, Ibadan, Nigeria, 15–19 August 1981, 12–15.

13. Given that Aidoo had not yet been to the United States and was herself writing from Ghanaian ideological assumptions about African-Americans, the representation of Eulalie is slightly *de-centered* throughout the play.

14. It is ironic that during the four or five years immediately preceding the publication of *The Dilemma*, Ghana had a Republican constitution, formal press censorship was introduced, a Preventive Detention Act had come into effect, the nation became a one-party state, and the price of its major foreign exchange export, cocoa, was rapidly falling in the world markets controlled by the West. A further irony becomes evident when we realize that Nkrumah was both agent and victim of the same ideological and economic forces that then beset Ghana, and that he described in *Neocolonialism: The Last Stage of Imperialism* (1965; reprint, New York: International Publishers, 1972). It might be said that Ghana was a school for anticolonial and neocolonial struggles, with Nkrumah conducting the lessons. See Basil Davidson, *Black Star* (New York: Praeger, 1974).

15. Wole Soyinka, *The Lion and the Jewel* (London: Oxford University Press, 1965), and *The Road* (London: Three Crowns/Oxford University Press, 1965). See Abiola Irele's discussion of *The Lion and the Jewel* in *The African Experience in Literature and Ideology* (London: Heinemann, 1981), 189–93. Of particular significance is Irele's discussion of Soyinka's use of Yoruba orature as it turns upon the metaphysical, and the playwright's positing of the artist, represented by the character of the Professor, as outside history. Another revealing commentary is Biodun Jeyifo, "The Hidden Class War in *The Road*," in *The Truthful Lie*, 11–22. In a manner comparable to this study of Aidoo's work, Jeyifo applies a "materialist, dialectical reading of *The Road*, . . . [to rectify] the displacement, in dominant abstractionist and idealist criticism and scholarship on the play, of the concrete material passions and aspirations of the play's characters" (12) revealed in Irele's criticism, for instance.

16. Mildred A. Hill-Lubin, "Storyteller and Audience in the Works of Ama Ata Aidoo," *Neohelicon* 16, 2 (1989): 221–45.

17. Ngugi wa Thiong'o, *Homecoming* (1972; reprint, London: Verso, 1980), 65–66. Ngugi and Jeyifo arrive at similar conclusions in this respect, though Jeyifo may appear more understanding of Soyinka's predicament ("Hidden Class War," in *The Truthful Lie*, 21).

18. Ama Ata Aidoo, *The Dilemma of a Ghost and Anowa* (1965, 1970; reprint, Harlow, U.K.: Longman, 1985), 7. For the remainder of this chapter, citations of

this source will appear in the text by page or line numbers only.

19. John Willet, trans. and ed., *Brecht on Theatre: The Development of an Aesthetic*, 2d ed. (New York: Hill and Wang, 1979), 192.

20. The micro-nation of the Fanti or "Fan-tse," which means "the breakaway part," journeyed southward until they reached the sea to escape their more ferocious kin, the Brongs and the Ashantis. They were led physically and spiritually on their journeys by "the Three Elders."

21. Frantz Fanon, *Black Skin, White Masks* (New York: Grove, 1967), 232.

22. Meyer Fortes, "Kinship and Marriage Among the Ashanti," in *African Systems of Kinship and Marriage*, ed. A. R. Radcliffe-Brown and Daryll Forde (London: Oxford University Press, 1950), 276.

23. See Ayi Kwei Armah, *Fragments* (New York: Collier, 1969), 225–27, for the theory of the role of the "cargo cult" in former colonial countries, particularly in its psychological effects. Also see William Lawson, *The Western Scar: The Theme of the Been-to in West African Fiction* (Athens: Ohio University Press, 1982).

24. I use the term *sujet-en-soi* to denote the neocolonial's existential and ideological status; more particularly, her or his captive consciousness, which precludes both a critical understanding of the neocolonial realities of these times and the precipitous action needed to assert one's *self* as fully conscious and free subject, agent, or sujet-pour-soi.

25. Louis Althusser, *For Marx* (London: Verso, 1979).

26. Orlando Patterson, *An Absence of Ruins* (London: Hutchinson, 1967), 1.

27. Ngugi wa Thiong'o, *Decolonising the Mind: The Politics of Language in African Literature* (London: James Currey/Heinemann, 1986), 3.

28. Dapo Adelugba, "Language and Drama: Ama Ata Aidoo," in *African Literature Today, No. 8*, ed. Eldred D. Jones (London: Heinemann, 1976), 72–84.

29. Amilcar Cabral, *Return to the Source: Selected Speeches* (New York: Monthly Review Press, 1973), 43.

30. Gloria Naylor, *Mama Day* (1988; reprint, New York: Random House, 1989), 23.

## 2. *Anowa:* In History

1. Ama Ata Aidoo, *The Dilemma of a Ghost and Anowa* (Harlow, U.K.: Longman, 1985). All references to *Anowa* are from this edition and are indicated in this chapter by page number in the text.

2. By a "wholly African trade," I refer to the pre-fifteenth-century trading patterns of the Akan people, including the Fanti. This trade extended east to the Kingdom of Benin, west to the river Bandama in the present Ivory Coast, and north to connect with trans-Saharan caravan routes. Sea trade was negligible.

3. For more detailed discussions of the European slave trade and its impact on Africa in general and this region in particular, see Walter Rodney, *How Europe Underdeveloped Africa* (1972; reprint, London: Bogle-L'Ouverture, 1973); Basil Davidson, F. K. Buah and J. F. A. Ajayi, *A History of West Africa—To the Nineteenth Century* (1965; reprint, New York: Doubleday, 1966); Robert July, *A History of the African People* (1970, 1974; reprint, New York: Scribner, 1980); J. F. A. Ajayi and M. Crowder, *A History of West Africa*, vols. 1, 2 (London: Longman, 1974); and A. A. Boahen, *Ghana in the 19th and 20th Centuries* (London: Longman, 1975).

4. More information about the Ashanti, Fanti, and European encounters during this period may be found in D. Forde and P. M. Kaberry, eds., *West African Kingdoms in the Nineteenth Century* (London: Oxford University Press, 1967); David Kimble, *A Political History of Ghana: 1850–1928* (Clarendon, 1963); W. E. F. Ward, *A History of Ghana* (London: Allen and Unwin, 1958); and K. Y. Daaku, *Trade and Politics on the Gold Coast* (Oxford: Clarendon, 1970). Ward's account is marked by an implicit Eurocentric (Anglophile) ideological bias, which masquerades as "reasonable objectivity."

5. The Ashanti had, by their victory over Denkyira in 1701, procured what was popularly known as "the Note"—the rental agreement originally signed by the Dutch and the chiefs of Komenda before they fell under the control of the Denkyrahene. See Davidson et al., *A History*, 242–52.

6. Henry S. Wilson, ed., *Origins of West African Nationalism* (New York: St. Martin's, 1969), is particularly useful as a source that brings together contemporary eyewitness and participants' accounts and explanations of significant events during the latter half of the nineteenth century. We are able, therefore, to make more informed responses and analyses of the attitudes and positions of the people (especially the Fanti and the English) engaged in ideological and material struggle. For a more detailed account of these wars and the vacillating British government's haphazard path toward colonialism, see A. A. Boahen, *Ghana*, and his "Asante, Fante, and the British, 1800–1880," in *A Thousand Years of West African History*, ed. J. F. A. Ajayi and Ian Ipsie (1965; reprint, London: Ibadan University Press and Nelson, 1969), 346–63.

7. Generally speaking, this kind of distinction neutralizes the effectiveness of the play, encouraging the sort of uncritical reading to which so many non-Western texts fall victim. This is precisely the problem discussed in the introduction to this study, also addressed by such critics as Edward Said, *Orientalism* (New York: Random House, 1979).

8. These provisions put the English in the position of policing the annexed Fanti region for the Ashanti; however, the British governor did not relish this job, and, despite another treaty in 1819, Ashanti-English relations went from bad to worse.

9. In this regard, I strongly disagree with the rather disingenuously loaded "hu-

manitarian" motivations J. K. Fynn, "Ghana-Asante [Ashanti]," in *West African Resistance*, ed. Michael Crowder (New York: Africana, 1971), 19–51, attributes to the British government's attitude toward the issues of power, profit, slavery, and other commercial activity in the region. For a more balanced account of the events of this entire period, see Kimble, *A Political History of Ghana*, and John Mensah-Sarbah, *Fanti National Constitution* (1902; reprint, London: Frank Cass, 1968).

10. What is particularly significant about this arrangement is that it is very similar to *panyarring* (originally from the Portuguese), the practice of kidnapping "a townsman of a debtor as security for debt and to get the relations of the man panyarred to put pressure on the debtor to pay up. From this, the practice developed of selling the man panyarred into slavery if the debt was not paid in time, and this could also develop into indiscriminate kidnapping of traders" (Boahen, *Ghana*, 363).

11. W. E. F. Ward, *A History of Ghana*, gives a rather detailed account of the events at this time, which enables one to better appreciate the complexity of the constitutional, economic and socio-political effects of the machinations of the British government and the English merchants.

12. In 1843 the British government had passed two acts, the Foreign Jurisdiction Act and the British Settlements Act, which gave the process of colonization its British constitutional legality.

13. For the full text of the bond, see W. E. F. Ward, *A History of Ghana*, 194; for a brief and excellent commentary about the bond, see Boahen, *Ghana*, 361.

14. John Mensah-Sarbah dominated Gold Coast politics during the early decades of the twentieth century, and his death marks the end of a period in which rising Fanti nationalism, primarily in reaction to overt British domination, underwent a gradual transformation from parochial petty nationalism(s) to become, relatively speaking, more "pan-Africanist." Thus his death marks the start of a qualitatively different kind of nationalist struggle in the Gold Coast, as opposed to the protectorate of Fanti states.

15. From a report by the Select Committee on Africa (Western Coast), the House of Commons, London, 1865, in *Great Britain and Ghana: Documents of Ghana History: 1807–1957*, ed. G. E. Metcalfe (London: Thomas Nelson, 1964), 208–20.

16. Ghana Information Services Document, Ministry of Trade and Tourism (Accra: 1979), 4 (hereafter GIS).

17. Efua Sutherland, "New Life at Kyerefaso" in *Ghanaian Writing Today*, 1, ed. B. S. Kwakwa (Accra: Ghana, 1974), 80–86; and Amos Tutuola, *The Palmwine Drinkard* (London: Faber & Faber, 1952).

18. I am by no means attempting to "voice over" Aidoo's eloquent presentation. I am suggesting that her authorial project and my parallel critique entail a clearer

understanding of the polylectical nature of the confluence of the ideological and material forces that impinge upon the personal and public histories of "actors" engaged in the daily struggles of survival in a neocolonial context.

19. Claire C. Robertson, *Sharing the Same Bowl* (Bloomington: Indiana University Press, 1984), defines the "corporate kin mode of production . . . as the cooperation of kin in a hierarchical labor-intensive organization of production" (13). To this broad definition I might add that the forces tending toward the individual ownership of the means of production and the products themselves are always-and-already being challenged by forces tending toward a more communally cooperative circulation of the wealth so generated. (The same would hold true if the relations of dominance were reversed.)

20. See Kwame Nkrumah, *Consciencism* (New York: Monthly Review Press, 1970), 12–14.

21. A "spirit child" is one who does not wish to be born into a particular *now;* having nevertheless had the misfortune to be born into such a *now,* the child dies as soon as possible. Nigerian poets and writers John Pepper Clark and Wole Soyinka have both treated the subject in poems titled "Abiku." Also see Aidoo's "A Gift from Somewhere" in *No Sweetness Here,* discussed in the next chapter. Such spirit children are fated to a cycle of early death and rebirth to the same mother. It is only by expiation or sacrifice that the child can be made to live a normal human life span in the *now* into which he or she has been born.

22. I am here borrowing heavily from Louis Althusser's theoretical interventions presented in *For Marx* (London: Verso, 1979) and *Reading "Capital"* (London: Verso, 1979). Even though he refers to "structure à dominante" and "structure toujours-déjà-donnée" in the context of socioeconomic relations and activities within and between the superstructure and the economic base of a given society, I contend that Althusser's interventions may be used most effectively in "reading" Aidoo's *Anowa* and, more generally, other texts, given the kind of qualifications expressed and elaborated upon in my whole text.

23. Nicholson's characterization of Anowa is somewhat similar to my own description, in chapter 1, of the "asthmatic old hag / Eternally breaking nuts / . . . whose actions are unproductive." Despite the seemingly "unproductive" nature of Anowa's struggle, Nicholson's insistence that we see Anowa as a *feminist* model reflects what might rightly be called "womanism." See Chikwenye Okonjo Ogunyemi, "Womanism: The Dynamics of the Contemporary Black Female Novel in English," *Signs: Journal of Women in Culture and Society* 2, 1 (1985): 63–80.

24. In the context of traditional and precolonial society, the priesthood would perform a function similar to that of Louis Althusser's characterization of *fetishism,* providing a formal means for occluding the dominant ideological structures and

their relationship to other practices. For a literary treatment of the once-central role of the priesthood in the face of the dislocating presence of British colonialism and Christianity, see Chinua Achebe, *Arrow of God* (1967; New York: Doubleday, 1969).

25. Kofi Agovi, "Is There an African Vision of Tragedy in Contemporary African Theatre?" *Presence Africaine*, 1st and 2d quarters (1984) 133–34, 61–63. Although I am reluctant to make the mother vs. daughter issue central to the "tragic" dimension of *Anowa*, I fully endorse Agovi's characterization of the titular heroine as one "possessed."

26. Although referring to the Ashanti, Meyer Fortes's remarks about kinship and marriage explain this practice and hint at the problems it might create in a marriage: "Ashanti custom provides no collectively approved means of giving expression to the underlying hostility in sibling relationship. . . . It is therefore merged in the other suppressed hostilities aroused by those obligations. The accepted expression for these is the belief that witchcraft acts only within the lineage. . . . *Illness, death, barrenness, economic loss, and other misfortunes are often ascribed to witchcraft, and those accused are most often close matrilineal kin of the sufferer, especially a mother or sister*" (Fortes, 275).

27. Lewis Nkosi, *Tasks and Masks: Themes and Styles of African Literature* (London: Longman, 1981), 180.

28. See Eagleton, *Criticism and Ideology*, specifically chapters 2 and 3.

29. Nkosi seems to conflate the textual and authorial ideologies of the drama. His prescriptions for the "improvement" of Aidoo's play might be valid if *Anowa* was grounded within a Western dramatic tradition and presented its intent and content as a straightforward opposition between contemporary Western and traditional African practices. Nkosi's somewhat orthodox Marxist reading is exactly what Althusser eschews in his article " 'Piccolo Teatro': Bertolazzi and Brecht— Notes on a Materialist Theatre" in *For Marx* (129–51). Further, the affinity between Nkosi's theoretical difficulties with Aidoo's text and Pierre Macherey's critical model is evidenced when Nkosi quotes from Macherey's *Pour une théorie de la production littéraire* (Paris: François Maspero, 1978), 128, before he discusses Aidoo's work (Nkosi, 177). In fact, both Macherey and Nkosi fail to view the text as specifically and inexorably aesthetic-ideological products.

30. Michael Etherton, *The Development of African Drama* (New York: Africana, 1982) 234; also see 227–32, 236–38. Etherton's analysis generally goes further than Brown's, Nicholson's, or Nkosi's and confirms much of my analysis.

31. James Africanus Horton, *West African Countries and Peoples* (1868), extracts included in Wilson, *Origins of West African Nationalism*, 175–76.

## 3. Back to the Present; or *No Sweetness Here*

1. Page references in this chapter are to the 1971 edition: Ama Ata Aidoo, *No Sweetness Here* (Garden City, N.Y.: Doubleday, 1971).

2. Ezekiel Mphahlele, "Introduction," in Ama Ata Aidoo, *No Sweetness Here*, 2d ed. (Garden City, N.Y.: Doubleday, 1972), xix–xx.

3. K. W., "Review Article," *West Africa*, 30 January 1971, 133.

4. Ama Ata Aidoo, "Sisterhood Is Global," *Essence*, March 1985, 137.

5. Donald Burness, "Womanhood in the Short Stories of Ama Ata Aidoo," *Studies in Black Literature* 4, 2 (Summer 1973), 21–24.

6. *Fefewo* is an Ewe word that signifies the totality of a story-telling event—performance *and* reception.

7. The discovery of this way of looking at Aidoo's collection of short stories came with the realization that post-1972 editions of *No Sweetness Here* were formatted differently. Gone were the original divisions between the "acts" or phases of the fefewo. The earlier editions of the collection signified these divisions by a blank unnumbered page, much like a pause or lacuna in the action. Obviously the economic considerations of the publishers superseded the aesthetic demands of the work itself.

8. Kwesi K. Prah, *Essays on African Society and History* (Accra: Ghana Universities Press, 1976), 22–23.

9. This is a reference to the Congo crisis and the aborted Katanga secession of 1960–61. For an informative history of these events, see Conor Cruise O'Brien, *To Katanga and Back: A UN Case History* (New York: Grosset & Dunlap, 1962).

10. Ruth Finnegan, *Oral Literature in Africa* (Oxford: Oxford University Press, 1970), 328–29.

11. I am referring to the integration of ethnographic or culturally specific information within the narrative. In both Aidoo's and Achebe's case, such information is unobtrusive; in terms of Western critical practice, however, this style is almost wholly interpreted in anthropological or sociological terms—the African writer is still the "native informant" for the benefit of Western scholarship—rather than in aesthetic-ideological terms specific to an African art.

12. For an informative discussion of the role and function of these Mallams and their more traditional counterparts, see Eugene L. Mendonsa, *The Politics of Divination: A Processual View of Reactions to Illness and Deviance among the Sisala of Northern Ghana* (Berkeley: University of California Press, 1982).

13. Wole Soyinka, *The Trial of Brother Jero*, in *Collected Plays*, vol. 1 (Oxford: Oxford University Press, 1973); Sembene Ousmane, "The False Prophet," in *Tribal Scars*, 1–7; and Andrée Chedid, "The Long Trial," in *Unwinding Threads: Writing*

*by Women in Africa*, ed. Charlotte H. Bruner (London: Heinemann, 1983) 202–8. Chedid's short story is useful from a comparative perspective. In contrast to Aidoo's character, Chedid views Hadj Osman's role, because of the religious conservatism he espouses, as contributing to the continued oppression of women as mothers and to the general underdevelopment of Egyptian peasant society.

14. Ngugi wa Thiong'o, "Minutes of Glory," in *African Short Stories*, sel. and ed. Chinua Achebe and C. L. Innes (London: Heinemann, 1985), 71–84.

## 4. For Lovers and Others, Not Just Another Version

Epigraph: Chimalum Nwankwo, "The Feminist Impulse and Social Realism in Ama Ata Aidoo's *No Sweetness Here* and *Our Sister Killjoy*," in *Ngambika: Studies of Women in African Literature*, ed. Carole Boyce Davies and Anne Adams Graves (Trenton, N.J.: Africa World Press, 1986), 155.

1. Ngugi wa Thiong'o, *Writing against Neocolonialism* (Wembley, Eng.: Vita, 1986), 14.

2. Sembene Ousmane, *The Last of the Empire: A Senegalese Novel*, trans. Adrian Adams (1981; London: Heinemann, 1983).

3. Efua T. Sutherland, *The Marriage of Anansewa & Edufa* (1975; Harlow, U.K.: Longman, 1987), 5.

4. Ngugi wa Thiong'o, *Matigari* (London: Heinemann, 1989); first published in Gikuyu (Nairobi, Kenya: Heinemann Kenya, 1987). The note "To the reader/ listener," ix, underscores the affinity to the works of Ousmane and Aidoo; in addition, by not writing of this work in English, Ngugi stresses his desire to create an *African novel*.

5. There are a number of Western critical explanations of Aidoo's style. See Ogunyemi, "Womanism," 71–79; a book review by Rand Bishop, "The Only Ones Who Need To Know," *Obsidian: Black Literature in Review* 6, 1–2 (1980): 251–54; and the exceptionally stimulating article by Femi Ojo-Ade, "Female Writers, Male Critics," 158–79.

6. To refine the definitions still further, both *No Sweetness Here* and *Our Sister Killjoy* may be described as *nyakpakpawo*. This implies that the narratives are serious and demand critical contemplation by the reader-audience. In Ewe, we may distinguish between these two works by defining the former as *fefewo kple eme nyakpakpawo*, a collection of dramatic prose narratives for the audience-reader's contemplation. I use the English term *episode* to describe the individual short stories in the fefewo *No Sweetness Here* to distinguish them from "A Love Letter." *Our Sister Killjoy* may be described as *fefewo aloo nutinyawo kple eme nyakpakpawo*, a collection of prose-poetry narrative performances and a meditation for the audience-reader's contemplation.

These translations are meant only to convey the sense of the original. I will use *nutinyawo* as the term that best describes *Our Sister Killjoy* in its entirety; *nutinya* (singular) to describe each of the three sections written-spoken by the Bird of the Wayside; and *nyakpakpa* (singular) to refer to "A Love Letter," since it is her meditation that is also meant for our thoughtful consideration.

7. Ama Ata Aidoo, *Our Sister Killjoy: Or, Reflections from a Black-Eyed Squint* (New York: Nok, 1979). Subsequent references to this work are indicated in this chapter by page or line numbers in the text.

8. Roger Genoud, *Nationalism and Economic Development in Ghana* (New York: Praeger, 1969).

9. "Where," "When," and "How" are each placed about one third of the way down on separate pages. "How" faces the title of the next nutinya, "The Plums," also on a separate page and followed by a blank whiteness before the narrative is continued.

10. Ayi Kwei Armah, *Why Are We So Blest?* (Garden City, N.Y.: Doubleday, 1973), 283–88.

11. Emile Habiby, *The Secret Life of Saeed, the Pessoptimist*, trans. Salma Khadra Jayyusi and Trevor LeGassick (London: Zed, 1985).

## 5. Poetic Interlude—Retrospect and Prospect

1. Aidoo's second collection of poetry is *An Angry Letter in January* (Coventry, U.K.: Dangaroo Press, 1992). The reasons for the delay in the publication of the first collection, and the subsequent change of title from *Dancing Out Doubts* to *Someone Talking to Sometime*, is ironic. The very neocolonialist concerns that have informed Aidoo's writing were the principal cause of the holdup.

2. Brenda F. Berrian, "Bibliographies of Nine Female African Writers," in *Research in African Literatures* 12, no. 2 (Summer 1981): 216, is a good starting point for a listing of Aidoo's early poems. For a more recent update see the chapter on Aidoo in *Fifty African and Caribbean Women Writers: A Bio-Bibliography*, ed. Anne Adams (Westport, Conn.: Greenwood, forthcoming).

3. Robert Fraser, *West African Poetry: A Critical History* (Cambridge: Cambridge University Press, 1986), 141, 153.

4. Ama Ata Aidoo, *Someone Talking to Sometime* (Harare, Zimbabwe: College Press, 1985). Subsequent references to this work are indicated in this chapter by page number in the text.

5. The magnitude of this problem is obvious when one notes that an estimated 50 distinct living languages are spoken in Ghana alone. David Dalby, in *A Provisional Language Map of Africa and the Adjacent Islands* (London: International

African Institute, 1977), calculates that the sub-Saharan region of West Africa hosts approximately 1,250 discrete languages. Even the conservative figure of 800 separate languages for the whole continent estimated by J. H. Greenberg in *Languages of Africa* (Bloomington: Indiana University Press, 1963) and strongly disputed by Ruth Finnegan in *Oral Literature in Africa* indicates the difficulty of continental communications.

6. For an extended analysis of the poetics of dirges in traditional orature, see the excellent work by Kofi Anyidoho, *Oral Poetics and Traditions of Verbal Art in Africa* (Ph.D. diss., University of Texas at Austin, 1983). Although Aidoo's poems cannot generally be classified as dirges, some of them reflect the spirit of that traditional form.

7. Kofi Anyidoho, "Henoga Domegbe and His Songs of Sorrow," *Greenfield Review* 8, 1–2 (1979): 55. This article includes introductory notes and translations of some of Domegbe's songs. Anyidoho's poetry is greatly influenced by that of his mother, Abla Adidi Anyidoho, of his uncles Agbodzinshi Yortuwor and Kwadzovi Anyidoho, and of Vinoko Akpalu and Kofi Awoonor. For more discussion of Anyidoho's work, see Robert Fraser, *West African Poetry*.

8. Atukwei Okai, *Oath of the Fontomfrom* (New York: Simon and Schuster, 1971) and *Lorgorligi Logarithms* (Accra: Ghana, 1974).

9. This is borrowed from Sembene Ousmane's *The Last of the Empire* and describes the spurious theoretical asseverations of some present-day defenders of negritude. Central to their claim for negritude is an essentialist, ahistorical foundation that authenticates the uniqueness, the emotionality, and so forth, of all "black" people.

10. Highlife is a popular musical art form that originated in Ghana (then the Gold Coast) at the beginning of the twentieth century. It "is a blend of traditional Akan rhythms and melodies with European musical instruments and harmony. It encompasses a variety of artistic expressions: music, dancing, story-telling and theater": Sjaak van der Geest and Nimrod K. Asante-Darko, "The Political Meaning of Highlife Songs in Ghana," *African Studies Review* 25, 1 (March 1982): 27–34. This short article, though cursory, is particularly instructive as an introduction to the complex articulation of this cultural product with its ideological and economic origins, which give it its popular significance.

11. Naomi Chazan and Victor T. LeVine, "Politics in a 'Non-Political' System: The March 30, 1978 Referendum in Ghana," *African Studies Review* 22, 1 (April 1979): 177–207, is a good descriptive analysis of this period of Ghana's history, i.e., the late seventies and early eighties.

12. Kwarteng Mensah, "The December Intervention and the Current Situation in Ghana," *Race and Class* 24, 1 (1982): 71.

## 6. A New Tail to an Old Tale

1. For translation and definition, see chapter 4, note 6.

2. Ama Ata Aidoo, *Changes—A Love Story* (London: Women's Press, 1991). Subsequent references to this work are indicated in this chapter by page number in the text.

3. Quoted in "Profile: Sharp-minded Progressive," *West Africa*, 22–28 April 1991, 593.

4. In this light, we may dismiss Zoë Fairbairns' remarks that Aidoo's "near-apology in her preface is unnecessary" (review in *Everywoman*, May 1991, 25) as symptomatic of her understandable desire to "universalize" and thus appropriate the text as more completely accessible by *her* Western readership.

5. The title of my concluding chapter, "A New Tail to an Old Tale," was the working subtitle of *Changes*. I use it to represent the major thrust of Aidoo's literary-ideological project; namely, to provide her audience-readers with new and radically challenging interpretations of "old" tales, old ways of perception, in order that we might realize that the actual point of all these tales is to *change* our world rather than just to interpret it.

6. Bola Makanjuola, "A Modern Woman's Dilemma," *West Africa*, 1 7 April 1991, 474.

7. Ama Ata Aidoo in an interview with Maya Jaggi, "Changing Her Tune," *Guardian*, 2 April 1991.

8. Ama Ata Aidoo in an interview with Deidre Forbes, "Change of Art," *Voice*, 9 April 1991, 18.

9. See chapter 3 for a discussion of Aidoo's use of the eavesdropping style in "For Whom Things Have Not Changed," "No Sweetness Here," and "Something to Talk About on the Way to a Funeral."

# BIBLIOGRAPHY

## Works by Ama Ata Aidoo

*The Dilemma of a Ghost* and Anowa. 1965, 1970. Harlow, U.K.: Longman, 1985.
*Anowa.* 1970. Harlow, U.K.: Longman, 1985.
*No Sweetness Here.* London: Longman, 1970; New York: Doubleday, 1971, 1972.
*Our Sister Killjoy: Or, Reflections from a Black-Eyed Squint.* New York: NOK, 1979; Harlow, U.K.: Longman, 1988.
*Someone Talking to Sometime.* Harare, Zimbabwe: College Press, 1985.
"The Girl Who Can." *Ms,* March 1985, 99–101.
"Sisterhood Is Global." *Essence,* March 1985, 12–13, 15, 134, 137.
*The Eagle and the Chickens and Other Stories.* Enugu, Nigeria: Tana, 1987.
*Birds and Other Poems.* Harare, Zimbabwe: College Press, 1987.
"– for Kinna VII." *West Africa,* 6–12 March 1989, 357.
"Nowhere Cool." *Callaloo* 13, 1 (Winter 1990): 62–70.
"Whom Do We Thank for Women's Conferences?" *Ms,* January/February 1991, 96.
"Modern African Stories 1" and "A Path in the Sky or 7 A.M. and Airborne." *Literary Review,* Summer 1991, 434–36.
*Changes—A Love Story.* London: Women's Press, 1991.
*An Angry Letter in January.* Coventry, U.K.: Dangaroo Press, 1992.

## Secondary Sources

Adelugba, Dapo. "Language and Drama: Ama Ata Aidoo." *African Literature Today, No. 8,* edited by Eldred D. Jones, 72–84. New York: Africana, 1976.
Agovi, Kofi. "Is There an African Vision of Tragedy in Contemporary African Theatre?" *Presence Africaine,* 1st and 2d quarters (1984): 133–34.
Althusser, Louis. *For Marx.* London: Verso, 1979.
Althusser, Louis, and Étienne Balibar. *Reading "Capital."* London: Verso, 1979.
Anyidoho, Kofi. "Henoga Domegbe and His Songs of Sorrow." *Greenfield Review* 8, 1–2 (1979).

———. *Earth Child*. Accra, Ghana: Woeli, 1985.

———. *A Harvest of Our Dreams*. Accra, Ghana: Woeli, 1985.

Armah, Ayi Kwei. *The Beautyful Ones Are Not Yet Born*. Introduction by Ama Ata Aidoo. New York: Collier, 1969.

———. *Fragments*. New York: Collier, 1969.

———. *Why Are We So Blest?* Garden City, N.Y.: Doubleday, 1973.

Bascom, William R. *African Dilemma Tale*. The Hague: Mouton, 1975.

Bell, Roseann P. "The Absence of the African Woman Writer." *College Language Association Journal* 21, 4 (1978): 491–98.

Bell, Roseann P., Bettye J. Parker, and Beverly Guy-Sheftall, eds. *Sturdy Black Bridges: Visions of Black Women in Literature*. New York: Doubleday, 1979.

Berrian, Brenda F. "The Afro-American West African Marriage Question: Its Literary and Historical Contexts." Paper presented at the African Studies Association Conference, Los Angeles, 1 November 1979.

———. "Bibliographies of Nine Female African Writers." *Research in African Literatures* 12, no. 2 (Summer 1981): 214–36.

Bishop, Rand. "The Only Ones Who Need To Know." Review of *Our Sister Killjoy: Or Reflections from a Black-Eyed Squint. Obsidian: Black Literature in Review* 6, 1–2 (1980): 251–54.

Brown, Lloyd W. "Ama Ata Aidoo: The Art of the Short Story and Sexual Roles in Africa." *World Literature Written in English* 13 (1974): 172–83.

———. "The African Woman as Writer." *Canadian Journal of African Studies* 9, 3 (1975): 493–501.

———. *Women Writers in Black Africa*. Westport, Conn.: Greenwood, 1981.

Bruner, Charlotte H. "Child Africa as Depicted by Bessie Head and Ama Ata Aidoo." *Studies in the Humanities* 7, 2 (1979): 5–12.

Burness, Donald. "Womanhood in the Short Stories of Ama Ata Aidoo." *Studies in Black Literature* 4, 2 (Summer 1973): 21–24.

Cabral, Amilcar. *Return to the Source: Selected Speeches*. New York: Monthly Review Press, 1973.

Césaire, Aimé. *Discourse on Colonialism*. New York: Monthly Review Press, 1972.

Chazan, Naomi, and Victor T. LeVine. "Politics in a 'Non-Political' System: The March 30, 1978 Referendum in Ghana." *African Studies Review* 22, 1 (April 1979): 177–207.

Christian, Barbara. *Black Feminist Criticism: Perspectives on Black Women Writers*. New York: Pergamon, 1985.

Condé, Maryse. "Three Female Writers in Modern Africa: Flora Nwapa, Ama Ata Aidoo, and Grace Ogot." *Presence Africaine* 82 (1972): 132–43.

Cooke, Michael G., ed. *Modern Black Novelists*. Englewood Cliffs, N.J.: Prentice-Hall, 1971.

Davies, Carole Boyce, and Anne Adams Graves, eds. *Ngambika: Studies of Women in African Literature*. Trenton, N.J.: Africa World Press, 1986.

Eagleton, Terry. *Marxism and Literary Criticism*. Berkeley and Los Angeles: University of California Press, 1976.

———. *Criticism and Ideology*. London: Verso, 1980.

———. *Literary Theory: An Introduction*. Minneapolis: University of Minnesota Press, 1983.

Etherton, Michael. *The Development of African Drama*. New York: Africana, 1982.

Fanon, Frantz. *Black Skin, White Masks*. New York: Grove, 1967.

———. *The Wretched of the Earth*. London: Penguin, 1967.

Fraser, Robert. *West African Poetry: A Critical History*. Cambridge: Cambridge University Press, 1986.

Grant, Jane W. *Ama Ata Aidoo: The Dilemma of a Ghost—A Study Guide*. Harlow, U.K.: Longman, 1980.

Gunner, Elizabeth. *A Handbook for Teaching African Literature*. Exeter, N.H.: Heinemann, 1984.

Head, Bessie. *A Question of Power*. London: Heinemann, 1974.

———. *The Collector of Treasures*. London: Heinemann, 1977.

Heywood, Christopher, ed. *Perspectives on African Literature*. New York: Africana, 1971.

Hill-Lubin, Mildred A. "The Relationship of African-Americans and Africans: A Recurring Theme in the Works of Ama Ata Aidoo," *Presence Africaine* 124 (1982): 190–201.

———. "Storyteller and Audience in the Works of Ama Ata Aidoo." *Neohelicon* 16, 2 (1989): 221–45.

Holloway, Karla F. C. *Moorings and Metaphors: Figures of Culture and Gender in Black Women's Literature*. New Brunswick, N.J.: Rutgers University Press, 1992.

Horne, Naana Banyiwa. "Ama Ata Aidoo." *Twentieth-Century Caribbean and Black African Writers*, edited by Bernth Lindfors and Reinhard Sander, 34–40. 1st ser., vol. 117. Detroit: Gale, 1992.

Irele, Abiola. *The African Experience in Literature and Ideology*. London: Heinemann, 1981.

James, C. L. R. *Nkrumah and the Ghana Revolution*. Westport, Conn.: Lawrence Hill, 1977.

Jeyifo, Biodun. *The Truthful Lie: Essays in a Sociology of African Drama*. London: New Beacon, 1985.

Jones, Eldred Durosimi. "Ama Ata Aidoo: *Anowa*" (review). *African Literature Today, No. 8*, edited by Eldred D. Jones, 142–44. New York: Africana, 1976.

———, ed. *African Literature Today, No. 8*. New York: Africana, 1976.

Jones, Eldred Durosimi, Eustace Palmer, and Marjorie Jones, eds. *Women in African*

*Literature Today, No. 15*. Trenton, N.J.: Africa World Press, 1987.

Julien, Eileen. "Of Traditional Tales and Short Stories in African Literature." *Presence Africaine*, 1st quarter (1983): 125.

July, Robert. "African Literature and the African Personality." *Black Orpheus*, 4 (February 1964): 33–45.

———. *The Origins of Modern African Thought*. New York: Praeger, 1967.

Killam, G. D., ed. *African Writers on African Writing*. New York: Africana, 1973.

Kilson, Marion. "Women and African Literature." *Journal of African Studies* 4, 2 (1977): 161–66.

Little, Kenneth. *African Women in Towns*. London: Cambridge University Press, 1973.

———. *The Sociology of Urban Women's Image in African Literature*. Totowa, N.J.: Rowman and Littlefield, 1980.

McCaffrey, Kathleen. *Images of Women in the Literature of Selected Developing Countries (Ghana, Senegal, Haiti, Jamaica)*. Washington, D.C.: Pacific Consultants Contract afr-C-1197, Work Order 36, 1977.

Marx, Karl, Friedrich Engels, and V. I. Lenin. *On Historical Materialism*. New York: International Publishers, 1974.

Memmi, Albert. *The Colonizer and the Colonized*. Boston: Beacon, 1967.

Mensah, Kwarteng. "The December Intervention and the Current Situation in Ghana." *Race and Class* 24, 1 (1982): 71.

Metcalfe, G. E. *Great Britain and Ghana: Documents of Ghana History, 1807–1957*, 188–220. London: Thomas Nelson, 1964.

Nagenda, John. "Generations of Conflict: Ama Ata Aidoo, J. C. de Graft, and R. Sharif Easmon." *Protest and Conflict in African Literature*, edited by Cosmo Pieterse and Ian Munro, 101–8. New York: Africana, 1970.

Nandakumar, Prema. "Another Image of Womanhood." *Africa Quarterly* 13, 1 (1973): 38–44.

Nasser, Merun. "Achebe and His Women: A Social Science Perspective." *Africa Today*, 3d quarter (1980): 21–28.

Ngugi wa Thiong'o. *Homecoming*. 1972. London: Verso, 1980.

———. *Writers in Politics*. London: Heinemann, 1981.

———. *Decolonising the Mind: The Politics of Language in African Literature*. London: James Currey/Heinemann, 1986.

———. *Writing against Neocolonialism*. Wembley, Middlesex, Eng.: Vita, 1986.

———. *Matigari*. London: Heinemann, 1989.

Nicholson, Mary Naana. "The Affirmation of African Womanhood in the Works of Ama Ata Aidoo." Master's thesis, University of Florida, 1983.

Nkosi, Lewis. *Tasks and Masks: Themes and Styles of African Literature*. London: Longman, 1981.

Nkrumah, Kwame. *Class Struggle in Africa*. New York: International Publishers, 1970.

———. *Consciencism*. New York: Monthly Review Press, 1970.

Odamtten, Vincent. "Ama Ata Aidoo." *Fifty African and Caribbean Women Writers*, edited by Anne Adams. Westport, Conn.: Greenwood, forthcoming.

Ogundipe-Leslie, Molara. "The Function of Radical Criticism in African Literature Today." Lecture at the Annual Ibadan African Literature Conference, Ibadan, Nigeria, 15–19 August 1981.

Ogunyemi, Chikwenye Okonjo. "Womanism: The Dynamics of the Contemporary Black Female Novel in English." *Signs: Journal of Women in Culture and Society* 2, 1 (1985), 63–80.

Ojo-Ade, Femi. "Female Writers, Male Critics." *African Literature Today, No. 10*, edited by Eldred D. Jones, 158–79. London: Heinemann, 1979.

Okai, Atukwei. *Oath of the Fontomfrom*. New York: Simon & Schuster, 1971.

———. *Logorligi Logarithms*. Accra: Ghana, 1974.

Okonkwo, Juliet I. "The Talented Woman in African Literature." *Africa Quarterly* 15, 1–2 (1975): 36–47.

Ousmane, Sembene. *God's Bits of Wood*. New York: Doubleday, 1970.

———. *The Money-Order with White Genesis*. London: Heinemann, 1972.

———. *Tribal Scars*. London: Heinemann, 1974, 1987.

———. *The Last of the Empire: A Senegalese Novel*. Translated by Adrian Adams. London: Heinemann, 1983. Originally published as *Le dernier de l'empire* (Paris: Editions L'Harmattan, 1981).

Owusu, Kofi. "Canons under Siege: Blackness, Femaleness, and Ama Ata Aidoo's *Our Sister Killjoy*." *Callaloo* 13, 2 (Spring 1990): 341–63.

Peek, Philip M. "The Power of Words in African Verbal Arts." *Journal of the American Folklore Society* 94, 371 (January–March 1981): 19–43.

Pieterse, Cosmo, and Dennis Duerden, eds. *African Writers Talking: A Collection of Radio Interviews*. New York: Africana, 1972.

Prah, Kwesi K. *Essays on African Society and History*. Accra: Ghana Universities Press, 1976.

Radcliffe-Brown, A. R., and Daryll Forde, eds. *African Systems of Kinship and Marriage*. London: Oxford University Press, 1950.

Rea, C. J. "The Culture Line: A Note on *The Dilemma of A Ghost*." *African Forum* 1, 1 (1966): 111–13.

Ridden, Geoffrey M. "Language and Social Status in Ama Ata Aidoo." *Style* 8, 3 (1974): 452–61.

Robertson, Claire C. *Sharing the Same Bowl*. Bloomington: Indiana University Press, 1984.

Robinson, Cedric. "Domination and Imitation: Xala and the Emergence of the Black Bourgeoisie." *Race and Class* 22, 2 (1980): 147–58.

Searle, Chris. "A Common Language." *Race and Class* 25, 2 (1983): 65–74.

Simonse, Simon. "African Literature between Nostalgia and Utopia: African Novels Since 1953 in the Light of the Modes of Production Approach." *Research in African Literatures* 13, 4 (Winter 1982).

Sjaak, van der Geest, and Nimrod K. Asante-Darko. "The Political Meaning of Highlife Songs in Ghana." *Africa Studies Review* 25, 1 (March 1982): 27–35.

Soyinka, Wole. *A Dance in the Forest*. London: Three Crowns, 1963.

———. *The Lion and the Jewel*. London: Oxford University Press, 1965.

———. *The Road*. London: Three Crowns/Oxford University Press, 1965.

Stewart, Daniele. "Ghanaian Writing in Prose: A Critical Survey." *Presence Africaine* 91 (1974): 73–105.

———. "New Life in Kyerefaso." *Ghanaian Writing Today, 1*, edited by B. S. Kwakwa, 80–86. Accra: Ghana, 1974.

Sutherland, Efua. *The Marriage of Anansewa & Edufa*. 1975. Harlow, U.K.: Longman, 1987.

Taiwo, Oladele. *Female Novelists of Modern Africa*. New York: St. Martin's, 1984.

Vincent, Theo. "Form in the Nigerian Novel: An Examination of Aidoo's *Our Sister Killjoy* . . . and Okpewho's *The Last Duty*." Paper presented at the African Studies Association, Philadelphia, 7 October 1980.

Walker, Alice. *In Search of Our Mothers' Gardens*. New York: Harcourt Brace Jovanovich, 1983.

Ward, W. E. F. *A History of Ghana*. 1948. London: Allen and Unwin, 1958.

Willet, John, trans. and ed. *Brecht on Theatre: The Development of an Aesthetic*. 2d ed. New York: Hill and Wang, 1979.

Wilson, Henry S., ed. *Origins of West African Nationalism*. New York: St. Martin's, 1969.

# INDEX

Accra, 14, 22, 43, 91, 92, 98, 160
Acheampong, General Kutu, 151,
    188*n*11
Achebe, Chinua, 1, 22, 100, 185*n*11
Africa, 15, 33, 36, 38, 84, 128, 129, 132,
    134, 136; as "Dark Continent," 38;
    precolonial, 11, 21, 40; struggle of
    people of, 81, 159
African, 21, 32, 36, 83; American, 21,
    22, 38, 114, 145, 151, 179*n*13; critics,
    3; literary criticism, 1–3; literature,
    1–3; in London, 84; male writers,
    16; men, 8; revolution, 6; trade,
    43, 180*n*2; womanhood, 16, 17, 81,
    185*n*5; women, 4, 33, 125; women
    writers, 2–5; writers, 5, 6, 117
Afrocentric, 3
Aggrey, King, of Cape Coast, 48
Aggrey, Kwegyir, 10
Agovi, Kofi, 64, 75, 184*n*25
Aidoo, Ama Ata: characteristics of style
    of, 11–13, 133–38, 177*n*18; concerns
    of, as a writer, 17–18, 81, 82, 133–34,
    161; education of, 8–10
Akan (people), 22
Alienation, 25–26, 76, 78, 95
Althusser, Louis, 33, 180*n*25; and
    "always-already-given structure," 55,
    183*n*22

American, 33, 36, 38, 39. *See also* United
    States
Ananse, Kwaku: folktale, 20, 118; as
    trickster, 62
Anansesem, 118, 186*n*3
*Anowa*, 9, 12, 43–79, 81, 85, 88, 90,
    98, 102, 104, 112, 113; and dilemma
    tale convention, 45–46, 50; as legend
    based on popular folktale, 45, 48–
    49, 53, 58, 182*n*17; structure of,
    50
Anyidoho, Kofi, 136, 145; 188*nn*6, 7
Aristotelian, 40
Armah, Ayi kwei, 9, 30, 81, 86, 109,
    125; *The Beautyful Ones Are Not
    Yet Born*, 9, 109; *Fragments*, 30, 86,
    180*n*23; *Why Are We So Blest?*, 125
Ashantehene: Oyoko Clan Kings, 44;
    Osei Bonsu, 45
Ashanti (Asante): defeat of, 77; expan-
    sion of, 44–48, 60
Audience, 21, 25–26, 41, 52, 53, 65, 74,
    78, 91, 96; as critic, 24, 26, 58; as
    internal (textual), 93; as participant,
    25, 60, 77; as primary, 7, 42, 50, 90,
    134, 165, 176*n*14; as reader, 82, 83,
    109, 118, 124, 131, 132, 133, 161

Bascom, William R., 19, 25, 178*n*8

Been-to, 30–31, 86, 87, 180*n*23

Bird of the Wayside, 50, 51, 85, 99; as actor-raconteur, 96–97; character of, 24, 26, 40, 77, 95; as double narrator, 102–4; as familiar, 160–73; as narrator, 24, 26, 81, 82, 88, 90, 91, 101, 104, 106, 185*n*7; in *Our Sister Killjoy*, 120–24, 126, 127, 129–30, 131; as poet-guide, 136–59

Blank of whiteness, the, 120, 131, 134, 140, 145, 147, 166

Bond of 1844, the, 48, 56, 60, 78, 182*n*13

Bourgeois, 3, 25, 29, 31, 38, 42, 57, 78, 105, 121, 124; oppression, 87; romances, 106; stereotypes, 107. *See also* Ideology; Petit bourgeois

Brechtian, 25, 176*n*14, 180*n*19

British, 44–48, 51, 52, 71, 72, 77; colonialist, 90; empire of, 71, 86

British Company of Merchants (BCM), 46–47

Brown, Lloyd W., 177*n*19; on Ama Ata Aidoo and orature, 21, 23; on *Anowa*, 49–50, 57–58, 75; on *No Sweetness Here*, 94, 98, 105–6

Busia, Dr. Kofi, 79

Cabral, Amilcar, 36; *Return to the Source*, 152, 180*n*29

Cape Coast, 24, 40, 95, 96, 98

Capitalism, 38, 52, 73, 99, 109, 134, 149, 158

Caribbean, 44

Carmichael, Stokely, 137

Central Intelligence Agency (CIA), 78, 142

*Changes: A Love Story*, 7, 12, 67, 160, 161, 189*nn*2, 5

Chapman, Karen, 14–16, 178*n*2

Chauvinism, 39, 66; national, 158

Chedid, Andree, 102, 185–86*n*13

Chichidodo, 109

Chorus, 50, 52, 53, 55, 62, 64, 67, 88. *See also* Audience

Class, 18, 36, 41–42, 52, 97, 117

Colonialism, 10, 17, 18, 37, 40, 43, 45, 46, 47, 51, 52, 53, 83, 84, 97, 125, 126, 141, 143, 147; and army, 89, 99; and authority, 96; end of, 88; era of, 85, 106; experience of, 114; legacy of, 139. *See also* Neocolonialism

Congo, 89, 185*n*9

Conrad, Joseph: *Heart of Darkness*, 120

Corporate-Kin Society, 52, 183*n*19

Critics, 1, 4, 15, 178*n*3

Culture, 31, 33, 36, 37; precolonial, 89; schizophrenic, 21, 148, 179*n*12

"Dark Continent," Africa as, 38

Death, 48, 72, 102, 118, 151

Dede Akaibi, 54

DeGraft, Joe, 133

*Dilemma of a Ghost, The*, 9, 12, 42–43, 45, 49, 51, 53, 59, 62, 65, 67, 68, 88, 99, 113, 119, 160, 163; as play, 14–18, 20–41, 112, 179*n*14

Dilemma tale, 18–20, 22, 23; convention of, 11, 15, 41, 82

Drama, 14, 15, 24, 28, 34, 39, 41, 46, 49, 52, 55–56, 59–60, 65, 67, 68, 73, 77, 81, 163. *See also* Performance

Eagleton, Terry, 20, 69, 178*n*11, 184*n*28

Eavesdroppers, 99, 110, 169, 189*n*9; eavesdropping as narrative strategy, 100

Elmina, 43, 44; Junction, 40, 53, 66
English, 44, 74, 82; pidgin, 84; prudery, 169
Etherton, Michael, 73, 184n30
Europe, 40, 43, 86, 88, 120, 121, 127, 141
Ewe, 185n6

Fanon, Frantz: 23, 29, 86, 180n21; *Black Skin, White Masks*, 86
Fanti (Fantse): 45, 46, 47–48, 51, 52, 55, 57, 100, 180n20; language, 82, 93, 136; traditional society of, 64, 66, 75
Fefewo, 81, 82, 83, 86, 91, 96, 99, 104–5, 110, 111, 131–32, 160, 162, 185n6, 189n1
Feminism, 3, 4, 9, 12, 16, 18, 49, 58, 72, 80, 162
Finnegan, Ruth, 91, 185n10
Fortes, Meyer, 29–30, 180n22
Fraser, Robert, 133, 187n3
French, 44, 120; hypocrisy of, 169; school, 166
Freud, Sigmund, 69
Freudian, 72, 125

Gates, Henry Louis, Jr., 3–4, 175n6
Gender, 18, 36, 41, 42, 77; manipulation, 113; oppression, 46, 85
Geopsychic nightmare, 129
German, 83, 109; government, 121; mother in "The Plums," 123
Germany, 122, 126
Ghana, 8–13, 21, 22–23, 27, 29, 40, 42–45, 56, 60, 78, 86, 87, 93, 97, 114, 122, 136, 145, 162, 166–67; dirges of, 151, 154; family in, 36, 38; intellectuals of, 22, 23, 28, 39, 149;

nationalities of, 83, 185n8; novel in, 160; politicians of, 88; society of, 41; sociologists in, 89; urbanites of, 93
Ghost, the, 25, 39, 41, 51, 53, 77
"Ghost, The," 27, 28, 41
Gold, 40, 129; mining, 110
Gold Coast, 8, 10, 22, 40, 45, 46, 52, 54, 71, 78; corps, 83, 89
Gordimer, Nadine, 2
Grandmother, figure of, 29–30

Harlem, 36
Heterosexual, 125
Highlife: songs, 151, 188n10
Hill-Lubin, Mildred A., 22, 178n3, 179n16
History, 1, 8, 12, 30, 33, 41, 43, 57, 71, 72, 88; and *Anowa*, 43–60, 64, 65, 73, 76; and *Our Sister Killjoy*, 120
Horton, James Africanus, 74

Ibadan, 14
Ideology, 11–13, 20, 23, 69, 83, 84, 87, 101, 155, 158
Imperialism, 81, 117
Independence, 87, 90, 92, 113, 114; of women, 9
Insanity, 78
Ironic, 56

Jesus Christ: and the feast of Ahor, 101
Jews, 83
Jeyifo, Biodun, 18, 23, 178n7, 179n17
Jim Crowism, 122
Johannesburg, 122

Kenyan novel, 132
King, Martin Luther, Jr., 147
Kumasi, 43; Central Hospital, 169

Lagos, 14, 122

Language, 85, 133–34, 135–36, 172, 187–88n5

Lautre-McGregor, Maxine. *See* McGregor, Maxine

Laye, Camara, 10, 177n21

Leadership, 27

Lesbianism, 125

London, 84, 86, 87, 93, 107, 126, 166, 167

Macarthy, Sir Charles, 47

McGregor, Maxine, 45, 82

Macherey, Pierre, 69

Maclean, Capt. George, 47–48, 182n11

Madness, 29, 48, 69, 72, 78, 112. *See also* Insanity

Makanjuola, Bola, 162, 189n6

Malcolm X, 137, 147

Mallam, 102, 103, 185n12

Marginalization, 38, 81, 106. *See also* Women

Marriage, 21–22, 53, 60, 63, 71, 77, 161; monogamous, 67; polygamous, 165

Marxism, 11, 12; nationalist, 49, 68–69

Matrilineal: society, 8, 9, 62–63, 70–71, 73, 113; gerontocracy, 51; law, 100; matriarchal figure in, 113

Mensah-Sarbah, John, 48, 182n14

Mohanty, Satya, 5, 176n12

Monogamy, 67, 71. *See also* Polygamy

Mphahlele, Ezekiel, 80, 185n2

Muslim (Moslem), 88, 90

Nana Yaw Fama, 10

Narrator, 19, 24–27, 34, 35, 53, 81, 82, 86, 92–95; as outsider, 100–102; as participant, 54; raconteur, 27. *See also* Bird of the Wayside

Nasser, Merun, 16–17, 178n4

Naylor, Gloria: *Linden Hills*, 3; *Mama Day*, 37, 180n30

Negritude, 10, 11, 15, 152

Neocolonialism, 5–8, 17, 18, 21, 31, 37, 39–41, 43, 46, 87, 114, 117, 125, 134, 141, 147, 164; elite of, 105; era of, 84; illusion of, 106; reality of, 131; society of, 93, 94, 159; and state, 106, 142; and subjects, 8, 85; sujet-en-soi, 33, 86

Newark, 148

New Orleans, 145

Ngugi wa Thiong'o, 5–6, 23, 33, 107, 116–17, 119, 176n10; *Decolonizing the Mind*, 180n27; *Homecoming*, 179n17; *Matigari*, 132, 186n4; "Minutes to Glory," 107, 186n14; *Writing Against Neocolonialism*, 5–6, 116–17, 186nn1, 4

Nicholson, Mary Naana (Naana Banyiwa Horne), 16–17, 58–59, 75, 98, 104–5, 114

Nigerian: novel, 100; pidgin, 127–28; urban population, 22

Nkosi, Lewis, 68–69, 184n29

Nkrumah, Kwame, 10, 22, 78, 142, 154; 179n14

*No Sweetness Here*, 80–82, 117, 122, 134, 162, 185nn1, 2; "Certain Winds from the South," 82, 97–99, 105, 144; "Everything Counts," 81, 82–83, 84–87, 107, 126; "For Whom Things Did Not Change," 81, 82, 83–85, 87–91, 92, 97, 103, 162; "A Gift from Somewhere," 82, 101, 102–4, 105, 108, 112, 144; "In the

Cutting of a Drink," 81–82, 91–
95, 107; "The Late Bud," 82, 107,
140, 144; "The Message," 82, 95–
97, 105; "No Sweetness Here," 82,
99–102, 103, 104, 144; "Other Versions," 111, 113–15, 140; "Something
to Talk About on the Way to the
Funeral," 82, 110–13; "Two Sisters,"
82, 104–7, 148, 164
Nutinya, nutinyawo, 119–20, 121, 123,
126, 131, 160, 165, 169, 172, 186n6
Nwankwo, Chimulum, 116, 132, 186n
Nyakpakpa/Nyakpakpawo, 129, 131,
134, 140, 186n6

Ogundipe-Leslie, Molara, 4, 11, 176n7,
179n12
Okai, Atukwei, 145, 188n7
Orature/Oral literature, 13, 22–25,
57, 89, 91, 117, 179n16; and radical
reading, 8, 177–78n15
*Our Sister Killjoy*, 6, 9, 12, 109, 116–
17, 119–132, 133, 134, 135, 136, 150,
160, 171, 172, 176n12; "From Our
Sister Killjoy," 126–29; "Into A
Bad Dream," 120–23, 129, 131; "A
Love Letter," 129–32; "The Plums,"
123–26, 141, 146–47
Ousmane, Sembene, 19, 102, 116–
19; *The Last of the Empire*, 117–19,
186n2; *Tribal Scars*, 19, 178n9,
185n13
Owusu, Kofi, 2–3, 175n4

Paternalism, 14, 71
Patterson, Orlando, 33, 180n26
Patriarchy, 2, 4, 74, 85, 106; ideology
of, 87; myopia of, 95; and privilege,
114

Peasantry, 27, 29
Performance, 26, 46, 50, 118; dramatic,
81; and narrative, 81, 82, 91; oral,
95. *See also* Drama; Orature/Oral
literature
Pessoptimism, 132, 134, 187n11
Petit bourgeois, 82; intellectual, 39–41,
42, 86, 141, 142, 148
Polylectic, 5, 50, 51, 155, 176n9; criti-
cism, 5, 13, 21; examination, 117
Portuguese, 43, 44
Power, 71, 96, 122, 123, 127, 156;
pauper's, 129
Pra (river), 44
Prah, Kwasi, 85, 89, 93, 97, 148, 185n8
Priesthood, 54, 56, 61, 62, 183–84n24
Prison, 99, 142
Prodigal, 40
Prostitution: and child labor, 93; and
concubinage, 88

Queen Mother, 8, 54
Queen Victoria, 56, 71, 76, 78

Race, 16, 18, 33, 36, 41
Racism, 14, 22, 130, 146, 147
Raconteur, 11, 24, 52, 117; as actor, 91.
*See also* Narrator
Rape, 88, 164–65
Rawlings, Flt. Lt. J. J., 155, 188n12
Rea, C. J., 14, 178n1
Resistance, 7, 88, 102
Revolution, 6, 85, 90, 156

Sanity, 63, 70
Schipper, Mineke, 2, 4–5, 175n2
Sekondi-Takoradi, 43
Senegal, 118
Senghor, Leopold Sedar, 10, 177n21

Sexism, 37
Sexual: excitement, 94; impotence, 68; oppression, 45; politics, 85, relations, 72
Sikaduro, 67, 68, 77, 112
"Skin Trade," 72
Slaves, 19, 40, 66, 83; offspring of, 22, 38
Slavery, 22, 46, 68, 72–74; domestic, 46, 47, 60, 66, 72–73, 77, 112, 147, 182*n*10; international, 47, 60; subjection of women, 61; trade, 44, 46, 52, 83, 89
*Someone Talking to Sometime*, 12, 160, 165, 167–68, 172; "Kwadwom from a Stillborn Kingdom," 154–55; "Legacies," 151–53; "New Orleans: Mid-1970s," 145–48; "Of Love and Commitment," 137–45; "Reply to Fontamara," 150–51; "Someone Really Talking to Sometime This Time," 153–54; "Someone Talking to Sometime—Routine Drugs," 148–50; "Tomorrow's Song," 155–59
South Africa, 122, 128
Soyinka, Wole, 22–23, 102, 179*n*17, 185*n*13; *The Lion and the Jewel*, 22; *The Road*, 22
Spirit Child, 54, 183*n*21
Stereotypes, 17, 178*n*5
Subject, 34, 46, 50, 79; colonized, 114; feminized, 91; neocolonial, 8. *See also* Neocolonialism
Suicide, 46, 47, 69, 78
Sujet-en-soi, 30–34, 37, 55, 60, 75, 86, 129, 180*n*24
Sujet-pour-l'autre, 94, 107
Sujet-pour-soi, 50, 64, 75, 129, 140
Sutherland, Efua, 10, 21, 133, 177*n*19

Tarkwa, 110
Texas, 140
Three Elders, 27, 180*n*20
Trading, 66
Tragedy, 46, 54, 59

United States, 16, 21, 36
University of Cape Coast, 133
Urban environment, 92, 165

Victimhood, 131; valorization of, 105–7, 110
Violence, 28, 39; and sexual excitement, 94

Ward, Cynthia, 20, 176–77*n*15
Watts, 148
Wayfarer, 34, 35, 40, 51, 67, 76, 77
West, 38, 40
Western, 10, 11, 12, 21, 30, 34, 85; contribution, 91; critics, 22; cultural practices, 93; literary genres, 13, 39, 95, 117
Witchcraft, 55, 67, 73, 77
Wolseley, Sir Garnet, 48
Women: autonomy of, 8, 9, 16; marginalization of, 45, 71, 81; record of, 97; resistance of, 101; socialization of, 77
Working classes, 29, 42. *See also* Class
Wright, Edgar, 1, 175*n*5

Yaa Asantewa, 54
Yebi, 48, 62, 66, 67, 74, 75, 78
Yoruba: orature, 22, 179*n*15; people of, 22

Zongos, 89